Books by Diane Ackerman

On Extended Wings

ON EXTENDED WINGS

Diane Ackerman

ATHENEUM   1985   NEW YORK

Library of Congress Cataloging in Publication Data

Ackerman, Diane.
    On extended wings.

      1. Ackerman, Diane.   2. Air pilots—United States—
Biography. I. Title.
TL540.A28A36 1985   629.13′092′4 [B]   84-45606
ISBN 0-689-11540-7

Portions of this book were previously published in the *New York Times* magazine.

Lines from "Blanche McCarthy" and "The Well Dressed Man with a Beard" in *The Palm at the End of the Mind*, by Wallace Stevens, edited by Holly Stevens, copyright © 1971 by Holly Stevens. Reprinted by permission of Alfred A. Knopf, Inc. Lines from Louis Simpson's "Unfinished Life" are quoted by permission of the author.

Published simultaneously in Canada by Collier Macmillan Canada, Inc.
Composition by Heritage Printers, Inc., Charlotte, North Carolina
Manufactured by Fairfield Graphics, Fairfield, Pennsylvania
Designed by Kathleen Carey
First Edition

For Martin

Acknowledgments

So many people contributed to the writing of this book, without their knowing it, that it would take pages to single them all out. I'm especially grateful to the regulars at the Williamsburg, Virginia, airport, and to Frank Jongepier, for their inspiration and companionship. That world has changed completely since I was there, as things do; but it remains intact in my memory.

At a later date, in Missouri, professional pilot Larry Pedersen read the manuscript for inaccuracies, and I am grateful for his help.

Some chapters of this book first appeared in the *New York Times*.

Most of all, I'm thankful to Paul, a "Vortac Widow," as he put it, when I disappeared into the sky for afternoons on end; he has guided me through the straits of many fevers.

Contents

An Autumn of Airplanes Called November

1

You are seated tensely in the cockpit of a single-engine plane, one hand crushing the control wheel as if it were a test of grip strength at a fair, the other half-opening the throttle with a tentativeness that has nonetheless sent you charging down the runway at 40 mph, toward the thick, wreck-hungry forest edging the airport, called Sapsucker Woods. Half the runway is spent behind you, the air is a single loud growl of straining engine, the end of the runway is lunging up at you like a punch, and, at your right, an instructor is screaming, *It's now or never!* You jolt the throttle forward as far as it will go, the plane rears up on its haunches, and suddenly numbers float under you: 32, your age, but also the compass heading for the runway,

3

320 degrees, painted in white. Less jagged now, the engine fills the cabin with a steady surf that doesn't seem to break. For the first time, you feel the seat full against your back, and above the uptilted hemisphere of the instrument panel only clouds are visible. Leveling off, you can see the horizon jumpy with haze. The stick and rudder pedals move under your hands and feet in ghostly procession, and you are banking away from the skunk-backed macadam of the runway, and heading toward the north shore of Lake Cayuga, into a piece of sky designated a Practice Area. Oddest of all, you are walking there, left foot, then right on the rudder pedals to keep your nose straight. And, underneath you, the plaid of crops looks like a bar of campaign ribbons stretching flat in all directions at once. There is no longer the intimacy of details, but much perspective, and the air itself is thickly present, almost a lens.

The first lesson is a contest between your instincts and your will. Nothing is what it seems. You steer with your feet, not just with the wheel. Pulling the wheel back will make you go up a little, but mainly slower. The throttle isn't for making you go faster, but up and down. When you try to turn handily by using a combo of the wheel and rudder, you blurt the controls in such a panic that the smooth airflow over the wings breaks, and it feels as if you've stepped into a peat bog in the sky as you skid and slide.

Getting the "right picture" is everything, you're told. You thought flight was a long, lyrical chorus of ever-changing views of the planet, and now you discover it's a series of stills. Because you can't trust the instruments with your life, you must learn to judge whether you are

4

climbing or diving, or at the correct angle for landing, or at a stall, or at the proper angle for takeoff—all by knowing what picture of the nose vis-à-vis the horizon will equal a specific airspeed. *Fix the picture*, the instructor urges, ordering you to fly straight and level, and yet, without meaning to, or even noticing that a minor trend has begun, you have let the wheel pull backward a shade and are slowly, effortlessly nosing toward a stall. He brings the plane back level on the horizon. *Keep this picture!* he commands, and for the tenth time since takeoff, he drags your right hand off the wheel. This time he makes you sit on it, so you'll be forced to fly left-hand-only-on-the-wheel; the right hand is used for throttle and flaps and trim and radio and all the paraphernalia on the right side of the plane.

Everything you do is wrong. And there's no remedy, for as soon as you concentrate on one of the six pieces of coordination it takes to fly, the others go. Just when you get the right picture (or airspeed), you aren't minding the throttle and drop 100 feet. The instructor erupts, becomes stern as an Old Testament God. In the air, 100 feet is nothing. But at 50 feet over the runway, it's death. Just when you get the throttle setting right, you lose control of bank and heading and are tolling across the sky. The dials are strange and difficult to read, the altimeter running both backward and forward, so that you must be able to tell whether the hands flexing between numbers are really 1:30 (only 500 feet high), or 2:30 (1,500 feet). A garbled message on the radio is addressing you. And when the instructor hands you the mike, you hold its black bakelite heart, press, and talk into the wrong side. He rearranges it in your shaking hand, as if showing you how

5

to hold a fork for the first time. *Relax,* he says, *try to relax.* Then you repeat after him words your brain refuses to understand, so much of it is overextended in the auslands of dials and coordinated limbs, and in the desperate, pulse-gunning pump of adrenalin that stiffens every muscle and keeps your heart revving. Again he tells you to tell the tower your name—"Cherokee Warrior six-one-two-two Juliett" (with two t's), as it says on the panel—and that you're five miles northwest of the airport and wish to land. The tower replies with a noisy smear of information. "Twenty-two Juliett," you answer to confirm his message, though you didn't even hear him clearly, let alone decipher his instructions.

The controls continue to move without you, though your hands and feet rest lightly on them, following their dance moves, trying to fathom their logic. All that is expected of you today is this moment, this willingness to follow, an introduction to the shape of the movements that you will make, not how or why or when to make them. Your job on landing is walking the rudder straight so that you stay on the middle line of the runway, and it seems like a sop tossed to you, until, at touchdown, you swerve and skid over the line almost to the grass, and then back again as the instructor begs you louder and tougher to steer the plane back to center line before you spin round and smash a wing.

Safely down and taxiing, you pull your hands and feet off the controls as if from separate fires, and give control back to the instructor, who had never relinquished it. Your muscles have been flexed hard and tight for half an hour without release, and now ache from the isometric lock they were in, some twitching so badly it's hard to climb out of the cockpit.

There is so much to remember, it's overwhelming. There's so much to be mastered; perhaps you can't master it, perhaps it requires a mathematical bent foreign to you. You were so much out of control. Your mind was sluggish, and it stammered, as eye muscles sometimes do when trying to make fast focus changes from far off to up close. Now you understand how terrifying it will be, and also how addicting. The pilot's seat is one of the few places on earth where one's life is truly one's own; there are no hideouts, compromises, misgivings, victims, benefactors. In a cavalcade of minute, urgent decisions, you must choose your fate. You can't risk being a passenger. But even if this existential itch weren't true, even if Nature weren't packed with wonders only viewable from aloft, and even if my curiosity weren't howling like a caged dog, I would still need to fly.

I don't feel particularly daring. To me, real courage is metaphysical and has to do with keeping one's passion for life intact, one's curiosity at full stretch, when one is daily hemmed in by death, disease, and lesser mayhems of the heart. Still, I am compulsively drawn to pastimes most people would find frightening. Some women consciously pursue danger, as a way of touching the fabric of their mortality. Daredevils, I mean, who need to live close to the edge to feel fully alive, who need to experience a constant state of rescue or reprieve. For me, it's just a case of my curiosity leading with its chin: things fascinate me whether they are dangerous or not. I don't need to fly because flying doesn't frighten me; I need to fly *even though* it frightens me, because there are things you can learn about the world only from 5,000 feet above it, just as there are things you can learn about the ocean only when you become part of its intricate fathoms.

It isn't that I find danger ennobling, or that I require cheap excitation to cure the dullness of routine; but I do like the moment, central to danger and to some sports, when you become so thoroughly concerned with acting deftly, in order to be safe, that only reaction is possible, not analysis. You shed the centuries and feel creatural. Of course, you do have to scan, assess, and make constant minute decisions. But there is nothing like *thinking* in the usual, methodical way. What takes its place is more akin to an informed instinct. For a compulsively pensive person, to be fully alert but free of thought is a form of ecstasy.

Being ecstatic means being flung out of your usual self. When you're enraptured, your senses are upright and saluting. But there is also a state when perception doesn't work, consciousness vanishes like the gorgeous fever it is, and you feel free of all mind-body constraints, suddenly so free of them you don't perceive yourself as being free, but vigilant, a seeing eye without judgment, history, or emotion. It's that shudder out of time, the central moment in so many sports, that one often feels, and perhaps becomes addicted to, while doing something dangerous.

At first, the only and ultimate fright is of trusting, releasing yourself to the present. Flight is nothing but an attitude in motion. If you're shaped right and go fast enough and tilt your nose to where you'd rather be, you can't help but leave the ground. Your wheels will dance, your wings will stray a bit, and then you will levitate as no fakir ever could, thanks to the reliable sorcery of nature. All things are transmutable when they break down to their lowliest components of cell and atom. A wing is only rigid and awkward on the ground; in the sky it is a rapid knife so sharp and delicate it can slice through interfolding tissues of air. The real terror is in the letting go, the willingness that first time to run the throttle full open and race down the runway, with hangars and trees and cars blurring helplessly at the edges of vision, to abandon everything known, safe, and significant, and leap into the terrible invisibility of the sky. The sky that could fall in fairy-tale hysteria, the sky in which Heaven is pictured and gods of all nations are enthroned, the sky that leads to the blackness with which one envisions infinity and the unimaginable subtraction of sensuousness we call death. The first terror is the oldest and most rugged: the fear of leaning into nothingness.

2

AFTER THE FIRST FLIGHT, you find yourself in a sandstorm of your own ignorance. It begins simply with the instructor, who has been trained to teach Socratically, asking you to solve problems, each phrase and term of which is an unknown.

"How does an airplane fly?" he asks.

"Lift," you answer brightly.

"What does that mean?" He looks at you with blue eyes on which soft contact lenses are floating like lost continents. You pause to collect your thoughts.

"That the wing is more curved on the top, flatter on the underside, and so the air goes faster on top, which causes uneven pressure on both sides . . . "

"Uh-huh," he says, smiling. "Now how does an airplane fly?"

The speck of information about lift you somewhere learned is irrelevant. A lecture in physics for toddlers begins that will leave you stunned by your ignorance of the natural world, and swamped by implied graphs and formulas and terms for mechanisms as hard to fathom as Greek used to define Greek. When he draws a graph to explain an important principle, you realize to your alarm, and embarrassment, that *you can't read graphs*. Repeat the explanation, you ask, but differently, in analogies, in images. In words this time, he draws you back to the graph, the same abstract terrain where it is so simple, so elegantly clear in the argot of the tradition out of which he has come.

"I haven't got it," you say weakly, covering the graph with one palm. "Use words."

Again he tells you, this time using the analogy of holding your hand out of your car window as you drive up the steep highway winding along the lake. He holds up his own large hand, as if out of the speeding car, and you notice how suntanned it is from basking in the cockpits of planes all day, how the blond hairs on his hand and arm look almost white in contrast.

"Is there more pull against your hand if it's palm against the wind, or fingertips to the wind?" He demonstrates.

"Palm."

"Right. Why is that?"

"Drag?" you offer hopefully.

"What's that?"

"I'm presenting a larger surface to the wind."

"Only incidentally, but I'll let that pass for the moment. Does that make your hand go faster or slower?"

"It goes the speed of the car."

"Does it?"

"No. It gets blown backward. It goes slower." Surely tutelage was terraced just like this in ancient Greece. The simple, demonstrable laws of nature.

"Why is that?"

"I don't know."

"What happens to the airflow around your hand when it's straight into the wind. . . ?"

From hands held from speeding cars, you move to wings, and the journey is as laborious and baffling as trying to learn algebra in sixth grade. You are afraid to tell him that you still don't know your multiplication tables. When you sit down and he draws a compass on a sheet of paper, asking, "What direction is o degrees?" you tell him fast and straight that you don't know.

"It's north. All right. Then what direction is 90 degrees?"

Your heart races. "About east?" The half-hour lesson has already staggered into an hour's ground school, and he tries to conceal his combined amazement and frustration.

"*Exactly* east," he says. "So, if you have a runway whose number is 32, and you know that they always drop off the last zero when talking about runways—that it's really 320 degrees—what direction is it in?"

It's sixth-grade algebra. Your mind freezes. "I don't know."

"Look at the compass," he says tensely running a

finger across his light, groomed mustache. "Zero is north. How many degrees in a circle?"

It's come to that. "360."

"Then what direction is 320 degrees?"

Painfully slow, you go through the cardinal directions. "Northwest?"

"Right." He says the word as if laying down a piece of granite. "And if thirty-two is the runway in one direction, what is it in the other direction?"

I have no idea.

"Just subtract one-eighty from three-twenty, or eighteen from thirty-two, which gives you . . . ?"

Subtraction under stress was never your forte. Finally, you produce the 14 you're being asked for.

"So, the same runway out there, which is thirty-two at one end, if you're taking off at the other end is called fourteen. At most airports the runways have huge white numbers painted at where your wheels should touch down, right at the end of the strip, and the tower will tell you which one to use. Let's say the tower here tells you to take off one-four, which way will that be?"

You point to the left end of the airstrip.

"Which is which direction?" he asks.

You're lost again.

"Where is it on the compass? Work it out."

You press your attention into the pencil-drawn compass on the table in front of you. "The northwest."

"Is it?" Again you hear that cross-examining inquisitional inflection that will plague you mercilessly every time you guess wrong, as you do to seven questions out of nine. It will pick at you like a beak: *Does it? Will it?* Your progress is excruciating. There is so much to learn.

Lift, drag, thrust, weight. Elementary rules of physics, without which you can't fly, since the wind and plane and weather are always changing, and what will take you up safely on one day will crash you into a leafy umbrella on the next. You must understand *how* the sky works, and also all the simple improvisations humans have created as a way of getting from one place to another without getting lost. Lindbergh used to buzz highways and read their signs; the telephone wires and other cables never gave him pause. But aerial life is more complex today, with jets, gliders, and helicopters, and radio towers, and restricted fields that stretch from 3,500 to 85,000 feet straight up, and nuclear warhead dumps, and Terminal Control Areas, and swift military experiments-with-wings that go whoosh in the night.

3

IN THE CHARTER OFFICE, the walls are a thick white
styrofoam, grayed by the dense smoke frequently hanging like a weather system over the chairs and desk. Ceil-
ing-high potted plants look as ordinary as furniture. A
suited man is sitting at a table in the corner, selling life
insurance to two pilots. Dark corridors lead away from
the main room into the workshop or hangar or boss's office or lavatory, in which there are two stalls and a sink
with a mirror too high for most women to look into. I
know by now that the wind-stiff sleeve on a pole outside
is a wind sock pointing in the direction that I'll be taking
off from, since to take off in the shortest distance one always takes off into the wind.

For forty-five minutes, the instructor tries to explain a principle to me. *When relative speed increases, the angle of bank must increase in order to keep a fixed radius around a given point.* I am trying to understand the words, the diagrams, but am deeply confused. What, in daily terms, are *ground speed, angle, bank, radius, point?* And how do they translate into a principle that will guide me aloft? A fog pours in over my mind. When we take to the air, I fly badly, out of control, let the plane fly me until, in desperation, I give over the controls. Flying low circles around a barn, I can't remember where to go steep, where shallow. For half an hour, I fly arbitrary circles in the directionless flux, losing altitude every time I turn.

"Why are we diving?" the instructor yells, as we plunge to within a few hundred feet of a cornfield. I still haven't mastered the knack of flying level ("You just dropped a hundred feet! You were coming in to land, and you dived through the runway!"). Worst of all, I have the treacherous habit of not remembering which way on the control wheel is up, which down. The instructor commands me to speed up, because we're too close to stall speed, and instinctively I yank back on the wheel, bringing on the warning buzzer. Coming in to land, he says keep 80 knots at all costs, just keep the line on 80. When it creeps to 90, I forget which direction will bring it up again, and plunge the wrong way. I am having a ruinous phase of opposite response. I can't make controlled turns. I can't keep the plane up. I can't understand the explanations of what I'm supposed to do, and I can't execute them when I do understand them. I also can't take off. Landing, so much runway swarms up at me I can't figure out what *level* is. Twenty feet off the ground, I put the airplane's nose where I think level is, and I'm wrong, we're climbing, which, at that speed, will mean a stall.

"Why are we climbing?" the instructor yells, and seizes the stick solidly enough to be in control if I make an opposite response. But, no, now I'm diving at the runway. "*Gradual* changes!" he commands. We land in three bumps, each one requiring a burst of throttle from the instructor, and a slight nose adjustment to set us down safely at last.

At home later, dejected and bewildered, I study my flying manual and am almost crestfallen enough not to wish to continue. It's too much. It overwhelms me. I rethink the day's instruction, step by step, using a green model Fokker 111 from the hobby shop as an aid. After a while, suddenly it starts to come clear: when the wind is behind you, you have to bank steeply, or you'll be blown through the turn. Christ, I think, how can it be as simple as that? *Keeping a fixed radius around a given point.* I start to work on the other phrases I didn't understand. *Seventy-nine knots considers time, and 65 knots considers distance.* That had stymied me each time I tried to understand it. What does "consider" mean in this context? Literally it means "with the stars," an astrological consultation. And yet one considers a job differently than one considers what dessert to order. "Time" could be sidereal, circadian, chronicity; and "distance," all the delicate shadings between football field and subatomic particle. But ultimately, I make sense of that, too: if you want to get the plane up fast, 79 knots; if you want to get it up steep, 65 knots. Again, the principle is easy, but the terminology a logjam.

At the next lesson, before turning on the ignition,

I tell my instructor how demoralized I am. First of all, I'm being asked to learn so many things at once, without ever mastering any one of them. All that leaves me with is an ongoing, worsening sense of being out of control. Can't we just practice one skill and get it down, then move to another? I ask. And secondly—the more important problem—I come from a different tradition than you do, I explain, my background is mainly in the Arts and Humanities, and when you try to teach me with graphs and formulas or with phrases that are mathematical abstractions, I go haywire. For example, a little while ago, when we were practicing stalls, you told me that the angle of attack increased in a turn because of "the additional lift required to maintain the vertical component of lift." I don't even know what you mean by the notion of *increase* or *decrease* in that context. My mind compulsively solves language problems, and if you give it an abstraction in abstract language, it runs through all the possible meanings for each term, searching hopelessly for the one that applies in this instance. Example: you said that when we're downwind, if I find myself too low, I can *swap airspeed for altitude* by tilting the nose up a little, and that confused me utterly. To me a swap is a fair and even exchange. But what you mean, I understand now, is that I must give something away, sacrifice one thing to make the other work. I'll go slower, but I'll go higher; the opposite when I land. In my mind it's a different process. Nothing is *swapped* or *exchanged* or *traded*. If I think like that, I see the wrong process. Something is sacrificed, given up. Worst of all, I feel mentally alien, in a different universe. My realm is visual, descriptive, full of sensory overload. I'm very good at pinball machines, but terrible

18

at video games—too abstract. I need things to be as specific, down-to-earth, thingly, and visual as possible. Mathematics was always a nightmare for me in high school. I feel overwhelmed, demoralized, and possibly unfit for learning these kinds of things, too much a right-hemisphere brainstormer, too specialized.

"All right," he says, with a public relations smile, "all right, I'll try to talk more simply." But his eyes are saying: *What a dame! Nothing but excuses and demands. Why can't she learn the way everybody else does?* A question that she wishes she had an answer to, too. "If you want to be cured, first you must expose your wound," as Boethius said, and I do so willingly, if it will help shake down the cloud of engineer-speak that makes me feel like a toddler in a synchrotron.

4

NORTHWEST OR SOUTHWEST, the runway is the same, but we pretend it's two ways out, as we pretend the tower man, who is also the ground man on a different radio frequency, did not drive to work in the same car this morning, is not smiling at the soft, uncertain, female voice conjuring him by numbers more permanent than an address. Numbers she is clearly reading from the panel, but which he knows by heart. It is a small voice in the endless ether.

"Ithaca Ground, two-two Juliett. Cayugair. Taxi," I say.

Half lost in the deep, rough vibrato of the engine, his voice floats around the cockpit like an hallucination.

He is correcting me, calling me by full name: "Cherokee Warrior November six-one-two-two Juliett." I have been too casual; we have not been introduced yet. In a noisy smear of information, he is telling me that the winds are from the east at 20 knots, gusting to 25 knots (they will blow me hard left as I take off if I'm not careful), that the altimeter is 30.01 (I set it to airport elevation, 1,100 feet), and that I will taxi to the runway facing Sapsucker Woods.

It is a voice wholly without physiognomy, and alert, cheerless, automatic. I lift my mike, press open the lock between us, and want to ask him, the disembodied voice in the cockpit, more important things. Three thousand years ago, a woman ordered her life by the counsel of gods speaking like this, wireless over the mind's planisphere. I want to ask him how mere matter led to us, about despoiling the Earth, how to make love stay, about the incubus of disease. I want to ask how flight began in animals, from the ground up or the sky down, and about the innards of the atom, and the outlook for our solar system, and how to allow for the 1,000 mph added speed of the revolving Earth in the general equation of one's life, and what attitude will give one the longest lift for the greatest distance. Encircling and poised, it is a voice always where you need it to be, just where it last was, a wavelength smacking on the shore of your loneliness as you fly cross-country, silently solo. But it does not muse or consider. Only affirm, only direct. It does not comfort or sympathize. Only appear, armed with facts, in an electronic cloud, then vanish when you confirm the fullness of its message by uttering your own name, "Two-two Juliett."

I am downwind. I should be hearing a voice over the breeze. I lift up the mike, speak to its perforations, whisper to its black ear. Perhaps I have not uttered the right words. My chest is stiff as a fort where the small cavalries of the heart maneuver, as I wait for the voice to lead me from this calm desertion to a slow, necessary descent.

5

"Just routine cleaning," the charter boss explains about a barrel-bellied truck out on the airfield hosing down the runway with foam. As he sifts receipts, his voice is level and calm, a still ledger itself.

Only later, after my lesson, when I pick up a newspaper at the grocery store on the way home, do I learn the truth in a headline too horrible and crudely expressed to comprehend. And too silent. How can horror be that silent? Five Die in Worst Air Crash in 30 Years. They had been soaping off blood from the runway, and the metal parts scattered about like loose change, and the fluids unidentifiably human or machine. No one had spoken about it, not my instructor, who was all business as usual, not the mechanics, not the secretary. Though all had seen the crash: the twin-engine plane taxiing to the runway, with a seasoned pilot and four businessmen aboard. Then takeoff, and suddenly the plane banking stiffly onto one wing at 200 feet, stalling into its own shadow, killing the men on impact before it burst into flames. The pilot had been found with the control wheel shaft straight through his chest, the others' bodies heaped and burned like so much wood from the forest only a short drive away. The groundsmen all thought it must have been a chandelle the pilot was doing, a climbing candle walk on one wing, a form of almost-aerobatic dressage. To the last fraction of time in which the plane was no longer hovering—still, at the peak of its stall, but beginning to fall—they couldn't believe what they were seeing. The mind has a lag time for horror. And then the plane was crashing into the ground, and they were running toward it, unnecessarily, since no one could possibly live through the crash, running by instinct as the rubble exploded into a ball of fire. Afterward, they would cold-bloodedly revile the pilot's judgment, as a form of anti-hex on themselves. So much of a flier's life is metal and chance, so much of what appeals to one is self-reliance, that one would never fly if it seemed luck outweighed intuition. So it was pilot error, they all hoped, not an engine failure, not a freak wind, not structural fatigue.

In Boston, a year ago, a turboprop crashed on takeoff whose symptoms were identical: nose up to stall, one wing falls, one engine fails. Pilot error, the report had been at first, but recently the FAA released a new finding. The pilot's seat slide had been faultily repaired. Airplane seats are adjustable, like those in a car, and sometimes they pull free and slide back suddenly. When that happened in the

Boston turboprop, the pilot's feet flew off the rudder pedals, the control wheel pulled the plane's nose up as he fell backward with it. Could the same thing have happened here? Five men dead because of a bad seat fitting? Or was it none of that? They'd left just after lunch; perhaps he had been drinking. Perhaps he forgot to check the free movement of his controls, out of complacency or boredom or a rush to get skyward. You tell your wife you'll be home at three, and it's already four, and you still haven't taken off. You're thinking about the waitress whose pink handkerchief tucked in her white uniform's pocket you teased her about. You're wondering whether you should have bought that video game set for your daughter's birthday after all. The corned-beef sandwich you had is sitting heavily. The passengers are joking loudly, and you smile at a macabre joke about Henry Fonda. You don't think that you're going to die today in the worst aircrash at this airport in thirty years. You can't imagine that a mind as amply given to thought and feeling could just stop. How can a whirlwind stop? Suddenly your wings are not where they should be. Out of the corner of your eye you see your shadow on the ground, like a small bat or a starling. You are looking straight into it, and descending six feet more to where the clouds wrap one tight and ceiling is limitless. You had the wrong attitude, and the Earth is unforgiving, as the new robin, flying its solo into our pool to die, wings spread but windless, learned that same night when men flamed in the bent anger of steel, and time vanished as they crossed the dateline of the heart.

A piece of my mind nags at me. I know I will have to know what caused the crash, as if the knowing could itself be a talisman against danger. It's a morbid imperative to carry to each lesson. The news reports are all vague and contradictory; we'll have to wait until the carcass of the plane reveals something like an answer, though I shudder to think on what clues that might depend.

5

How EASY IT IS TO LAND when you're on the ground, using a folded map for a runway and a hand for a set of wings. The mind makes its own fiction, in which you touch down like the eagle or tern you will never be, touch down with the round tedium of wheels, exactly on the numbers at the runway's threshold. Again you swoop your finger-feathered hand low over the mock runway, float level, then stall into a fine landing. The mind views the entire scene from above with such simplicity that it seems impossible that there could be any distance between thought, unburdened by the demands of the body, and action, when sensory overload jams all the circuits. Today's lesson is about the aim point, the magic spot just off the runway twenty feet or so, worn away by all the urgent eyes that have sought it, in our case a yellow spot of poor growth in the grass. Aim for that spot with something on the airplane—the cowl, a speck on the windscreen, a screw—and glide will be smooth, a perfect 80 knots. But you must hold it in perspective between the runway and the plane, not receding, not approaching, lock it into place with your eyes, that perfect balance between where you are and where you wish to be. As practice, you hold your hands in front of you as a frame, in whose exact center is a chair leg across the room, then walk toward it keeping it steadily centered and unmoving while the rest of the room seems to flood away from it on all sides. Leonardo doesn't mention this exercise in his notebooks, as he does staring at walls spotted with stains or mixed stones until they become landscapes, battle scenes, faces, or costumes, how "really marvelous ideas" may come from scrying ashes or clouds or the clanging of a bell, anything blurred, which the mind then instinctively struggles to make sense out of. Judging the exact center of an arch was no problem for him ("merely a strength made from two weaknesses"), nor other knacks of assaying proportion and space. He must often have held his hands just like this, to fix on a perspective. I like the idea of using body parts to test the mind's assertions, in an age when slide rules are already antiques.

As the pup instructor, Brad Lammergeyer, talks about an aim point, my mind skips to the crash point, the spot just off the runway where the twin-engine plane went down, and how spooked I'll be when, coming in to land, I see it, and know all the trauma invisibly present in that section of grass parallel to the runway. Suppose my mind, on its own private vector, aims for *that* spot? I shake my head, know I am just picking at a mental scab it's hard to leave alone.

A meticulous, almost exquisite dresser, Brad has not put on his usual tie and coat to teach in, trading formality for comfort in the 80 degree haze. Saddled with the full burden of instructing me, he is expecting an ordeal, his manner brusque and easily exasperated, and I don't disappoint him.

Trying to turn the engine over a dozen times, I finally flood it; what's worse, it makes a strange rasp before it quits, which sends him for a mechanic, returning only to find the phantom sound gone. He turns the engine over smoothly, on the first try, wipes a roil of sweat from his forehead, and buckles himself in again. After calling the ground three times, in full address, on the wrong frequencies, I find the right one. Brad's eyes roll. We taxi out onto the tarmac. I set the altimeter wrong, but the compass right. Brad is yelling at me to keep on the center line, yelling at me to throttle more evenly, not in gulps and spits, yelling at me not to use brakes and power at the same time. And, when I search his face, tanned cocoa-brown, slender and unlined, for the source of such commotion, he tells me to get my eyes back on the taxiway, where they belong. At run-up, I get the tower frequency wrong. And then we are set to take off, briskly, since a plane is close behind us. Wheels lift off before I realize it, and I am pulling the nose up into a stall. Brad yells at me to get into a lower nose position, 80 knots, for climb-out, to pick up speed over the runway as lift increases. Suddenly we are airborne again, but in a bell jar full of haze; water droplets make the air glossy, like a taffy, iridescent in places, and soon the airport, runway, and ground disappear, as if vaporized.

"When are you going to make your turn?" Brad yells at 800 feet.

A quick look for oncoming traffic in the haze, then I bank left, still climbing toward 2,000 feet and then shooting through it because I haven't changed the plane's attitude and reduced the power at the right time. Furthermore, I am supposed to be flying a rectangle around the airport, and already I'm arcing far toward the lake.

"Why are we out here? Where are we going?" Brad yells. "And why are we climbing?"

Flustered, I bark back, "I don't know!"

"Do something!" he yells. "Don't just sit there! Do something!"

I cut the throttle back to a setting I think will fetch me 90 knots, and bank sharply toward the airport again. It's a terrible bank; the turn-indicator ball tumbles far left. Brad yells about it. Confused and out of control, I can't talk to the tower, so Brad tells him that we are coming in for the *option,* either a *touch-and-go* or a *full stop,* depending on how poorly I do or what emergency I cause. But already I am losing altitude and trying to keep an even airspeed, jockeying the controls; my wings aren't level, and I am much too close to the airport to make a shallow turn. I am asking him what to do, out of caution, and he counters only with imperatives: "Figure it out! What do *you* think?" "Stop talking! Act." "Do something." At last I turn toward the airport, curving wide instead of making a clear crisp turn.

"We're supposed to be flying this base leg at a right

angle!" he snaps. "And are we too high or too low to make the runway?"

Too high? Too low? How high is *too* high? How far away are we really, how quickly will we settle down onto the telephone wires hemming Route 13? Or are we so high we won't be able to land at all? "I don't know," I say helplessly.

"Do something!"

I throttle back, and we drop dead toward the telephone wires. Brad whitens, but says nothing, his hand poised above the throttle.

"Obviously, we were too low," I say, gunning the throttle open. Now we are going to be too high. I see the aim point, but need flaps to steepen our descent, and even then come in hard and fast and, worst of all, not on the center line but at an angle.

"Fix it!" Brad barks.

I try pedaling: right rudder, left rudder, right rudder, left rudder. Nothing happens.

"Don't just jiggle the rudder, use it! We're leaving the side of the runway! Get us back on center line with our nose straight! Now! Fast! Fast!"

As the runway looms up under us at ten feet, I try to level out the nose, as he commands, only to find him yanking the stick back hard and settling us in.

"Diane," he says in a voice that is a storm cloud, "this plane is not designed to land on its nose. It can land on its back wheels, it can even land on all three wheels at once, but it can't land on its nose! You were *diving* at five feet off the ground!"

For the next four takeoffs and landings, I am even

31

tenser, more jittery and overwhelmed. For the life of me, I can't figure if I'm coming in too high or too low, something an aphid, a moth, a bird would know in an instant. Brad covers up the airspeed indicator, to teach me not to chase the dials, but I can't keep the plane's nose at the correct angle. My coordination blurs, and I make major changes in pitch, low over the ground, when life or death depends on delicacy. The control wheel moves 90 percent of its distance only in the last seconds at touchdown; the entire glide in and landing up until then are tiny changes, delicate moves along the long octave of flight.

Taxiing back to the hangar, I'm crestfallen and frustrated, unnerved at being yelled at so much, and full of pent-up adrenalin I can't release. Brad has turned flying into the sobriety of a war game. More frightening than all the alarms of the last half hour is how suddenly flat and bored I feel. There wasn't a single moment free from harassment, or any *thought*, only reflex, or any sense of the sheer rapture of flight that had brought me to the airport in the first place. Accomplishment was never my goal, but igniting a necessary passion. And now all I feel is dread. If this is what the summer's lessons will be like, there is no point in returning.

Brad looks equally angry, derisive even. How can I be so stupid? How is he going to put up with me all summer? His thoughts are on his face, over the suntan, under the sweat. One more shot, I figure I'll give it one more shot, but I am too mad at him even to talk, as I write out the check for the lesson and fix a time for the next go. He pulls out a spiral diary, checks its stepladder entries.

"I know this is tough work for you," I say in the uneasy silence.

"My pleasure," he says, forcing a smile, as he jots down my name in an opening two days away.

"You said that with great poise." I hear a tense laugh as I walk out the door. At that moment an empire jet is touching down at the end of the runway. I hear jets arriving and taking off six or seven times a day, but rarely see them floating in, pterodactyl large, to roll out the full 5,280 feet of airstrip. Inside there will be seventy-five people, all sitting in exactly the same position, and a pilot perched high in the cockpit, flying mainly on instruments, since the narrow wraparound windows don't afford much of a view. On takeoff, the pilot sees nothing but sky. Not that it matters. Flying jets is the height of mastery to which professional pilots aspire, but when they get there all the sensations of flight that first attracted them are gone. Bank a small plane steeply, and the horizon swims round instantly, the nose drops, and you dive. You can hear the air, feel the vibration, see the ground rushing underneath you. But in a jet there is little sound or turbulence or sense of motion. Things happen in a languorous, self-enclosed blur, and most of the flying is done on autopilot. The actual speed is awesome, but, from all accounts, what one really senses is a profound slowness. At the end of the runway, the jet pivots and taxis down a ramp toward the terminal. I feel sorry for the pilot, who learned to fly seat-of-the-pants, in a Cessna, Piper, or Beech trainer, and now is isolated from that primal thrill by power. And sorry for myself, who may have to endure a nightmare of abuse, as I did today, just to keep the thrill intact.

7

"BRAD, I think it's time we had a soulful discussion." I swoop low into the left-hand seat of the Warrior. His face is young and suddenly uncertain in its muscles, his beard imperfectly shaven. He is wearing a proper shirt and tie today, a touch of formality. But his aviator sunglasses are the only thing mature about his look, as if it were necessary for him to grow into his eyes.

"You're not going to yell at me quite so relentlessly today, are you?" It is not a question.

He smiles as if he weren't quite sure how to.

"It makes me confused and frantic."

"It isn't the instructor who makes you flustered," he

bluffs. "You do that. You do that because you're afraid you're losing control of the airplane."

"That may be, but yelling at me without letup isn't the solution. I don't suffer from a lack of adrenalin, as you may have noticed."

He laughs clumsily. Such head-to-head candor is a strain he doesn't know how to deal with, and it's a relief to hear me make a joke about how revved-up I am. I'm the lesson he puts at the end of the day, because my nervous energy and irrepressible banter make the hour doubly taxing.

"And I sure as hell don't need an adversary in the cockpit. If I try to do everything at once, I'll mess up on everything at once, and get confused—yelling is no way to teach me. It's no way to teach anyone, but it's positively no way to teach *me*."

"I just talk loud from being in planes," he says tensely. "I wasn't really yelling."

"Let's just take it up," I say after a long silence.

Up is higher than where you were, a neighborhood you are leaving, but no crossroads at the inn of your disposition somewhere below the clouds. *Take it up to 2,000 feet and level off at cruise speed*, Brad demands, and hard at 2,000 I begin to push the nose down and throttle back as the altimeter leaps through its rainbow arc. One of the oddest fancies of knowing is watching the numbers continue to lunge forward long after you have commanded them to stop, to fix the airplane at the layer of air you want. Still the numbers are moving and, looking out of the left window, down along the farmlands, you too are moving at the longest arm's length from the cows and the new corn and the greedy ledgers of the struggling farmers. *You shot right through it! For the last five times, you shot right through 2,000 feet.* DON'T DO IT AGAIN.

Up is such a wide, drafty, and buoyless ocean, where only you are what marks the twains in the current. You are what makes the sky visible. And in the ardent, down-rushing twilight, you climb again the stairs of flight to where 2,000 feet is, with a teddy bear of safety tucked under your arm in the form of the instructor sitting just out of eyeshot, but breath-close in the cabin, a huff or sigh away. And this time you find the right corridor, but at the wrong speed, you feel your way in the clearest passages of light as if they were utterly dark and without guide walls, and trim wildly to catch your speed at just where you want it.

He is showing you how to rest your elbow on the arm-rest, so that only your wrist is operative and free to swivel. The arm and shoulder, with which you could print the wheel against the panel in your zeal, is limbless and cold against the door. Only two of your fingers are on the wheel, clinging to its folds like the pupae of a nearly extinct species gripping the glossy black bark of a hickory branch. Today he left the windscreen dirty, so you can use the Gettysburg of dead bugs as markers for steep turns. High over the practice area, you bank 45 degrees, and try to sweep round a complete circle, without diving for the ground, as the plane pleads, or climbing into a turning stall, because instinct tells you to grab the stick too hard against your chest. But grab it you must, for the plane wants nothing more, with its lift diminished, than to plunge for solid ground, and, in a turn as steep as those you inadvertently throw, horizon is a note scribbled in a solar opus, something like a seam on the sky over the panel. Your eyes flash to the dials, but that fast Brad is covering them with his hand. *No! Do it by sight.* You must find the right *picture* of sky, horizon, and plane.

The picture is a teakettle pouring into the cowl of the plane. The picture is an open angle whose legs are holding the gristle-colored sky. The picture is a fall down the steps when you are little enough to find the steps falling, not you. You check your altimeter anyway. You are climbing. Your nose was too high. You correct. You are diving. Your nose is too low. The moment you correct, you are through the correction. You smile.

The dials are only a trend, not an arrival. That is the real lesson. You are in a cabinful of instruments, and all they mark is *a sense of, a kind of* number. How can the air be specific? How can the air be a depot? The numbers tell you only what lane you were passing through before you veered right, or left or up or down, just enough to enter a side street or incline that was endless and steady, into the ground, into space, into the cardinal directions. It is a mode of motion, a tendency you pretend is exact. The way a society agrees that reality is such-and-such a set of perceptions about the world. It is only a tendency, an agreed-upon way of moving, given fixed points, as if there were something certain in the uncertain flux, these numbers, this perception of reality, these codes. To impose the rigid complexity of a plane on the surge and puff of the ether is an act of such mental desperation only humans would invent it. You laugh as you realize how complex we have made the thralldom of a moth, insect, or bird.

All day, you watched delicate shadows flit across the chaise on which you were sunbathing—spores, birds, insects casting their shadows as you cast your shadow in a plane, swattably small, on the Finger Lakes wine country far beneath you. *Far* is not like a journey or an era, but a short fall so close it stuns you with its clarity. Put your nose down into the book of the fields, and you are 1,900 feet lower than you were a thought ago, a shrug away from the cambered road you cannot land on, the potholes that will grab your wheels and leave you strutted like some canape on a toothpick as you wheel over and crash.

Brad is sending you back into the "close pattern" of the airport, whose tower you can see now through the sun diffracting off tiny scratches in the plexiglass that make it spray confetti at every turn. He is talking to other planes up for a spin on this rare clear evening in a town whose weather is only ever wet—hot wet or cold wet—and whose private pilots are taking advantage of the calm to gain time aloft. Before takeoff, you watched a U.S. Air jet taxi correctly down the taxiway toward takeoff point, and then a small plane, whizzing behind like a cleaner fish, swing onto the runway to *outtaxi* the jet. Out of what, impatience? some misbegotten ideas about wake? Impatience. Suddenly a small plane dived in for a landing, and crisis was like a hot treacle in the air: the taxiway full of jet, the runway full of prop, and another prop dead on collision course with the first. The taxiing prop swerved onto an off ramp, as the jet sped up to let it go by, as the landing prop landed without flying through as it should have, and the airport fainted into calm once again. But life after the tower closes in the coral reef of an airport sky is an object lesson in caution and nerve.

Brad is telling me to throttle down from 2,000 feet and glide in at 80 knots, and I am trying to, but already I have overshot the turn for the runway, and that fast, he grabs the wheel out of my hand, screeches a hard tight turn away and doubles back at a radical angle. Then he talks tensely, vehemently into the mike: *Turboprop on base leg, did you see the Cherokee Warrior ahead of you on landing approach?* I swivel round, see the plane that I'd missed sight of but Brad saw hot behind us, much faster, and on our glide path.

"Uh, roger, I got you in sight all right now," the turbo-prop pilot says with self-conscious-sounding nonchalance.

"*Now*," Brad says, as he banks us steeply into the landing. "Like hell he did." This is the third controversy in ten minutes, and it is wiser just to get off the sky than risk all the maypole twining and untwining around the airport on so surgically calm and arterial an evening in June. We are swaying like a delicate leaf widely across the runway, threading up its outer lines, and Brad is yelling that we cannot land like this, nose canted toward the bar at the U.S. Air terminal, wings doing a take-it-away-man sideslip, that we cannot land with the fuselage swiveled against the thrust of the aircraft, that we cannot land when we are drifting wide into the grass, lush now from all the rains but pitted with mammal warrens and uneven rolls and breaks. I try to fly the plane back on the center line, but at 10 feet off the ground that is madness, a dream, like searching for water or a haystack to land in when you fall from a plane at 5,000 feet. He is putting us back, nearer to center runway, all rudder, at least parallel, nose front, and we are floating even as we descend. *Keep flying, keep it flying*, he says, *don't let it land, keep it level.* But level is a state of grace in another universe, and I am climbing, I am diving, the stall warning buzzer screams a cappella, like something thrown up from the sunset, a banshee, a ghoul, and we land hard—*We just COLLIDED with the runway*, he says—hard enough to amaze me we are still on the right side of the ground. We shake a hundred ways to heaven, and veer off at the first taxiway, just as the turbo-prop behind us touches down, too early.

Later, in the hangar, rehashing the flight, we see the turboprop taxiing off the runway; it casts a wheel onto the grass as it takes a turn, then taxis straight into the hangar wall. Brad's mouth drops open wide enough to hold a walnut, and he curses. Another small plane lands, taxis in, and starts to circle the hangar in a strange, quiet chug. We have no idea why. "Lost his trail of bread crumbs?" I offer. Tonight it is all madness in the skies over Ithaca. A small plane pilot taxis in and asks where "check-in" is. Brad sends him the long way round to the office, which he knows perfectly well is empty. A grounds-man skulking around the hangar with a brunette I know isn't his wife casts me a tense greeting; it is so tentative and human I smile quickly to reassure him of my discretion, as Brad and I talk on. I am voicing my disquiet with the way in which he's teaching me, as rigorous skills to be mastered at yell-point. And he is making the case for cold hard safety. An hour later, we are workable partners, if not well-wed, and I repeat, "I was deeply angry with you."

"Everyone has a bad day. I'm no exception," he says. We leave it at that, a covert apology, and lighten the talk.

"How often should I be flying for maximum steady learning rate, Mr. Engineer?"

"Oh, about every three days or so, what you're doing."

He tickles the belly of an adding machine, to arrive at my fee.

"After half an hour in the air, I lose muscle concentration."

He nods. "That's right. It's about as long as a beginning student's good for."

"How long are you good for?" I ask, then realize what I've said.

"All night," he snaps back, and grins, averting his eyes.

By now the groundsmen are coming in to tend to evening chores, the last pilots are drifting in to tie down for the night, and Brad scribbles something in my logbook, a few numbers, a trend, nothing like a stage or an arrival, just a sense that I have been flying, just a note that for eight-tenths of an hour I have been moving with an air mass, with it but not of it, high above the planet.

3

"War 6122j/ In 2503.31/Out 2.31" the receipt reads in fiscal pidgin, as if it were the report of a broader skirmish. What was the controversy that could be clocked in tachometer numbers (the amount of propeller spin while you were in the air)? You were learning about drag, the force that holds you back from the level gift of speed, the war with the wind which you can only lose, though to varying degrees, and sometimes on purpose. The reason a car needs more power to go faster. The reason fish have evolved so streamlined and trim. Change the camber of the wing by putting flaps on, so that they cup the air as if to shield it from the flame of the sun, and the airplane's nose plunges up, your arm strains to force it down, and you lose altitude greedily. Drag has pitched you high toward a stall as you drop, and you learn to counteract it at once: power up, nose down. Drag is what will bring you in steep as a dream of falling in a nightmare, full flaps on, if you must land in a hurry, or over a tall tree or in a short field, bring you in on a down-slanted pillow of lift, safe but all-eyes at the runway beneath you.

That was the dream you had for the first month of flying, floating in steep, on a vapory clear day, your eyes fixed on the stitchery of the center line beneath you, peering into the descent you would soon become part of. That still moment of diving float, when the world stops in midair, time stops, and the central moment of any sport happens, you hang between the second-hand jumps, between tock and tick, too free-floating and beyond normal perception for language to capture. Words are like rudders in a plane; they veer your nose right and left from a point, usually unspoken but built into their etymology. It's no good saying the mind goes blank, because that is only a metaphor, implying an equally metaphorical counterpart. And it is not a subtraction. You are in a state in which those things simply do not occur. It's that shudder out of time that you woke with, in dream, every morning for a month. And now you realize, oddly, that you haven't had the dream for days. But you are living out the dream as you hang an edgeless moment over the runway, then nose up to level flight, and higher still to land.

Flying back over the practice area, you are snapped through commands again. Climb to a given altitude. Keep it at a given speed. Do not lose more than 40 feet. Change your altitude. Do not change your speed. Your back is a solid sheet of sweat, and you are puffing your cheeks, working the bellows of your will, without realizing it, occasionally crying out gently from the strain. *Want to take a break for a moment?* he suddenly says in a voice so normal it disarms you. You nod yes, and as he takes the controls, you press your hands flat against the ceiling and look up at its buff, perforated metal. Your mind is a table you sweep clear of sensation for a moment. Still jittery, you say, *Right, I'm ready,* and that fast he resumes. Flustered, you grab at the altimeter with your eyes, can see its hands sweeping round, but cannot make sense of them. Up or down? He is yelling at you, but you are freezing. A closet has opened in your mind, a closet stuffed with wiffle balls, all of which are pouring out at once. *This is how people freeze in emergencies,* you are thinking, *this is how the mind quits when salvation is still possible.* The instructor is yelling at you over and over to do something, do *something,* and you do, but so late that you already have dropped 150 feet, as low as a mine shaft had you been closer to the ground. He is flustering you on purpose, to judge the breadth and limits of your panic. Flying lessons are always training for the worst possible circumstances, always crisis maneuvers, not the level-headed, lonely wonder of cross-country flying, when you're looking for tasks to fill the stagnant hours.

Kept at red alert for half an hour or more, your mind stammers and lurches for some time after you've landed, thinks in a pidgin too scrambled to translate. People speak to you, and you answer, cheerfully, but like someone shell-shocked. You begin to slip into a verbal shorthand casual and arcane enough to be a linguistic anomaly, a dialect of flight. In Pittsburgh, it took you months to fathom local talk ("We're down at the Pitt Tavern drinking Iron and I'm wired, and when my lady starts rappin' to this dude, I just book; it was on her, you know?"),* and now you are mouthing the most extraordinary and unlikely things: "So we're climbing out at eighty, for close pattern, and we see this Bonanza doing chandelles downwind at two. . . ." You begin to read the weather reports differently; a 40 percent chance of showers means a 60 percent chance that it won't rain, and you can fly on schedule. Above all, you see the sky now as a place in which to be, and when the afternoon is glassy blue like the shallow waters over a Bahamian reef (or 80-octane aviation fuel), staying on the ground is punishment by default. Your ears pick up the sounds of breaking waves, which are planes, and the days you spend between flights you spend in a green waiting room, at the airport of your desire.

Returning from the downtown library, up Route 13, I see a light plane at about 1,000 feet in the distance, high-winged and slow. I can see the wing struts, the tricycle undercarriage, and my mood brightens. I press the gas pedal to the floor, hoping to get to the airport two miles down the road in time to see it land. In a moment, it has disappeared, turning base leg, I hope, as I cross the intersection of the airport road and Route 13, zooming through a green light. And there it is, a Cessna trainer, gliding in at about 70 mph. How floatingly skylocked it looks, wings trembling, though there is no wind to speak of, leveling off much too high. I laugh. It is so obvious from down below. The pilot corrects, sends the nose down again, levels off,

* "We're drinking Iron City beer [a local brew] at the Pitt Tavern, and I'm all keyed-up, and when my girl friend starts flirting with another guy, I leave fast; it was her choice/fault."

sends the nose down again, and lands shakily. By now, I am past the runway, past the nervous pilot who has no idea I was racing below to catch up with him exactly at touchdown, that my heart is buoyed up just by the sight of him. Will there ever come a time when flying doesn't thrill me instinctively, against my will almost? I am writing this at the moment when my wonder is a hot poker radiating from the fire in which it's plunged. Wonder is a kind of romance and, as Oscar Wilde rightly notes, the essence of romance is uncertainty. Worry about it, and there will be no present tense, no tense present in which the moment is a gift one presents to oneself, the act of living in the cloud-festooned sky as it develops.

Over the airport, the clouds tower enormous and thick, like the outgassing of some volcanoes on Titan or prehistoric Earth. I've gotten in the habit of driving past the airport runway threshold every time I go out, even if it's just to the post office, or in a different direction, in case a plane may be in the pattern or coming in to land. It's an odd, anonymous obsession, I suppose, driving at 45 mph on concrete, along a road in whose culverts thrive black-eyed Susans, wild heather, teasels, and daisies, despite the fumes from jets and light aircraft and clouds of wheel rubber. But I can't resist watching with stark-staring amazement that last moment when a tons-heavy plane, engine off, is all float and ongoing, cresting in on the vividly substantial air.

9

WHILE BRAD, AL (the chief mechanic), and I stand talking one morning, something extraordinary begins to happen at the threshold of runway 32. A green biplane, which moments before had taxied out, now *crosses* the runway and lines up parallel to it, but on the grass. Then it falls up into the air, at speed, in a tight climbing green arc, while its engine screams, loops once and lands right where it took off. Al laughs to see my eyebrows twisting, as I try to make sense of the winged roller coaster.

"What was that?" I ask.

"Poleskie," Brad says with a sneer.

"What's a *Poleskie*?" I ask. "A Polish aerobatic maneuver?"

"That's about right," Brad says, then adds, "You and he have a lot in common."

"Cut the mystery, gents. Who's Poleskie? . . . Wait a minute—there's a painter who lives around here named Poleskie, but . . ."

"That's him," Brad says. We watch as the biplane takes off again, trailing gristle-colored smoke, straight up into the hairpin dive and pinpoint landing. It's like watching a moth perform. "He's nuts," Brad says, and goes inside.

"How nuts?" I ask Al after Brad is out of earshot.

He shakes his head no. "He's a nice man, quiet. Flies well. An artist, like you." Two Channel 13 TV trucks drive onto the tarmac, as the biplane taxis back toward the hangar. "Come on, I'll introduce you to him," Al says sotto voce. "You may need a friend around here."

Engine roar, filling our ears with the same prop wash that sends dust and cinders and bits of grass across the macadam, acts as a polite buffer until we are right beside the plane, and the pilot shuts down the engine, as cameramen approach from the other side. Deeply suntanned from flying in the open cockpit, Poleskie is still unconsciously squinting as he greets us, hair blown about, looking ruggedly relaxed, as out of a flying movie—Gregory Peck in Indochina, flying to save the Asian missionary women who run an orphanage.

"Oh, yeh, you're the poet," Poleskie says, pleased, and stretches one hand out of the cockpit. "I heard you were learning to fly . . . Listen, we're going over to Mecklenburg to film some aerobatics. You're welcome to come along."

Behind him, a TV announcer waits like a piece of Swiss

chocolate, perfectly groomed and suited, so I accept hur-
riedly, reschedule my lesson for later that day, and set out
for Mecklenburg, a small town across Lake Cayuga.

By 1:00 P.M. I'm sitting with a small crowd alongside
Mecklenburg's grass airstrip. Overhead, Poleskie's green
Pitts Special biplane begins a penmanship lesson in sky-
writing: Morse code dots and dashes, connected looped
e's, a wide white infinity sign. All in Wedgwood white
on the pale blue sky. It is an obsessive writing; he returns
to dot i's and cross t's, and to bring an oval to its ultimate
conclusion, tail in mouth. Then Poleskie disappears from
view for a moment, perhaps only because he has turned
the plane slantwise and the eye must now find a double
razor blade on edge. But his engine's repertoire of grunts
and groans continues, loud, purposeful, and unintelligible,
like the voice of a Neanderthal trying to break through
to speech, a voice out of the blue. Now he is climbing
steeply on the tip of a white plume of smoke, an Aztec
feather. The white wake falters. "Running out of smoke,"
a cameraman says. It is always like that, puffing your
name at the blue until you run out of smoke. The cameramen are sighting on him with an unwieldy black box,
taking his azimuth. He circles the airport and begins a
tight, hard, rapid roll in an even circle around us, at an
even height, banking as he spins, rolling as he shallows
out, winding himself in the sheets of the air. Across the
yellow top wing are squiggles like those painted by prehistoric man in the Lascaux caves. Then he geysers straight
up, flip-flops, and flies a box entirely upside down. A thin,
overly groomed announcer, with a voice like white bread,
stands before the Channel 13 camera, talking into a hand-

held mike, as Poleskie dives at the runway and sweeps up behind him, climbing out only a few feet over his head, William Tell in a biplane. But the announcer sees none of this; he's too busy reciting his lines, eyeing the forever open eye of the camera, and judging the best angle to capture both him and the plane.

How disciplined they all are, the cameramen, the announcer, the chase pilot in a high-winged monoplane. It doesn't seem to them at all odd that there is a man doing maniacal things overhead, his hands, feet, and reflexes those of any expertly skilled worker, but his mind as unlike theirs as a jaguar's is a junebug's. He is their raw material, as they see it, the trigger for their ten-minute spiel on Six O'Clock News, not the experimentalist whose art is decomposition, not the pyrotechnical writer who rides his own firework. They are thinking only of how best to homogenize him: they will fit him into one of two categories—just an average guy, or ultrafreak. They are not wondering what would send a man into the sky to cough smoke over a pastel blue that can't be touched.

Finished now, he is flying back toward the Ithaca airport, just across the lake, on which sunlight staggers, leaving behind him a series of white ellipses, and a sky one remembers being carved by a gymnast whose wrists were smoke, whose heels were wings. "Look up into the terrible mirror of the sky," Wallace Stevens says in a sense-luscious poem, but do not enter the mirror and change the reflection. When world is everywhere exhaustingly plural, what would prompt a painter of landscape and figures to rush skyward, to change his sites, from inventing fully present artifacts to creating with paints designed to blow apart? Open up the canopy of the mind the width of the

Universe, and everything will fall into it; the bloodlines of category and seemliness begin to blur, as do object and process, and the mind swims in a rich miscellany of such imaginative nerve as powered Rabelais, Dylan Thomas, and others. But the reciprocal of that thought is that you can never sum it up, never reduce it, never choose the right contingency sample that will somehow *portray* the wild, booming, dark, iridescent madness of it, at times like sherbet, at times like radium. The only artwork ample enough to contain all of consciousness would be consciousness itself. Abandon the framed illusiveness, the pigments of defeat, all petty lusting after dimensionality through flatness, and rehearse the way even the tightest rigors break down. Scream into the sky, and leave behind the rigged austerity of clouds, fixing order on the blackness for the slimmest moment, a rival decomposition between the wakes of nothingness, as when a vivid memory fades, or in the tantrum of silence one becomes aware of the moment a fist pounding on one's door abruptly stops.

10

AFTER A MORNING OF those aerobatics, flying a Warrior sounds arthritic. But it's six-thirty now, dinnertime, and most of the local pilots are at home. That's the excuse I use when I fly just before the light fades, but actually there would be many fewer planes to avoid by radio or outswerve, if I flew during the day, when plane owners are at work in all the stressing professions that pay well enough to buy a small plane. The incoming airline and corporate jets are no problem; their civility in the air is so well practiced. It's the unruly pilots, grasshoppering around the local fields, who appear suddenly in front of you, pouring out of the sun like dandelion fluff, not knowing whether they are upwind or down. I tell myself

I fly at six-thirty because the airport is roomier, but the truth is how beautiful the sky is at that hour, a white haze with powdery smudges, and it is never more a fluid. Twilight is a pink moth whose wings tremble across the horizon, and, here and there, across the farmlands, a pond sparkles like rumpled gold. But mainly the air is dead calm, palpable and still. I can't resist just being up in it.

If you want to land, land; if you don't want to land, don't land; but don't do both at once, Brad says urgently, as we swoop down at the runway, too low. I add power and we level off, too high, floating evenly long down the center line. *To do nothing is also to act,* he adds, and that is the sucker punch, the last door of acquiescence slammed shut. Killing the power gently, we belly down to the runway at last, as I ease the nose upward barely enough. A rough, jumpy landing. *Right. Let's go,* he says abruptly, as if we were only at an intersection at which the light had changed. As if nothing special had taken place, no frantic climb out, no downwind leg spent creeping in toward the runway instead of staying parallel to it, no sunlight glittering off the lake in the distance like gold leaf beaten into an eagle's wing, no sun swollen red in the west, already stealing back the shadows from things like a shopkeeper taking in the wares at closing time, no final turn toward the airport too steep and too low, then time slowgaiting as we drift in for final approach, time broadening to a jungle river to be forded, time cringing to a hair. I remember Nobel physicist Hans Bethe gleefully describing the cosmic throb of a collapsing star: from a colossus 1,000 times as large as our sun to a ball the size of the earth—all in less than a second.

Right, let's go, Brad says so decisively. And round again

we fly, this time floating in too high at first, then dropping straight down, as I add power and we rear up, and drop back down again. I can hear the coarse ragged skidding of the wheels. *You're runway shy*, Brad says. *Do you want to land, or not? This isn't a coordination problem, it's a problem in your mind.* He's right, of course, which I know as soon as he says it. The mind makes its own convenient prisons. You seem to be willing, seem to be fully committed, when all the while there is a part of you that wants the opposite, that can't be fooled by your hand on the throttle. In a steep bank at 800 feet, you use the left rudder; then, frightened by peering straight into the ground, and knowing how dangerous that bank is at so low an altitude, you turn the wheel in the opposite direction. Not on purpose, not so quickly that you notice doing it. It just happens: the controls pull in opposite directions, because you don't really want to bank that steeply at all. "Turn or don't turn," Brad says, "but decide. To do both at once will get you killed!" Learn to let go, if letting go is what you want. If it isn't really what you want, then don't let go. But don't pretend to be doing one only to sabotage it with the other. Don't delude yourself, for instance, that you're living on the edge, a card-carrying voluptuary, a nonstop celebrant of fascinations and variety, a rapturous explorer of life—if what you want is the emotional safety net of a home, the reliable love of one man, your feet on the ground. To do nothing is also to act, because the forces of society work so hard to drag you down to the easiest common denominator. You know it's happening, you swear you won't let it happen, and it happens anyway. It's so acceptably easy for a woman not to strive too hard, not to be too adventure-crazed, not to take too many risks, not to enjoy sex with full candor, not to undress with her eyes every man she meets, not to live in a state of rampant amazement each day because she can't get over the shock of living—being here at all, in the midst of lichens and aromatic grasses and octopi and golden-shouldered parakeets. It isn't seemly for a woman to have that much zest. Nice girls aren't supposed to have an erotic relationship with the Universe. It's so much easier just to accept the package that has been arranged ahead of time; it is waiting for your arrival. It will put an end to all those cumbersome decisions. Why take the long way round? You'll get there eventually. Stray from the expected glide path, and women will resent you, men will be intimidated by you, parents will be mystified, then disappointed, society will be afraid to let you live on its moral outskirts, and, worst of all, you will be your own saboteur. You will not be able to fall in love with a skill or field of knowledge without falling in love with a man who represents it. You will not be able to stay self-reliantly single, without compulsively needing to be in a marriage or steady relationship. You will always be searching for a normalcy, a looked-afterness, a passivity, an agreed-upon good-girl acceptability that, in your heart, you despise. Despising it doesn't make you want it less. To do nothing is also to act. Everything you have done for the past heart-revving, terrifying, expensive, time-consuming, infuriating, curse-flinging, emotionally sapping month has led up to this moment when you are the only one in control of the airplane, bringing it in fast and low over the runway, partially unable, because—despite everything you have said, are saying, have learned, are swearing to—part of you really doesn't want to land.

JJ

FOR EXACTLY A LUNAR MONTH, I have been taking flying lessons, while the moon runs rings around my cells, and two chesty robins have been tending a nest at eye level in the evergreen at my backdoor. Since I was gone some of the spring, they assumed no one was home to bother them, and now they find me constantly to-ing and fro-ing only a foot away from their thinly protected brood. Occasionally, they make strafing runs at me when I lie on the chaise nearby, and I notice that as long as I am watching them, as long as they can see my eyes, they don't fly in with food for the babies. Only if I look away. On Saturday, as usual, I walked straight up to the nest to see how the three babies were doing and discovered that two had flown. The last one was perched on the edge of the nest, its mouth open in the avian semaphore for *feed me*. Both parents were nearby, in a tree and on a wire, alternately calling to the baby and flying close by the bush, to show it how. For nearly eight hours I watched them threaten, cajole, and try to lure the baby off the nest. Their conversations were continuous; soon, I could pick out the call of that specific baby and those specific parents from the other robins in the yard, and track them to each spot in which they arranged themselves to call. At times, the chick flapped onto a fork of evergreen needles, and once actually fell deep into the tree, only to fight its way back up to the nest again. Desperate, the parent birds started flying in with worms hanging from their beaks, nosing up into a stall just before they reached the bush, then flapping to stay aloft as they tempted the baby bird to lunge after them.

Close to sunset, exhausted and running out of ideas, one robin started flying straight into the nest, coming up behind the chick, standing on the nest for a moment, then gliding over the yard. *You put your legs here*, it was saying, *then you do this*. It was too close to my flight instruction. I started to laugh, then sobered up when I remembered the raccoon who prowls at eight every evening, and how he perched high in a tree, grabbing at birds. I myself had been flying only yesterday, though I wasn't designed to, and this creature, built for flight, whose hollow bones would save it if it only trusted them, was helpless. *Okay, enough of this*, I said to the yard at large, picked up my sun hat and went straight up to the nest, stared the baby robin in the face, nose to beak, and said, *If I can do it, you can goddamn well do it; let's go!* I scooped it into my hat, into which it promptly squirted, and carried it to the middle of the lawn. At once the sky filled with crows and jays and the parent robins vigilantly chasing them off. The shocked baby sat rigid as a lawn ornament. With gloved hands, I lifted up its wings, spread the soft still feathers an inch or so, until it hopped forward again, and this continued, absurdly, half way down the yard, until suddenly it didn't hop out of my hands but spread its wings and glided twenty feet to the base of a tree. Now what? In the open, it was an easy mark for predators. I lifted it into the air again, and this time it glided, flapped, and glided clear to the end of the yard and over a fence onto the limb of a well-protected sapling. After sunset, I could hear the separate calls of the chick and parent birds, checking, testing the night sounds for each other. If only a plane were that easy, I kept thinking. More moving parts, and they don't move as efficiently. Better not tell this to my flight instructor, I decided, that I spent part of the weekend teaching a baby bird how to fly. He would chide me for playing at flight instead of concentrating, for woolgathering instead of boning up, and probably make some crack about what a miserable groundling I was, when even a witless robin could fly.

"You take all the fun out of flying," I had said to him recently, after a particularly savage outburst at me, an outburst that ridiculed my spontaneous delight with the way you could make the wing tip hold a spot on the ground like a turning knife point.

"Fun?" he had sneered. "Fun? Flying isn't supposed to be fun. It's *dangerous.*" Then he went on to blister me up and down about how badly I was flying, how stupid I was, what a lousy memory I had, how daft, how thick I was. The more he screamed at me, the worse I flew, and the louder and more brutally he screamed, until finally I crumbled up against the window, crying, my spirit like a small, thin bone, broken; and I let him fly the plane back to the airport, deftly, as I knew I never could.

12

I don't want to fly anymore. No: I want to fly more than anything. But I can't fly unless I accept the instructor's loaded rifle toward me. It's too small a cabin in the sky for ballistics at close range; I can't take the rejection. All day I've felt my ribs pressing out through the meaty hovel of my chest. My heart is pounding so hard I can see it moving under my blouse like the *muscle* it is (Latin for the little mouse gladiators said ran under their flexed skin), and though I've studied the flying manual soberly, I can't ease my sense of dread.

Instead, I make an appointment with flying schools in two nearby towns. Most likely, their instructors will be less informed about the physics and engineering of planes, though they may be better teachers. But the drives will be terribly inconvenient. How shall I recover from not being able to zip over to the airport, only minutes away, watching the clouds overhead as I go, feeling the deliciousness of straddling two worlds like earth and sky in mere minutes? Or watching the Warrior churn overhead as I lie out in the sun, and know that I too will soon be up there, drifting over my own head. Last lesson, I left my sunglasses in the plane by mistake. I searched everywhere, and couldn't find them, but now I know that they have been in the sky for days without me. When I've looked up and the plane came between me and the sun, they were there, linking the earth with the sky through purple lenses.

With a burden of anxiety and regret I finally drive to the airport, but cannot face entering the shack. I'm so depressed I can barely walk, let alone feign emotional equilibrium, and certainly not fly. So, for half an hour, I sit moping on an old broken dinette-set chair at one end of the hangar, looking at the dust-caked miscellany of planes, in good repair mainly, but rather shabby. Such a variety of airfoils: it's like a glossy color page in a guide to types of moth. Piercing the wheels all along the bottom of one wall, sunlight decorates the cement floor with shimmery hex signs. I love the oily smell of the planes, and the puddles of spilt gas, and Poleskie's cheeky green Pitts Special biplane sitting snub-nosed in the very corner, as if it were a toy put away for the night. And, outside, the yellow wind sock blowing toward the northwest, its trunk straightening and dropping like a trumpeting elephant. And the dense forest all around the airport, the bird sanctuary overgrown by design and loud with birds (though the charter boss sends men out to shoot the starlings with shotguns). And most of all, I love the moment when the runway is all ahead of me, the horizon is so definite and far, as death is, always present; sometimes you can see it clearly, as now, and other times, when twilight settles, you lose it as sky and lake become a single figment. As the English nature poet John Clare did, you can walk all day, looking for the horizon, and never find it. But it is always there, absolute, a visual reminder. Life has a meridian. Life has an edge. You can fall off of it if you don't take care. You will fall off of it even if you do.

How can I fly? In my heart, I believe that were I to fly miraculously well today, and the instructor clambered out at the taxi ramp, saying, *Okay, take it round by your-self now*, I couldn't trust him to have my safety firmly in mind. I don't mean that he would consciously endanger me; no instructor would do that; but that subconsciously his desire to have me subtracted from his life is so great that I can't completely trust him. Six o'clock. Time for the lesson. Inside the office I find Melissa, a tall, cute blonde of unidentifiable age, who has tanned herself to the color of wood stain and is dressed in her usual flying outfit: a khaki-colored flame-retardant jumpsuit worn by pit crews at Formula One drag strips. Coming from a military family, she is learning to fly in the hope of being chosen by the Air Force as one of the ten women fit for pilot training each year. She smiles when she sees me and has been waiting to be a passenger during my lesson, an observer. Her lesson was earlier in the day, so this is double training for her, and the last thing I need in the emotional whirlwind I'm in is an audience. I find it hard to speak, move even; making conversation with her is an effort, spent mainly in revealing both my upset and my relief to hear that he's hard on her as well. But we are talking about a different degree and kind of response; I've flown jump seat during a lesson of hers, and his wrath is fixed exclusively on her flying judgment.

The screen door slams on its flimsy hinge as he arrives, and we all head for the tarmac, to sit on the plane wing for a few minutes, as he teaches us what things an engine needs to work: fuel, vapor, spark, and air. He is teaching me about engines so I'll understand what the controls I gyrate are really doing, so I'll be closer to the working mind of the airplane. Gas, I learn, ignites only as vapor, not as a standing liquid; hence the silliness of movies in which bandits shoot at a car tank and the car explodes. A lighted cigarette in a tank of gas won't set it aflame; which explains the boss's punchy, cowboy habit of ostentatiously checking the gas in each wing, with a cigarette lighted and dangling from his mouth.

"Wouldn't there be some fumes rising from the fuel that could ignite?" I ask, interested despite my funk.

"Absolutely," Brad says. "That's why we all stand back when he does it."

The throttle, I learn, does nothing but feed air to the engine, which makes possible larger or smaller combustions.

"You mean, when I'm closing in on the ground, goof suddenly, and add power fast to get the hell out of there before I crash, all I'm doing is adding air?" I ask incredulously. Suddenly I wonder all over again, with fresh insight, fresh marvel, But how does an airplane fly? And it's enough to rinse away my depression for a moment.

63

But not long enough; I feel like I'm carrying an andiron into the plane with me, as I gloomily take my place in the driver's seat.

Dutch rolls (swivels around a point), and exercises in stalling attitude, and speed control. Rough, undistinguished landings. As if in antidote to my upset, he is mild with me today, yelling very little, although his tone is all fractions. When the lesson is over, and I return to the taxiway and flip the switches off, depression is still intense. I will not be able to return, feeling such an object of his scorn. If I accept his knowledge absolute about flying, as I must to learn, how can I filter from that the message, belittling me, that rides with it? Why does it matter? Why don't I just ignore his attitude and take what he can teach me? Why does his civil acceptance have to be present for me to learn?

With a sky-blue pen, three stars on its barrel, I write out a check for the lesson, the last one I will pass over the counter into his hands.

When the others leave, before I leave for good, I say, "Brad, can we go someplace and talk for a couple of minutes?" He locks up the building, and I sit down in front of it, on the curb by my car, while he leans against the hood of his jeep van (coincidentally called a Cherokee).

"Would you mind sitting down, too?" I ask.

"Sorry, the teacher dies hard," he laughs, and sits down on the curb next to me, a yard away. And we begin a conversation that will last hours into the night. With a screw lying at curbside, I idly gouge a deep circle into the dirt and broken macadam, as I explain to him as best I can that I can no longer deal with his hatred of me. Failure yes, hatred no. His face is a study in angles and shadows. It is something I have invented, he says. I remind him of things said, how cruel and personal they were. He's shocked. How could I possibly think he felt that way when he spent so much time with me doing ground school, when he was paid so poorly to teach, when he gave me so much time and hard work during lessons? I uncover the bruises. Why, for instance, keep slapping me down whenever I say something colorful or funny or risqué or avid?

Before we know it, we are into a discussion of mentalities, the artist's versus the proper pilot's mind, which Brad is trying to "funnel" me into. I'm reminded of the Ernest Gann flying thrillers, in which real men held their liquor and real women held their altitude, and nothing in life was so precise as a real man's allegiance to precision, self-discipline, and blasé heroics. His men were all aura, unmoved by the soppiness or tears of womenfolk, untempted by ambiguity of any sort, romantic or esthetic, most alive when they were dominating something—a plane, themselves, other people. In the beginning, aviation attracted gypsies like Leonardo, the Wright Brothers, St. Exupéry, vivid minds drawn to a mystery that could be solved, drawn by beauty, wonder, and a kind of mental pout, in which prolonged ignorance is unendurable, and one yearns for that mountain peak from which the universe is finally scrutable. Their sane crazes mainly quarantined them to lives too strange to be fit for conventional human doings. They were the eccentrics, pestered by if's, who stared up into the sky, and said "possible."

Then aviation went through a military phase, out of which we still haven't fully evolved. The sky was no longer a mystery, but an invisible nation, territory to be tamed;

65

and planes were just machines, as the people who flew them should be: efficient, cool, stoic, strategic, regular guys, no namby-pambies, who imposed their will on lesser mortals, and knew that, even though the meek might inherit the earth, the strong would inherit the meek. We're coming out of that finally, now that a wider spectrum of people is attracted to flying, some of them quirky and eccentric as the original aerophiles. For them, mastery is a hollow reward, and discipline is not in itself an aphrodisiac. An instructor's boot-camp harassment won't change that kind of mental fantasia, just send it underground and make its custodian miserable. Terror teaching won't work on the decisively enraptured, or on anyone very well, except those who thrive on battle, but certainly not on the thin-skinned or sensitive; and there are professions in which sensitivity is built-in.

"You realize that you're trying to *funnel* a bouquet, an explosion?" I say.

"I can't have you flying the plane joking around, thinking how poetic the sky is," he argues. "Your attitude has to be more serious, more rigorous."

"Because I'll be a safer pilot? Because you can't be appreciative and rigorous at the same time? Because the skillful are only ever solemn? When you think about it, you know that what we're really talking about has nothing to do with absolutes, or safety, but just with different casts of mind, different ideas of beauty and decorum."

For him, an enthusiastic attitude is the wrong esthetic for flying; for me, it's the crucial one. To him, it seems extravagant and messy; to me, it's a refusal to let the universe be less than fully present in everything I do. As we talk, he begins to realize that by trying to funnel me into

66

the right attitude he's been attacking how I think, and that could only be construed as deeply personal, an attack on who I am. He was not aware of it. Most of all not aware that it could lead quickly to something like this, the two of us sitting like the shell-shocked after an air raid, with misunderstanding an unexploded bomb between us. For another hour we talk, until my depression is gone, in fatigue and reassurance, and we are comfortable again.

Orion is sparkling clear overhead, as I gouge a circle deeper and deeper into the macadam. The belt stars, Alnilam, Alnitak, and Mintaka—which I just can't think of as merely ϵ, ζ, and δ, as most astronomers do—are hard white sequins. Their names mean a sash of spheres and pearls, a girdle, the light-studded belt of a giant; although the Arabs used to call them collectively the Golden Nuts of Orion, and the curved dangle of white stars the Sword, swooping now toward Sirius like a glide path for a landing strip light years long. Finally, we stand up, brush the curb dust from our pants, and head home, in separate cars, by separate routes.

13

INTO THE OFFICE I BURST, primed with questions about wings and graphs and the airfoils of moths and the coefficient of lift. Brad is sitting in a faded gray T-shirt, looking a little hung over from the wedding party he went to the night before. Or so I assume; I read only his behavior, not his mind. Because of our talk the other night, I'm especially nervous, want to show my seriousness of intent. In the midst of asking questions, I somehow forget everything I've been learning so well for weeks, backslide on basic principles, and worst of all—as I discover only midconversation—am uttering all this nonsense with the boss in earshot. I thought he'd left early, as usual, but he's in his office a few yards away.

The flying I do is even worse than the ground school, thanks to a light wind and the instability of my overtrying. I mess up on ground-reference maneuvers repeatedly, relentlessly, while Brad yells a stream of disbelief, yells so long and so viciously that, at last, I give up control of the airplane, and lean my face against the plexiglass window, through which the ground is gently turning. All I want is to be out of the line of fire. "Shall we go back?" I mumble, suddenly hopeless. But he has heard me over the engine. "No," he says, "*don't* lose control of the plane! Try it *again*." Again I make the same mistakes, without understanding how to stop making them. Brad demonstrates the maneuver. But it's no use; when I take the controls, the plane is contrary and all over the sky. Brad is losing his temper again, in a biting rhetoric I find unendurable. *Why can't you do it? You know what you're supposed to do! You know you're not doing it! Why do you keep making the same mistake? Why don't you think for once! You're not thinking! Do it right this time, damn it!* Again I try, again misjudge it. He hurls some abuse at me and says in disgust, *Let's go back to the airport.* But my mind has stopped focusing for some time now, so much of it is trying only to escape, only to make the yelling stop, only to keep enough self-esteem to want to wake up each day.

The landings I do so badly that, even after we taxi back to the hangar and talk about them, we take to the runway again to shoot a few more. But every one is the same: I come in on approach fine and then, only yards off the ground, relinquish control of the plane. I should still be flying it down, not leveling off and just waiting for the ground to rise up at me. But worse than that were two particular mistakes, dangerous and unforgivable. Coming in too fast because I lost control of my airspeed, I rushed the throttle up full to the fire wall, which gained altitude but, unfortunately, also reared the nose up very close to stall, and at an angle extremely hard to fight down. Then I tried to climb out in that attitude, which was impossible. Brad seized the controls and made us stable again.

"Miserable landing," he says.

They are all miserable, miserable in ways complex and hopeless. At the last moment, it is so easy to abdicate control, to give life over to someone else, just to freeze your eyes and let the ground rise up. Why is that? Why is it so tempting to let go just at the moment it becomes most a question of finesse, but also most fixed, most settled? It's always easier to leave things as they are until you crash into the ground, than improvise hair by hair the way to glide in like a wing, thanks to the tiny increments of decision.

Post mortem lasts two hours. Dusk has fallen, and with it rain and poor visibility, in which no student pilot flies. A jaunty Texan arrives in a Mooney, a rakish sharp-featured little plane with a forward-slanting tail fin, which has become as much a cult object as a Seiko watch or a Farquar globe, and he arranges lodging for both the plane and his family. Brad yells at me for another half hour. Whatever happened to the truce we made the other night? There is no evidence of it today. I flew badly, and he's tough in rebuke. All it needs is for him to say, last thing, as I'm walking out the door, without lifting his eyes from the ledger even, "Listen, don't lose heart. I wasn't yelling at you personally, only at your performance. You'll do better next time." But nothing so sensitive comes. And I leave again in boiling defeat, nerves raw, feeling that I've been judged and found wanting. I've never flown so badly, nor has he ever been so brutal. At home, I pour a drink, sit down on the sofa, and start to cry. Nerves all ajumble, I lie awake most of the night, hurt, angry, and full of dread, and positive for the first time that I will never learn to fly, cannot learn, am only capable of failure. This is not necessarily destined to be a success story, as I know only too well, but a sortie into the lure of flight and what it teaches; it's entirely possible, despite my ardor, that I *can't* learn to fly, have no gift for it, will have to throw in the towel and somehow make peace with that disappointment. Not every goal is reachable after all, though some of us only discover that when we are swamped at midrapids, having set out with a confidence as buoyant as a bark canoe.

14

THE SKY IS A PALE BLUE LINEN. The sun has another yard of treetop to clear, so for the moment the yard is viewably lush. Freed from squint, the eyes can take in everything in a slow steady pan: the map of shadows on the sunlit lawn where a rabbit is eating a dandelion, stem first, flower as an afterthought. An anxious robin, startled from its nest two yards from me, is pacing around the patio with a stretched, Modigliani neck as it works up the courage to return to its brood. Some stewardesses, I recall, wear pins that have only one wing on them (unlike the pilots' two) to signal that they are only half-fledged. Gypsy-moth caterpillars are everywhere thickening up the weave of the grass, or creeping along the pool coping.

They're so fuzzy and toylike I must keep reminding my-self not to be too appreciative. Their crimes are visible from the air—vast brindled woodlands whose future has been sucked out.

The robin risks a fast steep flight into the nest at an angled stall, with a worm folded unevenly in its beak, and the new brood of baby birds, whose mouths are ever-open wedges, peep to be fed. Separate beads of water, caught on the yew needles from this morning's rain, are single colors in the sunlight—red, blue, and yellow—the same size, twinkle, and color of Arcturus, Sirius, and Capella through a telescope. Out of context, it's hard to tell the difference between a bead of water at noon and a ninth magnitude star. Or a piece of carbon evolving under stress to a canary diamond.

I've been reading Maxine Kumin's poised, keenly observant poems in *Our Ground Time Here Will Be Brief*, as I lie out in the 90 degree sun. *How can you be cold?* my companion, Paul, says of the steady sweeps of gooseflesh on my legs and arms. The chill Kumin speaks of is a weather in the cell, and my flesh hails when I read such beautiful lines about it. I suppose it's the delicate eulogy of defeat that makes these poems so moving. Lying in the sun, I have already accounted for the deaths of some things: ants and flies so tiny that when they land on any-thing wet they die—a damp soda can, a sweaty sun-lotioned arm. Death draws beings together against their will; there's no subtracting oneself from its service; it involves you anyway, atom by atom, until more of you is involved than not, enough of you to involve even that im-probable fever called *thought*. Example: a brown moth, fluttering around me for half an hour, has finally thrown itself against my sweaty leg and left enough of its brown dust to accomplish its doom.* Somewhere at half-flutter in the grass now, it will become a form of energy for some bird or frog. I want no part of such conversions; but I have no choice. I'm certainly not to blame; but wiping the brown powder from my leg—fractured ability to fly readable only as specks of brown dust—I feel as bad as if I were an accomplice. Innocence does not absolve you from anything. Morality has no place in Nature, only in Culture; but cultured beings amid Nature find it hard to draw the emotional line.

The Earth is not the same when you've looked at it from 3,000 feet. There are no intimate homely details of wild strawberries or clover or the stiff yellow combs on tiger-striped irises, or the smell of wild scallion after sunset, or the tipsy angles of a lawn chair leaning against a stucco wall, or looking into the white horn of a petunia. There is nothing as practical as learning to tell the sex of a garden hose, or how a siphon works. All the details are lost.

But the horizon is always with you, as you discover with some surprise. The higher you fly, the higher the horizon is. How could it not be on a round planet? There is no sense of falling off the Earth, only of Earth's being a shallow bowl in which you sit, contained, with the rest of its habitués, protected at whatever altitude. The horizon looks like a mountain range beyond which you can never go. You remember being five and listening to a red plastic record on a toy record player. You can still see the

* Probably a female, which are notoriously bad flyers, despite their namesake, the Gypsy Moth biplane, flown by famous women aviators.

yellow label on the record, and how raggedly it wore away at the spindle hole.

> "The bear went over the mountain,
> the bear went over the mountain,
> the bear went over the mountain
> to see what he could see.
>
> The other side of the mountain
> The other side of the mountain
> The other side of the mountain
> was all that he could see."

I have tried to be a modest watcher of the skies and of the daily mischief matter can get into, but there are some views of Creation only possible from certain perspectives. I've been thinking about balance, harmony if you like what the ancients called it, when all at once you grasp two incompatible ideas, and something else results, something that flies on nothing though it's heavier than air. Poetry does it all the time, using tongs of metaphor to drag an old idea into new light. Yesterday, for example, I was sitting in the departure lounge at Kennedy Airport watching jumbo jets lumber and pivot around the taxiways like mating mastodons. Cumbersome, inflexible, a slow-motion ballet. Imagine those tons-heavy hunks of grimy metal aloft on the sheer, soupy ebullience of air. It's not the same with our planet, 6 sextillion 588 quintillion short tons, hung on nothing, because the planet is falling, we are only ever falling (into the arms of the constellation Lyra), and it's just our good luck not to have to take that correction into account every time we stand upright or lean left or fly a plane. Still, there are days when I do put my hand down on the chair arm first as I sit down, just to make sure it hasn't swept by me at 1,000 mph while my back was turned.

15

Driving to the airport, I watch a plane skid through a 90 degree turn in the distance, loop twice, and grease across the sky. Then it roars into a hairpin climb, loops, and pulls out into a row of tight level rolls, screeches through another 90 degree turn, and does a fast diving run over the terminal, climbing out at the last moment into a series of tight spirals that continues the full length of the runway. Poleskie is out of his mind; his eyes must be marbles rolling around the cabin, his face must be flattened dough from the g's he's pulling, and why doesn't he black out?

Doubling back at speed, the plane pivots around one wing like a gyroscope, crosses and recrosses the sky in front of me, with turns sudden enough to rip its wings off. We think like that, losing wings as an insect might, but the wings would probably keep flying for a while; it's the rest of the plane that would drop. Anyway, this is definitely it: Poleskie has gone bonkers at last.

Near the U.S. Air terminal, my vision jumps, and I suddenly realize how duped I've been. It isn't a real plane at a distance, but a model remote-controlled plane closer in. The Flying Club (someone has removed the "F" from their hangar sign, so that it now reads "LYING CLUB, Gov. Approved") is having a "Flyin' breakfast," as they frequently do, to raise money, boost morale, and draw new members. So the skies will be full of high-winged Cessnas giving visitors brief rides, and homebuilt or re-stored planes from the area, and perhaps even an ultra-light or two. The air will be mobbed.

"It's too busy here today," Brad says, as he arrives in shorts, sipping at a can of root beer, rather than anything with caffeine. Small planes have no bathrooms (although, of course, men can improvise easier than women can). The cooler in the line shack has only fruit juices. *Breath-takingly humid all week*, the weather report said, and so far it's right, as both of our flushed, sweat-pouring faces show.

"We can do ground school," he says, "or we can go to Cortland."

Cortland? Of course, planes go places.

"Cortland!" I answer, and that sends us back in-doors for a sectional map of New York State, and my first lesson in navigation.

A sectional map is a little like a two-dimensional ver-sion of the paste-and-water maps children make for school.

The Adirondacks rise high and coffee-colored from the Sherwood-green forests and pale blue lakes. But there are also dark blue and magenta zones, delicately stippled, to show the limits of controlled airspace, unbroken magenta circles for terminal radar areas, unbroken blue lines for terminal control areas, magnetic compass roses in blue over some cities (such as Ithaca), and a stunning array of information about anything a pilot might conceivably use for navigation. The obvious: airports, in either blue (tower available) or magenta (no tower), showing which direction the runways run, how long they are, whether they're lighted or not, the elevation of the airfield, and what radio frequency is in use for both tower talk and, after hours, Unicom communication with other flyers in the area. Less obvious is the notion of site, not just the landforms, streams, lakes, and rivers, but forest towers, gravel pits, race tracks, glider areas, drag strips, saw mills (what does a saw mill look like from the air?), country clubs, ski areas, and, my favorite, twin drive-in theaters east of Utica, which look like two breasts, nipples pointing southeast and southwest. Power lines are also marked, and changes in elevation every seven miles or so. There is too much for any one eye gulp to capture, but such a palimpsest isn't meant for quick reference, unless, certain of a route or abysmally lost, one is hunting for special landmarks—an orchard or highway, perhaps, or something as large as the Hudson River. Otherwise, it's meant to be pored over, by someone less amazed than I to find towns called Sky Hook, Airy Acres, Jewett, Graphite, and Severance. I don't know what sort of people live in Zoar or Beckett or Canaan, but the itch to zoom over and nab a local for study, as aliens do in so many sci-fi stories, is mighty strong. Less than comforting is how many mistakes I find. Minor mistakes in radio frequency, spelling, services; three in less than five minutes' study is quite a lot, and you soon learn to use the map as what it is, a relic commemorating life as it was in Zoar only when the map was printed.

"As the crow flies" is no longer a tongue-in-cheek measure of the impossible we approximate by road. Our plane flies the birdways, and Cortland is only ten flight minutes away, up Route 13, which lies below us like a freshly ironed ribbon. The airport runway is 2,000 feet shorter than Ithaca's, so we enter the traffic pattern around it with a steep, slow descent in mind. With flaps on, the plane's nose tilts deep at the ground, and my hand is uneven and cold, an icepack on the stick, worrying it back and forth to an approximation of 70 knots, which I can't seem to find. 80 knots; 60 knots; too fast; dangerously slow. With a runway this short, you can't afford to float along it, but must land decisively right on the runway's threshold, or go round and try it again. There are no second chances if you land with half the brief runway behind you. My airspeed staggers all over the place, and I come in too fast, but, worst of all, at a ridiculous angle almost perpendicular to the center line. Touchdown, and we skid sideways on the wheels. I can hear the rubber screaming, as Brad curses in detail for the first time since I've known him. Quickly, he centers and straightens the nose. *Priorities, Diane! Land hard, land fast, drive it into the ground, but for God's sake don't land off the runway! Do you know how much damage we just did to the wheels? Do you know how fast we're landing? WHAT DO YOU THINK HAPPENS IF YOU SKID OFF THE RUN-*

WAY AT SEVENTY MILES AN HOUR? If you don't do anything else right, you've got to keep the nose parallel to the center line!

Climb out to 1,800 feet, a left turn back into the traffic pattern, my hand gripping the stick never to let go. When I hunt for 70 knots, leaning stiffly forward to scout the skies and runway, Brad puts a hand gently against my shoulder, says quietly, almost tenderly, *Sit back, relax. It's fun to fly, remember?* Breath leaves my mouth before I realize that I've sighed. I slump back into the seat, and my hand magically relaxes, finds the right airspeed. It's so easy, so easy. The runway rises below me, and with a paradoxical all-out effort I am concentrating only on being relaxed, not thinking about it, but releasing my body to the deepest calm I can imagine, and there is no problem with the stick. It doesn't bumble in my hand, it doesn't yank at my wrist, it moves by finger-light touch so delicate it doesn't seem to move at all. *Perfect approach,* Brad says. *Keep it coming down. Beautiful. Beautiful. Are you too high or too low?* Suddenly I see what I didn't see before, that I'm a little too high, and reach down for the flaps already on at two notches, still concentrating on the calm that will keep my hands steady. Then something goes wrong. The plane sinks a fast 50 feet, an elevator car dropping. Brad grabs control to steal us out of danger. I had done the exact opposite of what I meant to: took off the flaps I already had on instead of adding another notch. I had caged my mind on one thought—the airspeed, relaxing—and left no nomadic problem-solving part of it free to travel across the wide tundra of accident and improvisation. There is no need for Brad to scald me for such a mistake, so obvious and so stupid; I berate myself. He's remarkably quiet. *You're tired,* he says matter of factly, *let's go back to Ithaca.* He pushes me away from the instrument panel that I'm once again leaning stiffly against. *Sit back.* And deep into the seat. *Relax.* Everything falls into place, the controls, the direction. It was fun flying a new airport. Even if I did stall the plane on the taxiway and waggle across the center line every landing. I'd been able to relax a few moments at the wheel, able to savor the touchable sky again.

In the distant shimmer, a long white rectangle looks like white enamel, a sink or a ledge. The airport? My eyes fix it, try to read its contours. But, no, it is a building at the edge of the airport, whose runway jumps into focus dead in front of me. I *didn't* see it. The eyes are so stubborn about traveling around the landscape. They want to cling to something safe, not prowl. Late in the afternoon, the sky is still full of visiting aircraft. But I don't hear the voice of a woman in a Cessna, who flies every evening at twilight into our airport for touch-and-goes. I've come to recognize her careful, fastidious voice on the radio as she announces that she's a Cessna southbound from Cortland, and then states her position at each leg of the traffic rectangle, in a voice so fabricatedly calm, deliberate, unconfusing that I can almost see her neat clothing and hairdo, guess what she does for a living (high-skill, but essentially routine profession; a lawyer, perhaps, schoolteacher, or GP). Her clarity is almost an affectation, a self-definition. We are not the only creatures declaring their whereabouts in the sky. Below us, Sapsucker Woods is full of self-announcement, by frog, squirrel, chipmunk, and bird, each declaiming its bird- or frogness with sound. Bats in Peru have learned to hunt the plumpest frogs by the fullness of their croak. A vast song means death in Peruvian marshes, but not here, where haze is a mainstay of each evening, and scouting the skies for a small plane flying edge-on is like looking at Saturn when its ring plane is an exact tally line midplanet: invisible wide ribbons of snowball and rock.

A small low-winged training plane enters the airport traffic to my right, but I cannot tell whether it's coming toward us or going away from us. Even in daylight. *Where are you going?* Brad asks in disbelief as I turn the wrong direction for the traffic pattern, an invisible shoe box over the airport. *Which runway did you leave from?* he says acidly. I laugh to myself, knowing I've done this before in a car—turned off a highway into a gas station, and left in the wrong direction. A steep turn brings me back into the right pattern, and I land surprisingly well. Brad is appreciative, generous even, until the tower requests that I use the first taxiway, one rushing close to me, and, slamming brakes on, I skid around a corner. The wheels have had a rough afternoon, but I haven't. Brad has managed to straitjacket his temper today, even worked at relaxing me; it can only be a new strategy, one I've been pleading for. I feel my confidence climbing back again, and the most delicious excitement that makes me pace and twitch from rekindled thrill as we plan Tuesday's cross-country flight clear to Teterboro Airport.

16

By NIGHTFALL, the sky is a thick, dark curd; thunderstorms are predicted for early morning, with poor visibility all the way to Teterboro Airport, where I'm hoping to fly on my first cross-country. Six times in the night I wake, worrying about the weather, and then a seventh, when I give up being anxious, and lie awake thinking about weather in general.

Clouds are such strange apparitions to be staggering hugely across the sky, making weather mischief, foretelling calms, taken equally for granted by Innuit and Quechua. Look up into the blue awning, and they are almost always there, above the rain forests, above the mesas, above the store in Secaucus, New Jersey, called Hubcap

World, above the downed RAF tail gunner in World War II (who fell from his plane into deep snow and lived, to be discovered by a mystified German patrol), above the skies in which I fly, and sometimes below them. What an odd predicament for matter to get into. Jagged ice looking soft, tiny motes looming large, all of it sea-changing from fireball to thunderhead to diced ice-crystal smears iridescent as live fish. Variety is the pledge that matter makes to itself to try all the spindrift possibilities of a form. Take the idea of *ice crystal*, rotate it a thousand ways, and float it in the wide blue banner overhead.

Last February, milk bottles were exploding on doorsteps in England, the North Atlantic began to freeze, and, in Pittsburgh, subzero winds sounded like incoming jets, as they filled the streets with snow-djinns and mauled uncovered flesh. *Dangerously cold*, the weather people warned, *Don't go outside*. One evening I watched six cars, lobotomized by cold during the two-hour hockey match, hulk lifeless in the parking lot across the street from my apartment, then vanish from the landscape, whited over. Only the streets were visible: black macadam dashed with white lane dividers and zebra crossings, patterns we've all seen before, some in dreams: the timekeeping on antler bones of Cro-Magnon hunters, people into whose facemasks I've stared in museums, startled to think that we've not always been here, certainly not during the Riviera of the world when time was sweat and food the landscape. Only in the fiercest ice age did we thrive, inventing cold-defying arts like sewing and fire tending. We haven't always been here, but we've always been part of wintry unrest, always honed to iciest craft by ice. I keep trying to capture it, the quarry in my cells, the time before time was chronic, when fire was something living that could only be captured, art was a potion, and mulled by the harsh stratagems of winter, we drew ibex, fish, and flower on cave walls, to reconjure the spring, each hair luminously recalled, every fin exact, every gesture perfect.

At 7:30 A.M. Brad phones to say that thunderstorms all the way south have turned the sky into a pinball game. Even if we could fly, we wouldn't see any landmarks below; it would all be on instruments. Instead, I take U.S. Air into Kennedy, crabby and impatient, a backseat driver. A day later, he and his girl friend, Melissa, who have flown the training plane down for a jaunt, meet me in Manhattan, so I can fly back from Teterboro, a short cab ride across the Hudson River and one of the best kept secrets in New York. Not until you actually turn down the airport road is there a sign to tell you where the busy airport lies, packed with private jets and props, and charter planes available at close to standard carrier price, but at a less-congested, less-delay-ridden, easier-to-reach airport. In the front seat, next to the cab driver, Brad directs which routes to take through rush-hour traffic. He is all flying instructor.

"Turn right just after the tunnel, and follow that until you come to the junction with one and nine," he says in a tone that was lately saying *Right, take it up to three thousand feet and level off at a hundred and ten.* "Right, right, keep it coming RIGHT. . . ," he says to the driver, an old unflappable man wearing a peaked cap. "Keep it going right, I said, RIGHT." There are no controls for him to seize. In the backseat, Melissa and I are laughing as Brad instructs, revises, chides, and urges, clear out to Teterboro. Cowed, the driver does everything he's commanded to.

Nothing like the congested aerial Calcutta of Kennedy or La Guardia, Teterboro traffic is still thickly abuzz. A conga line of planes inches along the taxiway until we are only number six in line, creeping up close behind a twin-engine prop, to use some of its wash to cool down our overheating engine. Brad does all the radio, because the electronic jabber is relentless. The air traffic controller works constantly; his voice is the white glove of a traffic cop on a busy New York street corner, windmilling, sweeping, bringing things to a halt, then ushering a car through, halting again, and directing cross traffic.

"Uh, Cessna, wag your wings," the voice asks. We look to the sky downwind, where two planes are nose to rump at 1,000 feet. One of them wags its wings. "Right. Cessna, turn base, you're number two behind the Aztec. . . eight-seven Zulu, you're cleared to land. . . Number one, on six, what's your sign?"

Brad punches in the button on the mike. "Seven-one-four," he says.

"Warrior seven-one-four, taxi into position and hold," the tower continues, "Tomahawk five-niner Sierra, taxi to six. . . ."

We take to the runway, and wait, feet on the brakes, a long sprawl of concrete in front of us, whose middle a light, guppy-shaped airplane skitters across, from one taxiway to another. The Tomahawk. Fifteen minutes later, we are still waiting, thighs twitching from the strain of holding the brakes, as planes land and taxi across our runway. Oil temperature has risen steeply. Soon we'll have to turn the engine off, to cool down. The radio chat is relentless, full of inflection and reply, a numerical catechism. But the numbers change quickly, and even the air traffic controller forgets which plane is number one to take off. What stays constant is the rhythm, the inquiry and reply, the short clauses, the reverse synechdoche of words that stand for letters: Alpha, Bravo, Charlie, Delta, Echo, Foxtrot, Golf, Hotel, India, Juliett, Kilo, Mike, November, Oscar, Papa, Quebec, Romeo, Sierra, Tango, Uniform, Victory, Whiskey, X-Ray, Yankee, Zulu. It's a strange miscellany of words for piloting by. Alpha suggests the waves, electronic markers of mental calm. Echo, a form of location by submarine, porpoise, or bat. Juliett is spelled wrong, though Romeo is right. Delta, India, Uniform, Victory, Yankee, and Zula all smack of British and American imperialism. Foxtrot and Tango say more about when the list came into fashion than the others do. Golf is the puzzler. Why not Garnet, Goldfish, Garbanzo (too ethnic), Gargoyle, Galaxy, Galley, or Garbo? Golf seems such a yawn amid foxtrots and zulus. And isn't Sierra a confusing word when one is over the Sierra Mountains?

"Teterboro Tower, Focke-Wulf one-six-seven-five Quebec, five miles southeast, with X-Ray." Brad and I look at each other. There is a rebuilt German World War Two trainer in the sky somewhere over Queens, and "with X-Ray" means it has listened to a special channel of airport information, and thus knows the runway in use, weather conditions, and other ephemera the tower won't have to repeat. In the distant heat mirage, another three planes taxi across the runway on command from the tower. Two planes land, minutes apart. The cockpit temperature rises into the high eighties.

"Seven-one-four cleared for takeoff," we hear, casual as a wave through.

"Let's go!" Brad says, and I slide the throttle full open for takeoff, keeping low to the ground to pick up cooling-off speed before we climb out.

Rising high over the runway, we are higher still over nothing but housing developments. I've only ever seen them from above in Monopoly sets, or from the sound-stagelike cabin of a large airplane, and my pulse starts to run. What if we crash now; imagine the deaths. There is no place to land safely in an emergency, no field or empty road or forest. The best we could do is look for a wide truck going around 45, our stalling speed, and try to land right on top of it. A radio tower off to our left and close at eye level. Steer clear of it! For what seems the length of a movie, small houses set in even perpendicular rows pour underneath us, the same house side by side, street by street, mile by mile.

"Keep your eyes moving around the sky, for other planes," Brad cautions. "It's a busy airport. Keep looking. Check your speed, check your altitude, watch out for that radio tower, swing good and wide of it. Climb out at ninety knots, I said, to cool down. Ninety! Not eighty. You're acting like a trained monkey! Ninety!"

Then the city disappears into green felt, forest, and farmland, carpet and wood floor. We pull out the map, and my eyes stagger over it in small doses, then back to airspeed and altitude and heading, but already I've lost track of the site I found on the map, finding it again too slowly to get back to the instruments. Like separate stalks of broccoli, trees are bushy-topped, packed tight around the calm rigor of plowed fields, or sprawling inexhaustibly lush to eye's limit, more like a carpet of moss than a forest. Martin Heidegger saw in trees the slender daily link between earth and sky, carrying our eyes always from the mundane to the ethereal and back again. Green cathedrals. The limits of growth. That all changes when you view trees from above in summer, barkless, branchless, unaspiring, indecipherably maple, ash, or hickory, but only a deep-piled green or brown-green fur, as if the earth had a hide thick as a sheep's or wild pony's. The undulation amazes you, hills swelling close, touchably present, then plunging into what can only be a valley. A *valley*, you say to yourself, because it is the first time in your life you have ever fully understood it. If you were asked to define one, this is what you would remember, not a gouge in the land, but a falling away, a gentle pocket between two sloping hills or stiff, pluckable mountains.

"What's our next landmark?" Brad asks.

I consult the map. "A river."

"Where do rivers occur?"

"In valleys."

"Right. Where are you likely to find a valley?"

"How about over that mountain?" I point to a long, reclining figure in the distance.

"Sounds good. Let's look." The reclining figure becomes a rumple of clothes on a bed, flowing toward us, passing under us, and then a valley appears, through it a river snaking from one edge of vision to the other, disappearing behind hills, reemerging onto flatlands as bits of wire. How easy it would be to overlook. Northwest lies a large lake, one of many on the chart, all different sizes, but similar in shape, and I try to decide which one it is.

"If we passed over the transmission lines there, and the island in the river, when we were supposed to be north of it, and there's no city visible to the right, where this one on the map is supposed to be, except that we must be too far west, then is that lake this one to the west, or that one to the northwest, in which case I'm headed wrong to keep on the course we plotted." I fumble the map farther open until part of it blocks my view of the window. Brad pulls some of its accordioned folds back down again.

"Is that a question?" he says. "Look for landmarks. That watch tower, that bend in the river. What is the biggest landmark you've got between here and here?" He frames the latitudes with his hand. Then I see them, lozenges the color of Brownie uniforms, a mountain range. He points toward the sun, reddening up just now over an uneven horizon. Surely we'll have to climb, to breeze over the peaks. Wolfgang Langewische, the grand old man of flying technique, offers this simple rule of eye: if something appears to be moving closer to you, you'll miss it; if it's moving farther away from you, you'll hit it. They are moving closer, those pastilles on the horizon.

"How far away is it?" Brad asks.

"Thirty-five miles?"

He nods. "About that."

Moving fast in the opposite direction, thick puffy clouds pour overhead like time-lapse photography. We are somewhere between the moon and New York City, as the song goes, and if we are on course, Binghamton is just ahead, and a U-shaped section of the Susquehanna River, through which we should pass like an arrow through a valentine heart. Anyway, that's what the map shows. But the thing about a mountain is that it's a visual impasse, too. A range reveals only one valley at a time, unless you are high enough for a wide perspective. Low down, under 5,000 feet, there is a startling feel for how round the world is; one can never see past its gentle bulging. In the distance, a river spirals through the landscape, and I follow its meander through dense settlements to open field and back to settlements again. Floating over its middle, a saddle-shaped basin, I glance at the map, then down below, then at the map again.

That's it. The piece of world the chart maps. I am jumping all around, thunderstruck, trying to touch landscape with my eyes. Brad casts an indulgent glance back at Melissa. He imagines I'm thrilled to have identified the right landmark, to be on course, imagines I'm easily wowed again by a powder puff-like beauty, the blue symmetry of the river winding around the city.

But I am thinking about hydrogen, the simplest atom, consisting of nothing but a nucleus and one electron, or one positive charge and one negative, if you like, the positive 1,800 times as massive as the negative, the electron a mere insinuation of matter, its whereabouts iffy, somewhere within a radius of about 1.15 angstroms from the nucleus, a range scientists like to depict as shadow. Who can say where the electron really travels? You watch it the way you watch a cat run behind a slat fence. I am thinking about how hydrogen gave rise to everything in the Universe: limestone caves sweaty and cool in the summer, gladioli, ocelots, adenoids, jealousy, bombs, pulsars, star-nosed moles, pouting, the fetlock stars by which racehorses are frequently identified, video games, golden-shouldered parakeets, desire. Thinking about the cosmos before the Big Bang, when the Universe was all in one place and solid, a hard local object in an endless ether, which exploded into a prowling, radiant fog of hydrogen and helium, which collapsed into stars, some hot enough in their innards to forge the elements, and into planets, some cool enough to harbor life, in part because one of the elements produced was carbon, a molecular wild card. What a long, dicey, unlikely journey from that tough silky ball of hydrogen to this sac of chemicals that can contemplate itself, holding now a two-dimensional map in one hand, and translating it into the three-dimensional view far below, as we fly over the planet in a sheath of metal going 125 nautical miles per hour. No, I am not thinking of beauty, but of chance, though they have much in common, and how long ago, in some early chaos of the Universe, my atoms became possible, out of nothing more elaborate than hydrogen and motion. As I look from the flat map to the 3-D world below, there is too much to be said to say anything. If I change course to 104.5 degrees, the angle of bond of oxygen and hydrogen in a water molecule, we'll end up far east, in the Catskill Mountains somewhere, at altitudes higher than I've flown so far, with no airports to put down in when our gas gives out. Anyway, Melissa and Brad are tired, Ithaca is only a few minutes away, and there's no point in changing course so late, with the sun well down, and the light already fading.

17

From all accounts, this is the monster, the chief pilot with a jackboot for a voice and a temper that will fry you in your seat. Dark-haired, grinning, he leans against the wing, his arms folded, his body one long casual angle. Though it's only noon, his beard is already starting to grow in, and his cut-off blue jeans are frayed into thread haloes just above each knee. His eyes are hard brown lenses of aviator sunglasses—shaped like an insect's, you are thinking—and there is something at once inquisitional and nonchalant about his expression. Everyone has warned you about him: ex-student (*Bob screams like crazy*), new wife (*Bob's a sweet, quiet guy, but when he climbs into a plane he becomes a gestapo*), instructor (*If you think I*

94

have a temper, you ought to fly with our chief pilot; now
THAT'S *a temper*), secretary (*I'll just schedule you with
one of the "less aggressive" instructors*). But with Brad en
route to Atlanta for the weekend, if you wish to fly, it will
have to be with the man grinning in front of you, as he
speaks in a tone willing, ready, but also profoundly bored.
He has been here before, arms folded, the chord of the
wing pressing across the back of his waist, a student pilot
pacing nervously in front of him, has acted out this petty
drama so many times, it no longer challenges or ignites
him. A plane is landing, and then another, a high-winged
Cessna, a U.S. Air jet. Bob is the first instructor who
doesn't turn to watch, doesn't use it as instruction. The
clouds are rumpled and smeared overhead in a strange
combination against gunmetal blue; it's how a child would
make Christmas angels out of cotton, cardboard, and
paste. But he is not noticing the clouds or the hot, dusty
breeze, or any other significa of the day, or anything special
about what we are doing standing beside the accumulated
power of 150 horses three miles northwest of a long lake
pointing roughly toward the Bahamas. Brad is always
tense and meticulous about ground school and preflight,
all attention, all verbal run-up and mind-set. But Bob
checks only to see that there's gas and oil, then brushes
the air with one hand.

"Let's fly," he says.

"You've got quite a rep," I say, swinging into the left
seat.

He laughs. "I'm only aggressive when someone doesn't
work," he says, sliding his seat into position. "You've got
to experiment. Try something. If it doesn't work, try
something else. Try everything else. But keep experi-

menting, that's the only way you'll learn." He buckles the shoulder harness and relaxes into his seat, crosses his arms and waits, glances outside at the airport parking lot, into the hangar. I am keeping him from his newspaper or trimming his nails. By now the plane is turned on, the engine idling smoothly, and nothing remains but calling the tower. I can see the shadowy angle of his open eyes behind the glasses, as he watches a Bonanza taxi into a nearby bay.

"Shall I call the tower?" I ask.

"Do whatever you want to, I'm just along for the ride," he says, and I tell the tower who we are, and that we'd like to do touch and goes, then we taxi toward runway 14. The tower is all gab today, asking me to wait before I get to taxiway Charlie, so the U.S. Air jet can leave first, then clearing me to taxi up to runway 14 but adding something I can't quite decipher.

"What did he say?" I ask Bob.

Bob shrugs. "Ask him to repeat himself. That's what he's there for."

By now the jet has rushed down most of the runway, leaving a fine black residue in the air behind it. I hold the ridge of the microphone against my upper lip, press in the button with my thumb.

"Ithaca tower, twenty-two Juliett, say again please."

After a moment, the cockpit fills with voice: "Twenty-two Juliett, taxi to one-four, caution wake turbulence."

"Twenty-two Juliett," I reply, to signal my understanding, then ask Bob to make sure: "They're telling me to wait three minutes until the wake clears?"

"When does the wake begin?"

I think of boats flying through the water. "At takeoff."

"Right. You should have been watching for the moment of rotation, and then planning to take off before you reached that spot on the runway."

The tower calls again, nagging. Why aren't I busy taxiing, and do I plan a run-up, to test the engine, before takeoff? I do, press the heart-shaped mike against my mouth, and say so. After run-up, I request clearance for takeoff, but the tower tells me to wait exactly where I am because a Cessna is on final. A glance left: 300 feet from the runway threshold, a high-winged plane is gliding in slowly. I'd forgotten to look. When it lands, the tower tells me to *taxi into position and hold*, then, once I'm square on the numbers, clears me for takeoff. It seems like it's been a long conversation, all at the level of pouring pebbles.

"Ready?" I ask Bob.

He nods. "Wheel all the way back."

In seconds we are airborne, though only just, inches above the runway and climbing into a low stall, then falling to the runway again and taking off, touching down and taking off. Bob is laughing.

"Think of Yosemite Sam—pointing his six-guns down, shooting at the ground, and saying, 'Dance, pardn'r.' I want you to dance the controls, dance your feet, dance your hand on the wheel. Keep it all in motion until you see what works, keep it fluid."

Opposite the spot on the runway where I wish to land, I put on the fuel pump, and cut off my power entirely, then slow up to the proper airspeed for gliding in.

"Are you too high, too low, or just right?" he asks.

"Don't know yet. I'll wait a second to see."

"Okay. You get a little nervous, huh?"

97

"Why?" I ask, though the answer would be obvious if I could only see myself leaning stiffly forward in the seat, my mouth open and puffing gently, as if I could blow the plane down to earth like a soap bubble.

"Your hands are shaking like a machine gunner's." He sounds so calm.

I am too high. I put on one, then, two, then three notches of flaps. I am too low, reach for the throttle. His hand gets to mine first, pulling it away. As I remove the flaps I've only just put on, I am still too low, so I reach for the throttle again, and this time he doesn't stop me, as I add a spurt of power, enough to clear the row of red lights fringing the runway. *Why has he not been screaming?* I wonder, just as he begins to talk nonstop.

"Where are your feet? Rudders, rudders! Keep it coming down. Dance your feet. Dance your hand. Keep working on it. Don't give up. Keep working it down. Move your feet!"

Leveled off too high, the plane drops to the runway, then lifts off again; as I ram the nose down, it bounces up again, and I pull the nose up; it falls back down and reels up again.

"You're using a sledge hammer," Bob says. "Use a ball-peen instead." Finally the plane sticks to the runway, but only after a long roller coaster that's undoubtedly left the tower men cackling. "Listen," Bob says quietly, "you can't *force* a plane to land. It can only land itself. You can't land it. You have to permit it to dissipate its energy. That's the only way it can land."

I am thinking about poems, and how the best of them land, dissipating their energy completely only by the last line, how you cannot force them into a new attitude in the closing seconds, or try to sum up all the preceding commotion, or leave them hanging, level, at 6 feet off the ground, or plunge them toward a point they should have been drifting toward all along. And I am thinking of the balsa airplane I fly in the backyard, how it swoops and stalls and works its way down to a smooth landing, all by itself, through one excursion and crescendo after another.

"Take off." He sits back and folds his arms again.

We are sprinting down the runway, as I glide the wheel lightly in and out until it grabs hold, and we are up. My feet are dancing, too. How can this combined apoplectic seizure lift 2,000 pounds of metal into the air? It seems like such a twittery act, Obeah, not physics. *Voodoo*, an early plane was called; *Vampire*, another one; only later, in aviation's no-nonsense maturity, were planes named things like *Cruisemaster*, *Airtourer*, *Agtruck*, or *Traveller*, and the full run of Indian names, *Seneca*, *Apache*, *Cherokee*, etc., but nothing like the original names that tagged the hocus-pocus of flying, the inexplicable marvel behind even the cleanest-boned and most lucid explanation, the mystification that comes only after complete understanding, when you realize that there are questions left that have no inflection at the end, no words like "Why" or "How" or "What" to begin them, but a nuggety amazement at the *thatness* of life, that its forces and processes and forms should be what they are, even if you understand how they are. The rouge of mystery under the whiteface of explanation.

More takeoffs and landings, with Bob speaking only at the outer edges of a mistake, never en route to it, or preventatively. In between, he is cool, nonchalant as a paratrooper sitting on a stool at a drugstore counter. My feet are lazy when I land; I haven't figured out how to tap-dance and juggle at the same time. I am axing the runway to death, instead of letting the plane slice through the air at its own tempo. But he is not haranguing me. At least I am trying, ad lib, to land more smoothly than a dump truck pouring a crash of hot metal onto the runway. *Keep it dancing, keep it moving,* he urges as I come in to land again. And I'm reminded how different he and Brad are as instructors and in attitude, even though they're both obsessed with combating the same horror: passivity. Everything else is acceptable—error, bad judgment, ignorance, lack of skill—everything but passivity. Otherwise, life stops; life is motion. Otherwise chance gives way to fate. Lack of action is for zombies, for life's passengers, not for those the Universe doesn't scare into stupefaction. Their implicit attitude is clear: born astride the grave, as Beckett says, we move from one helpless state to another. But between them runs all the pant and lather of a life, spent mainly responsively and responsibly, or spent mainly in a long dulling wait—waiting to be told what to do, waiting to be buffeted by one breeze after another, waiting limply between two wakes.

The art of flying is overcoming the lure of passivity. It's that simple, but also that chilling. Some pilots, like Brad, see it as a form of agitation: get out and assassinate, form parties, take action. And some, like Bob, are more ontological: just keep attentive, keep moving. But the enemy is only ever the same, with its potion of inertia and mask of quiet. Quiet is a form of trauma; there is no real quiet on earth. But given the hurdy-gurdy raucous spell of life, inexplicable, explosive, jetting away at every angle, the idea of quiet is so riveting; it's tempting just to lie still and wait, mentally camouflaged, for the next command.

18

THE VOICE IS A BLUNT INSTRUMENT, and there are times when nothing is fuller than an absence. I sit calmly in the copilot's seat of Poleskie's Apache, floating at 9,000 feet, between two completely different layers of cloud, in the sky but out of the combat zone of my instruction. And the instrument IFR sky, over the clouds or in bad weather, is nothing like the experience of sky a visual VFR pilot has, when one's eyes are tethered to the ground, and every glimpse of the clouds and wide blue canopy overhead has a ballast of farmlands, mountains, and rivers. Above a thick cloud deck, but below an even smear of high cirrus clouds, there is a corridor of teal-blue, an unsky tint which one can only see as a distant accumulation of color, not as something we are part of from the point of view of another plane looking at us. The thick clouds below have geography, as the land beneath them does, and you can see the forming systems broken by occasional blue sink holes, which look oddly Caribbean. The horizon is uncertain, a tinge between the clouds, but there is a definite sense of where up is, in the frieze of cloud nebuli overhead, not in the thick, churning *weather* below us.

Now I can understand the Samuel Barber program music, "Night Flight," based on the novel by St. Exupéry, in which a pilot's loneliness is relieved by a single sound, the radio beam, his numerical name echoing across the sky to human eyes. A winking green light on our panel says it's working. *Squawk Ident*, an air traffic controller will say as we enter his airspace, and when we press the small flashing green square, he will know things are as they should be for tracking us. The squeaky radio blips are constant, too, as if a porpoise were loose in the cabin. But mainly there is noise, the squawking of a demented mynah bird, the sound of musclemen ripping doors off their hinges. Not just the static, but the voices of pilots and tower men and women, all jagged and loud enough to scour out your ears. Turn the radio down, and their message won't be clear from the background of shaking glass. There is a vocal path through the overgrowth, but finding it means chopping away insignifica with one's mind, searching for what is landscape, what figure, what figures seem to be moving on which roads. Knowing what to expect is the secret. Poet Howard Nemerov confessed once that his early RAF days were spent "just beginning to understand what they'll say, certainly not what they've said," a good warm-up for the tougher deciphering of the muses that would follow.

On his lap, Poleskie keeps a small tablet, and a ballpoint pen tucked under one thigh. As each checkpoint gives him numbers, he jots them down, as if he were taking orders in a small Italian restaurant in Manhattan, so he can repeat them to the speaker before entering them into his instruments. The voiced numbers are his lifeline when the earth is whited over, and in some ways it makes the job of flying much easier than for a VFR pilot, who has charts to consult every few miles, and is flying low enough that he may run straight into a fog or storm he can't climb over. Instrument flying means being led into an airport along invisible routes by an Ariadne in a tower at an unseeable airport. *Vectors*, they're called. In a fog outside Green Bay, Wisconsin, we follow a vector down through the clouds. Poleskie sets the *slave* on his autopilot, a tiny claw that fastens onto a heading, and the plane turns itself; the tower changes our vector, Poleskie changes the claw, and thus we steal through the soup toward a runway which appears like a dream from the blind reality of the clouds.

From time to time, he points to my altimeter, meaning, *You take over. All you've got to do is keep the right altitude*, as he studies an accordioned IFR map on his lap. Holding the control wheel by thumb and pinkie, as if it were a stein of beer, I struggle to keep us exactly at 9,000 feet; the controls are ultrasensitive, the weather's rough, and it's a tough job. But what's astounding is how minutely attuned he is to changes in pitch. If, by accident, I begin a trend that will result in a change of as little as 20 feet, his hand automatically flashes out from the charts, makes a small precise adjustment that brings us level again, and disappears without his eyes ever looking up. Twice I do it, just for fun, to watch his instincts at work. It's only much later that I learn how I've been over-exerting myself, and that a well-trimmed plane requires only a tap one way or the other, the moment a trend begins, to bring it back into line. A point of honor with him is being exactly where he says he'll be, at 9,000 feet, not 9,010 or 8,990, so those who follow him on radar will see him as an unwavering line across his flight path, meticulously in control.

For one week in August, in a sleepy, many-siloed city in Wisconsin, the skies swarm with prehistoric shapes. Over three quarters of a million people from as far away as Australia, Singapore, and Vietnam pour into motels called Budgetel and Pioneer, take rooms in modest houses edging the exhibition grounds, or camp out in sleeping bags under homebuilt planes, whose wings make sundial shadows on the grass. The pastures, normally full of Wisconsin's economy, are mobbed by thousands of planes, each one tied down as if it would otherwise escape. The air is constantly abuzz, aroar, agrind, or awhistle. Odd configurations float across it: flying hex signs, a pair of scissors, bat wings with a lawn chair underneath, a skew-ered egg, stalactites between two tongue depressors, a rigid white swan dive. For miles along the highways, cars are pulling off the road and people standing beside the cornfields, mouths agape, staring at the beautiful mad-ness in the skies over Oshkosh.

The annual Experimental Aircraft Association (EAA) Fly-In Convention and Sport Aviation Exhibition began as a way to organize and celebrate the forms of flight outside the FAA's jurisdiction—aerobatic flying, antique planes, warplane replicas, ultralights, racing planes, and homebuilt planes of varying levels of sophistication and imagination. Now it's the largest aviation event in the world, a crossroads for inventors, a soapbox for the EAA (whose concerns are safety, legislation, and education), and a medieval fair for visitors, who find brightly striped tents for exhibition and refreshments, talks by NASA astronauts, tethered blimps and balloons, nonstop air shows, planes being raffled, award ceremonies, rides in a hulking green-black antique trimotor, vendors selling mugs, T-shirts, and full-size executive jets, evening concerts by John Denver and other performers obsessed with flying, and a gorgeous miscellany of thousands upon thousands of shiny, groomed planes. There are also thirty forums, with technical papers delivered by researchers from NASA's Langley, Ames, and Lewis Aeronautics Centers, and hundreds of educational workshops and exhibits.

But mainly there is the atmosphere of mass obsession and undiluted wonder. There are none of the many wars now at full spate around the world. There is no inflation or crime rate or existential despair. There is only flight, one of the oldest puzzles, equally amazing to the Laplander and the Bantu, the constantly astounding thralldom of a bird, moth, or aphid. What's extraordinary about the Oshkosh Fly-In is the innocent relish at the heart of it, a free-floating thrill identical in the children present, who are being dragged out of cockpits into which they've climbed when no one was looking, as in seasoned pilots who, despite their thousands of hours aloft, still make *buzz-buzz, putt-putt* sounds when they talk about some plane's performance. It draws overweight, varicose couples with folding chairs, carrying plastic tote bags, handed out by the Air Force, that say "We Guard America's Skies." It draws ponytailed, bare-chested, heavily jewelried young men in a time warp from the Sixties. It draws voluptuous, and corn-fed, entrants in the Miss and Mrs. EAA beauty pageant. It draws the self-reliant backyard builders of small planes (from scratch), who are walking around with tool kits, hoping to be rallied to action. It draws film-makers and dentists and owners of used-car lots. And, of course, it draws the inventors of planes, corporate or out-in-the-garage variety, who fly their sometimes improbable-looking crafts to the grounds and put on displays in the daily airshows at 4:00 P.M.

There are no jugglers and clowns, but there are wing walkers, and formation flyers and daredevilry. The serious international aerobatic competitions take place in Fond du Lac (fifteen miles away) in the week after the Osh-kosh Fly-In, and some of the aerobatic pilots fly (for free) at Oshkosh; most of them are strolling around and gawking like everyone else.

None are gawking more than we four; my companion, Paul, and I, and Jeanne and Steve Poleskie, who invited us to fly out with them in their Apache.

"Do you miss your Pitts, dear?" I hear Jeanne say to her husband, who is watching a Pitts Special biplane do snap rolls, hammerhead dives, and other maneuvers, while trailing smoke. Poleskie shakes his head, without shifting his eyes from the airplane, but his right hand is moving unconsciously through an eight-point hesitation roll.

There are two classes of spectators, those with and those

without a line pass, which allows you to walk right up to all the planes and inspect the workmanship or eye the controls. Anyone involved in aviation, and therefore alert to caution and courtesy around planes, can get one; even a student pilot's third-class medical card (required to begin lessons) will do, though, of course, it only states the bearer's good intention, not accomplishment. Other visitors must stand back a bit farther to admire the big black glossy Stinson Reliant, with a bat's face and high hunched wings, or the cheeky little lemon-yellow Fly Baby, or the row of candy-apple red aerobatic biplanes from Arabia, the Royal Jordanian Falcons, or the pink War-Hawk with a toothy grin painted on and a bright red nose. One bullet-shaped homebuilt with an engine at the rear, the Vari-Eze, is so popular that whole fields are packed with them. Resting nose down on the grass, to make boarding easier, they look like rows of elephants kneeling for their riders.

The Fly-In lasts a week, and many of the planes that left early are still "present" at the week's end: on the muddy, much-walked-over ground are the grassy silhouettes of planes, now winging back home, that stood long enough to protect a T-shaped piece of pasture from mower, thunderstorm, and feet. These grassy ghost planes are the softest spots to sit to watch the air show, and it makes an odd apparition of real passengers on vanished ships.

Planes take off from the 6,700 foot runway at one-minute intervals all day long. It's a little like Obeah: in a far field, a small jet or a World War Two Mustang or a Wizard-of-Oz Tin-man-looking Trojan gets religion and taxis down to the access road paralleling the runway, just as a sailplane or Gypsy Moth may be taking off. It's a bustle of fascinating planes for the onlooker, but a nightmare for the air traffic controllers, who work in overlapping shifts, at what for eight days is the world's busiest airport, four times busier than Chicago's O'Hare Field. So many private planes pour in that at most times two must land simultaneously, one at the threshold and one halfway down a strip used for that purpose. And that while the air-show planes take off and land on the main runway. All of the planes must somehow be shepherded clear of one another, which is why there are special, neon-yellow pages, in one of aviation's guides to airports, with nothing but elaborate instructions on how to approach Oshkosh by small plane during the Fly-In week.

Bizarre accidents and fatalities do sometimes occur. In 1982, a woman's feet were amputated by the propeller of a runaway plane, left unattended with its engine going, which taxied into the tent she was sleeping in. A light plane crashed into the rear window of a moving car in the 1700s block of a suburban neighborhood. Two planes locked wings as they strolled side by side in the air, plunging to the ground and killing both pilots. An ultralight ditched in someone's backyard when it lost its bearings in the fog. And various homebuilts made emergency landings in cornfields and along roadways, disoriented by the thick, curdlike clouds that soaked the exhibition for a day or two, made six-inch mud ruts, and sent some queasy flyers packing on the first good flying day. These accidents caused a stir, but they didn't drain the zest from the festivities. Controlled danger is part of flying's lure, and the mounting number of people and planes present was so great that most officials were relieved at how few incidents there were.

For sheer spectacle, few things in life are as dazzling as the daily afternoon air show at Oshkosh. It begins with two women, known as the Silken Chutes, parachuting from on high, spewing red smoke, while three biplanes wrap ever-widening smoke spirals around them clear down to the ground. An American flag waves from each chute; the National Anthem plays loudly. Updated, this is nonetheless echt Americana, the way all barnstormers began their programs in the 1920s and 1930s (Lindbergh himself began as a wing walker). What follows is a mass attack of World War Two "Warbirds," as an announcer recalls each plane's history, construction, and design.

Then the flyers who work the air-show circuit, like rodeo cowboys, do their cloud dancing, one by one, mainly in biplanes. A snap roll, a square loop, an infinity sign. A tail slide, in which the plane climbs straight up, cuts its engine, and falls spinning into its own smoke. The thunderstorms have passed, and now the skywriters leave their own weather system. Silent flight: the announcer demands quiet from the audience and waiting planes, then a biplane does gull-like maneuvers with its engine off; the only sound is a gentle, eerie whinnying of air through struts and over wings. Next a trio of Christen Eagles does hair-raising formation stunts, leaving smoke halos at the top of each parabola or hammerhead dive. An eighteen-year-old engineering student from Stanford wows the crowd with precision moves, like climbing on edge, in a famous biplane his father designed. A husband and wife perform a wing-walking act; his T-shirt says "The Wing," hers "The Walker."

People with camera lenses as long as their forearms, and babies holding inflatable planes too pudgy to fly, all gape stiff-necked for three hours, though by late afternoon some get a little blasé. "Not another wing walker," one young woman sighs. No one would dream of leaving before the finale's two dazzlers. First, a one-of-a-kind NASA swing-wing jet, that looks like a letter opener, unseals the air, zip, zip, over the grounds. Finally, the performance everyone's been waiting for: Bob Hoover, flying a twin-engine Shrike Commander, a twelve-seat plane designed to carry executives. The best aerobatic pilot the United States produced in the Sixties, he starts high above the runway and treats the Shrike like an aerobatic sailplane, cutting one engine, then both, doing rolls and spins and stalls, and slow beautiful loops, all on nothing but momentum and nerve. Every movement he turns into a graceful gesture, a geisha's hand, demonstrating the laws of flight and aerodynamics. Calculating exactly how much momentum he will need to land, roll down the runway, taxi off the ramp, pivot, and stop, he does a series of breathtaking loops close to the ground, and winds up on the exact spot beside the runway where he began. The audience exhales in unison. Twelve-seat planes aren't supposed to be able to do that.

The last vision one has driving away from the Fly-In, the one that reappears in dreams, is of a swarm of forty brightly painted ultralights circling over a field of corn. There should be a buffalo carcass underneath. Instead there is a long conga line of cars, with exhausted passengers craning out of every window, still amazed, and staring straight into the setting sun for a last eyeful.

19

CALM AS A PITCHER from which the milk has been poured, Brad has been trying to teach me to land, for three lessons straight, with little progress. It seems always to be on my mind, this inability to connect with the ground in the right way, descending gently, gradually pulling the nose up into a polite stall a foot off the ground, just as the plane has spent most of its momentum, deftly parallel to or on the center line, back wheels touching first, front wheel touching after. It sounds so easy, but seems impossible. Often I wake too early in the morning, when the blackness I greet open-eyed is identical to the blackness of my eyes closed, and realize that in my sleep I have been doing landings, that I am becoming obsessed, that my psyche is hooked day and night now. I've begun hunting myself.

"I wish I knew how to land," I lamented one day, when Poleskie and I were shmoozing outside the Cayugair office.

"Everyone can't do everything," he had replied so matter-of-factly it startled me, and for a while that simple truth carried me through dozens of snafu landings. He was perfectly right, everyone *can't* do everything, or at least not the same things, and the main point about landing is getting the plane on the ground, somehow, anyhow, just as long as you can walk away from it. There's no contest, and there ought not to be any rush.

But we are all waiting, hoping, that each lesson I will solo. On Monday, my landings are good enough, not great, not smooth, not in the right attitude of back wheels touching first, but *acceptable*; I can get the plane down. My control of landing straight down the runway is terrible, though; I'm forever at an angle to the center line, diverging from it at 60 mph when I land, which will one day rush me off the macadam and onto the grass, possibly spinning round or toppling over, possibly igniting the fuel in each wing. Tough as it is to correct, landing crooked is *not* acceptable. On Wednesday, I land better, and my center line control is getting a shade better, too; we make landing after landing after landing. The tower starts clearing me to land before I ask for it, they're so used to seeing me crank around to the left. Coming round one more time, I misjudge my altitude and get so low so fast that unless I do something I'll land ten feet in front of the runway, in the grass and lights. Instinctively, I pull up the nose. And that is the end of soloing at least during this lesson, because I've made a classic mistake, a student pilot's mistake, guaranteed to get me killed. I've tried to stretch a glide longer than it can be stretched, according to the laws of physics. It is not negotiable. By pulling the nose up (the mind says: get back into the sky!), I added drag, which made me drop that much faster into the grass I wanted to avoid. When Brad yells, I do come in with power, but I have waited too long to decide to do it, and he can't solo me when I make mistakes like that. Which he says without thinking, because it's on his mind, because it's on my mind, because it's on the mind of the boss who, when I phoned up for a lesson on a day both instructors were away, said in only half-jest "You'll have to go up solo," because it's on the mind of the line men, one of whom, seeing me sweat-drenched and exhausted after an hour of touch-and-goes, said, "Another dozen workouts like that one, and you'll be off on your own," because it's on the minds of the tower men who have begun to give me precedence over other planes in the pattern, sometimes clearing me to land before I ask, always ushering me in to land ahead of approaching Cessnas or jets waiting to take off. I know it may be my second-guessing what sorts of things they will say, and my improving ear for radio-jabber, but they seem to be speaking more slowly to me, more obligingly. I am on their minds.

They have seen me go round and round on the combination ferris wheel and merry-go-round they conduct, and know I should already be up there by myself. They see me level off too high, barrel in too fast, miss my landing, and fly through, take off in recovered falls; and, if at first they may have laughed at my clumsiness, by now they are commiserating, urging me through my mishaps, cheering silently my small victories. In their lighthouse on the outer bank of the airfield, they are watching everything I do. They've heard my voice, at first stumbling, uncertain—and so quiet they had to ask me to repeat myself or, as they discreetly put it, "Please confirm that your radio is working; we're having a little trouble hearing you"—grow surer and bolder, relaxed enough now even to add courtesy. "Twenty-two J, what did you say?" the tower man asked the other day, because I had added a piece of information he didn't expect. I had thanked him. They are watching in their elevated eyes, with their binoculars that track me across the sky, and they are anxious, too. After all, they will see Brad climb out of the plane to solo me long before I call them. By now, after so much struggling, I am an underdog, and when at last I do solo, they will watch me closely, they will spirit me round with their eyes, they will reassure me with their voice, they will not breathe easily until I am safely down. In the beginning, I had made jokes about why there were three men in the tower at such a small airport—"One to hold the mike, one to push the button, one to speak"— but the truth is two of the men are trainees, as I am, and after watching my snail's progress, they must be feeling compassionate.

It's no big deal, of course. After solo, you still work with an instructor, even though you're allowed to go up and practice on your own. When it happens doesn't matter. But most people solo at around ten hours; some after four hours even. By twenty hours, I start to get twitchy about it. We all thought I would solo after each of the last few lessons, and now the tension is high, though no one talks about it outright. Today we begin by doing slow-flight maneuvers, to practice the right attitude for landing, then hurry back to the airstrip to do touch-and-goes. A half-dozen of them, better and better. Two of them in a row are good enough to solo on. As we go round one more time—climb out, turn left, downwind, turn left—everything goes according to plan, then rapidly falls apart. I forget to put on my flaps, which I need to insure landing at a slow, manageable airspeed. Then, finding myself too low, I decide not to put them on at all, but just land long and fast. Which is what happens; floating forever down the runway, I land at 80 instead of 50, just barely in control. Brad is exasperated. He says he can't solo me when I make a mistake in judgment like that. I let the plane determine what I had to do, instead of dominating it, gaining altitude, putting flaps on, and coming in the right way, if belatedly.

"What I'm looking for is *consistency*," he says in a voice that sounds genuinely sorry. "You've got to persuade me that you can land safely *every* time. Don't improvise; you're not ready to improvise yet. Your landings don't have to be great, but they have *got to be consistent.*" Sweat is running along his neck, as it is along mine. His face is a study in futility, which he tries to brighten as he reassures me about the things I did right. But we've both got the will-this-be-the-solo-day jitters; it's on everyone's mind, and I've let us all down. Especially, perhaps, the men in the tower, to whom I say sadly, "That's it for today," as I taxi off the runway and head back to the Cayugair office where, writing up the bill, Brad will once again have to fill in the space marked "dual."

At home I lie out in the sun, despondent, all afternoon, beside a pool whose water is the color of the sky and in which the sky is reflected: clouds, planes, birds, jet contrails, all trapped within the swaying lozenges of light, a symmetry of sunlight and wave mechanics. The day is flawless, 74 degrees and unending blue. But my gloom deepens every time I hear a light plane purr overhead.

20

THIS WILL BE THE DAY. Knowing that, I wake three times in the night, rehearse a few landings, then fall asleep again, waking up at last at seven-thirty, wishing the day would just get on with itself so eleven-thirty will arrive and I can get the damn thing over with. Butterflies all morning. My hands make nervous forays to nonexistent wisps of hair, or settle slipped sunglasses back into place, though I'm not wearing any. I take special care to eat protein, carbohydrates, and sugar two hours before flight time. Anything that may work the oracle. I just want to get soloing over with; the strain is terrible.

"I'm not despondent!" I say to Brad, as we climb into

the Warrior. "Very nervous, but not mopey. I'm going to do everything right."

"There's nothing to be nervous about," he says nonchalantly. "The real thrill is when you cross-country solo. The other's no big deal, just a formality. Anyway, we're just going to go up and do some power-off work today." His voice is calm and casual, but I've read enough accounts of soloing to know that that is precisely the tone instructors always use at moments like this. The I-have-confidence-in-you, anyway-it's-practice-as-usual monotone, accompanied by no eye contact and frequent yawns. He's studied the MO of *the instructor* well enough to have it all down pat, the cool prelude, the soon-to-be inadvertent moment when he says, "Taxi it over there and drop me off; it's too hot, and I'm getting bored; you take it round." My sweaty palms are moving by themselves, rubbing up and down a short length of each thigh. I notice that, for the first time, he has brought my logbook with us.

At the run-up, he has me lock his door, both latches top and bottom, as I will need to do when the seat is empty, and as I will need to remember should I ever have to climb out in a hurry. Bang the seat-belt buckle open, and reach both hands for the door latches. The tower clears us, and we are off easily, climbing to 2,000 feet, turning downwind. The radio fills with chatter.

"Where is that Apache?" Brad asks.

I don't know. And now another plane has entered the pattern; I hear the tower talking with him.

"Don't just do nothing! Where are they?"

I grab sections of sky with my eyes. Nothing.

"What else can you do? Think!"

It dawns on me. I lift up the microphone.

"Ithaca tower, twenty-two Juliett, how far did you say that Apache was from the airport, and I don't see the other plane in the pattern. Can you tell me where he is?"

The tower responds like a summoned genie: "The Apache, seven miles northwest, will be entering a right downwind for three-two; the Cessna is now on final, one mile. Have you got him in sight?"

"Not yet. Looking." I reply, as I slow the plane up to 70 knots, and extend my downwind leg far toward Elmira and a mountain. Then I see the Cessna already closer to the airport than I am and turn base leg. I know I will still be able to land before the incoming Apache.

"What else could you do instead of hitting that mountain we were aiming for?" Brad asks, with surprising calm.

"A little farther out, and I would have requested a three-sixty."

"Good."

In we fly. It occurs to me that I've just had my most elaborate conversation with the tower yet, used them as a resource, as I will from now on, until my plane spotting and radio eavesdropping get better.

When the runway looms up, I add flaps and kill the power, drifting in on a good glide path, add more flaps, and come in too steeply, drive the plane down to the ground, as Brad exhales audibly, and level out perhaps two feet over the runway, without pulling the nose up. In fact, I touch first on the nose wheel. It's a miracle the propeller didn't hit.

"Terrible!" he says, letting his open palm drop on the

panel, as if it were a falling door. It cuts up through the air. "Let's go!" he says.

The next two landings are also flat, and after the second one he abruptly ends the lesson. Today will not be the day. Things are far too wrong. I keep doing the same thing, over and over, gliding in well, leveling off, and then waiting for some magical coalescence of altitude and momentum before I yank back on the nose and get into a landing position. By the time I've waited for that magic transit, it's too late, we've landed flat and too fast. It is no longer a problem of understanding, or skill, but of determination, as he rightly says, quietly, patiently now, going over the step-by-step pictures in the manual, reading aloud from the text. We have been through all of this before.

21

THE BRIGHT, SUN-SCOURED MORNINGS, when the clouds are big as those outgassed by volcanoes, and the mornings so gray and turbulent that visibility is one mile, the length of the runway—all are weighed down by disappointment and defeat, attempts at landings muddled, misjudged, and misexecuted. Each day I return with freshly invented confidence, to try again to figure out how to land, and an hour later, turn the engine off, teary-eyed and depressed, having done everything wrong, without understanding quite what to do right. Occasionally I land well, but can't repeat it; it was sheer fluke. We no longer talk about soloing, we just go up and shoot two landings, and if I bungle them, as always I do, we go off to work on something else, slow flight, or VOR navigation. Under the best circumstances, learning new skills can be daunting, and with no reservoir of confidence and a daily booster shot of failed landings for a dozen lessons in a row, I feel at last that I've come to a fence I can't climb over, to the outer limit of my ability to learn to fly. There seems no way to go but down. At last, Brad is even-tempered with me, quiet, almost disinterested. He's run out of ideas for how to break through this impasse, and going round and round the pattern with me making exactly the same mistakes has become tedious. What began as a slight tendency not to land well has become worse, over the hours, as I never seem to progress, my hope plummets and I fly less confidently. Working around my jinxed landings is not so easy anymore; it's time I was up and practicing by myself. But there are VOR navigation exercises to do. Today the simplest problems were mazes I couldn't solve. Tonight I still can't solve them, though Brad has run through them with me over and over.

In desperation I went to the eye doctor this afternoon, a mustachioed young man wearing a white uniform suited more to a bakery. In addition to the usual tests—the puff of air fired at each iris for glaucoma, the iron mask that looks for incipient cataracts—he opened a thick leather primer before my eyes. On one page sat a large bee, wings spread so their full veil and filaments showed; on the next page rows of animals and rows of circles whose centers were dots (which looked bizarrely like a form of skin cancer or bull's-eye warts). *Touch the bee's wings*, he had said, and I reached my hands out to where the wings were, almost flat against the page. *Is there anything remarkable about these animals?* he asked. But there was nothing, except perhaps in an extra-ocular way: they all were in gestures suggestive of a Barnum & Bailey Circus poster. When he put corrected lenses over my eyes, the Universe changed. The bee's wings reared out from the page and hovered in midair; the animals were at different perspectives; one of the circles had a protruding dot as its hub.

"It may not be the only factor in your trouble with landings," the doctor said shaking his head, "but your depth-perception is *significantly* less than it could be."

Imperfect, my eyes are an odd duo. My left doesn't see past about sixteen inches, whereas my right sees "past infinity," as the doctor put it, and I must confess it sounded poetically just that I had one eye cued irrevocably to the tender mercies of what's local, and the other pounding out past infinity. It suits my mental landscape. But not the world's, where *real* can be measured on instruments. To see, my eyes work independently, the left for close work, the right for distance, rarely together. Well enough to drive a car or ride a horse or dive from a springboard, but perhaps not well enough for piloting from the left side of a cockpit. The prescription sunglasses I emerged with were so strong (pulling the right eye back, stretching out the left) that they will take some time to get used to, if get used to them I ever can. At the moment, I see everything double when I wear them. And, anyway, aren't there one-eyed pilots of tale and history, who did fine without stereo vision? Langewische swears that depth perception is incidental to flying. Ultimately, moving around the Universe is a relative thing: if your senses deceive you, just take into account the amount of deception.

The glasses were my last resort, I'd hoped they'd be

the answer. If they are, it's one I can't begin to use yet, it's so cumbersome and strange, a hall of mirrors. Tomorrow I'll go back to Cayugair, and once again not be able to do landings, and then I think I will have come to the end of my courage, by which I don't mean the courage to overcome one's fear of flying, but the courage to keep returning to the scene of rampant failure. I'll have to quit, and just admit defeat. But mainly I'll have to give up the beautiful mirror of the sky, which for a brief spell I was able to enter. *Everybody can't do everything,* Poleskie had reminded me. Isn't it enough that I can do all the other things I can—write poems, teach, scuba dive, ride horses, and such? Why do I need to fly planes? But, as e. e. cummings wrote, "the mind makes its own beautiful prisons." All my life I've wanted to fly, but never had courage and money enough at the same time to do it. And now, because I seem to have bumped my head against the ceiling of what I'm capable of, a bump I would have thought impossible in my twenties, I will have to give up, having wasted an entire summer in hard work and upset and long hours and $900, and psychodramas with my instructor, and constant bouts of rapture, jubilation, and torment, all adding up to worse than nothing: the memory of a soured attempt at something still wickedly alluring, even touchable in places—the fingers can glide along it and trace its contours, but never grasp it, hold it firmly, pick it up, lay it back down again.

22

A BEAUTIFUL SKY OUTING with friends. Jeanne and Paul chat in the backseat of Poleskie's Apache, if *chat* is the right word for the level of casual yelling it takes to be heard over two Lycoming engines. From the copilot's seat, I can see their lips moving, faces happily animated, as they talk about the ground scenery 3,000 feet below, or the cloud scenery only a few thousand feet above, or Paul's novel set in Atlantic City and Vietnam, or the article Jeanne's writing about formal gardens, or Poleskie and me in the front seats, like two playground pals, busily flying the airplane. More often they just snooze, each leaning against a window, or letting their eyes track over the galloping landscape. We snatch glimpses back at them, smile or wave, and resume a conversation that runs the full length of the flight, a tutorial, master to acolyte, but offered with such gentleness and patience I have no sense of ordeal, but of a gradual unfolding piece of paper on which a drawing becomes clearer and clearer. No autopilot today. No vectors. Not even Poleskie's headset microphone, which he operates by pushing a button on the wheel, like a machine gunner firing. No high altitudes and the large, clear vistas they permit. And no scolding when I do wrong. Coaxing and gently teasing, he teaches me about using the VOR for navigation; in his plane are two VORs, and a DME (which tells distance from a VOR beacon in miles, and flying time, as well as the airplane's speed—a handy gadget). Pilots in their sleep and senility must hear the words, *If that's such and such, and that over there is this, then that must be* . . .

"What's going on?" Jeanne calls, alarmed, as we pivot around one wing tip, right over the Wilkes-Barre VOR, a metallic white cone in a flat grassy clearing on top of a mountain. It looks extraterrestrial, and in some ways it is; like a mental magnet, it draws pilots from all directions to one of the invisible handrails in the air. Fastened to the ground, it is nonetheless of the sky, and one of its duties is to fill a small box on the plane's VOR indicator with the word TO or FROM. *Quo vadis?* (Whither goest thou?) it says en route to the beacon. And *Unde venis* (Look to from where I've come), it says once you pass over it. Round and round on needle edge the plane pivots, so precisely we seem to be on a cord, part of a toy a child is swinging.

"So how do we get back on course?" Poleskie asks,

smiling impishly, as the vista spins on its side, and I search my chart for a new heading that will send us straight to Poughkeepsie. Drawing it means using both sides of the chart, which can only be done on a work table, with a straight edge, a piece of 8½ x 11 paper, and endless curses at the sadists who invented such a clumsy way to plot a course. I fold the chart back into neat accordions.

"Pilotage," I say, which sounds like a form of dressage, how to ride all the horses yoked together by one engine. And it is in some ways, except that the barnstormers who flew it best would have found the term too self-consciously refined. They'd be equally put off by cosmetic, snooty terms like "flight deck" or "cabin attendant." To them, it was just seat-of-the-pants flying: scout the countryside and see what it tells you about where you might be.

"What's that water?" Poleskie asks, nodding to a bowl of blue to the north. "And what heading should we leave on? Choose one fast, the passengers in the back are getting hungry for lunch; they're going to start getting grouchy." Wide-eyed, the passengers in back look tired of being spun around a 60 degree bank to their left, bracing themselves against the window and each other, while we gab inaudibly up front. I choose a new heading of 120 degrees, and tell him the water is the Cannonsville Reservoir.

"Are you sure?" he asks, banking the plane around one more time, as if it were a gyroscope balancing on a pencil point.

"Positive. It's shaped like a ginseng root, it's north of the VOR, and we're right between it and that major highway that looks like a profile of Eleanor Roosevelt." I point to a highway bulging south, then curving east. "Also, those transmission lines are right."

"Very good. And 120 degrees will do fine. Now what's wrong?"

"Wrong? It seemed for a moment that things were right." He hands the controls back to me, and I feel the stick come alive in my hand.

"Yeah, but something's changed since we left Ithaca."

I give a fast, thorough look at the dials, all of which seem normal. What else could have changed? Outside. The landscape, of course. The weather has changed. The low ceiling has dispersed, and we can climb to 5,500 feet, where we wanted to be from the start. In any case, there are mountains in the distance that are definitely higher than we are, 4,200 feet, according to the chart. When you're lost, Poleskie explains, *always climb*; you can see larger areas, patterns start to emerge, and you get better radio reception, because you're not hidden from a signal by the bulging of the Earth.

Soon the Hudson River appears, like an open vein of coal, then an enormous cross right off one wing tip— something evangelical that must light up at night, with *Jesus Saves* glowing in blue over its cross-beam. "What is that?" I ask.

"An airport. Check your chart. How long is it?"

It's on the chart all right, but is too large to depict with the usual circle that signifies an airport. "Okay, it's this blue cross, and . . . an *eleven thousand foot* runway?"

"That's right. The seven-forty-sevens use it to do touch-and-goes. They have to practice somewhere."

All we want from Poughkeepsie is its airport restaurant, a good lunch spot with picture windows facing the runways and one small, bug-eyed window for plants ("or dining hunchbacks," Paul says). But we find the restaurant closed until 3:00 P.M., and the nearest one that's open a few miles' walk clear around the airport. Taxis are nowhere. Back in the plane, Poleskie starts up each engine, then calls the tower with an unusual request.

"Ah, Poughkeepsie tower, November three-three-six-seven Pop. I'm at the FBO, and I'd like to taxi over to that Exxon sign at the northwest side of the field. We're going to the restaurant just beyond the trees over there."

"Roger six-seven Pop. Taxi to taxiway Alpha, and hold short of runway three-three."

Leaving the FBO (where planes are rented, sold, and fueled), we approach runway 33, using our plane as a taxicab. The tower tells us to cross "without delay," and we scurry over, though probably not fast enough for the pilot in a small Cessna just crossing the threshold of 33 a short nightmare away.

A minute's hike through the woods, and lunch is turkey sandwiches on homemade bread, in a tavern whose decor is a television screen the size of a bed hanging over the bar and the unmistakable sounds of a wedding reception in a cordoned-off room. As ever, Poleskie has guessed right about where the restaurant must be. He echolocates like a bat, and I'm constantly amazed by how swiftly he understands *where things are.* An aerobat in the sky, who must know where each piece of the spinning jigsaw fits, he navigates the ground with a psychic's precision. In Green Bay, for instance, where we four stayed during the Oshkosh Fly-In, and where Poleskie had never been before, a young girl picked us up at the airport and drove us to our motel by a serpentine route. The next day, a rental car man fetched us by another route. And on the third day, as we drove back to the airport, Poleskie plotted a course based on where the airport must be, given the lengthy series of left and right turns, every one of which he remembered in exact sequence. It was clear to him at once how to balance all the changes of direction into a straight path to the control tower, and within minutes we saw it.

After lunch, we fly straight up the Hudson River, with its mansion overlooks, groomed farms, chic stables, commuters' maisonettes, and overwhelming miles of state forest, thick green and unsettled. We spot a bridge the chart says will have an airport on either side, and just beyond the easterly one, Old Rhinebeck aerodrome, where we're headed to spend a day watching an air show of World War I planes. Because the show's already in full swing, we can't land there, and anyway the runway is a grass strip too short and pitted by staged explosives to risk landing a twin-engine plane on. Nearby is a small strip (2,700 feet) called Sky Park, hidden among the hills and valleys, which Poleskie's practiced eye picks out after a couple of sweeps in a likely area. He makes a close steep circle around the runway, which is in very bad repair, with tall trees at either end, and a mountain the full length of one side. The pavement can't be more than ten feet wide. He checks the wind direction and the potholes, while we keep an eye on the dog-fighting planes nearby at Rhinebeck. On final approach, the ground disappears and reemerges in a line of small hills and valleys. Then, over the trees and ready for a steep descent, the plane is suddenly hurled toward the ground and thrown back into the air in a boiling motion as it blows quickly toward the mountain as well. Poleskie's hands are everywhere as the plane bucks and rolls and plunges. Just keeping level is a full-out war, so he flies the length of the strip, checking the wind at various points, and where the macadam has crumbled unusably, then climbs out steeply, and banks round for another go. In the backseat, Paul looks chastened, and Jeanne has both hands pressed tight against her eyes.

"I don't know whether we can land here," Poleskie says. "I don't want to do anything hair-raising with passengers aboard. . . . I'll just give it one more shot." He turns final. This time he's ready for the wind stew, and when we cross the trees and boil down, he rides it as part of a planned descent, landing fast, but rolling out within a few hundred feet, over cracked macadam and tufts of renegade grass. There are plenty of planes on the ground, but no other twin; a crowd has gathered outside of the hangars to watch us land. Dustballs blow in a gale across our wings, as does a disoriented monarch butterfly, part of a slipstream rushing over the leading edge of the wing as we secure the plane with ropes and blocks.

The taxicab to the aerodrome is an old Pontiac driven by a heavily bangle-braceleted woman of about sixty, who ushers us into the car, along with her Chihuahua. The backseat is littered with shoes, all the same style, but in different colors.

"One more," she says brightly, and I reach a hand behind me to what I thought was a seat belt pressing into the small of my back. I hand her the purple pump. The dog twitches into position on the armrest between the two front seats, and we are off to Old Rhinebeck, a fair of rebuilt World War I planes, lined up like prize farm animals along a sprawling midway. There are booths with cotton candy and souvenirs, as well, and men walking around in authentic turn-of-the-century flying duds. Cole Palen, the veteran barnstormer who imagined Rhinebeck into being, is a deeply suntanned and wrinkled man in flying helmet, goggles, riding boots, jodhpurs, leather jacket and white scarf, telling yarns about legendary pilots to an eager crowd circled around him. His teenage daughter hawks rides on a biplane, and other friends and relations run other concessions. It is a very Faulknerian scene. Overhead, a miscellany of glossy, brightly painted biplanes reenact World War I battles above a backdrop of French buildings, and fly after balloons, which they catch in their struts. The crowd of a thousand or so people, mainly families with children, are as amazed as their predecessors were when the So-and-So's Flying Circus came to town. Another show has less hoopla, and waits silently in the hangars at one edge of the grounds, where antique planes, some no more than a few struts and a bit of paper, are on display along with vintage posters about the Red Cross or the Huns.

"We will take you high or low, fast or slow, anyway you want to go," the barker is calling, as he hands out cotton flying helmets and plastic goggles to grannies, babes in arms, and everyone in between who have cued up for a ride in a green biplane whose wings are tilted into a broad parallelogram. Four people at a time can sit in the opera-box front seat; the pilot sits in the rear. But we, on the other hand, are prowling the hangars, looking at a 1911 version of the cross-country Blériot XI with a 70HP Gnome rotary engine, the elongated baby carriage on which Blériot became the first man to fly the

English Channel in 1909. The thing about Rhinebeck's planes is that they actually fly, most of them weekly during the Saturday and Sunday afternoon plane concerts. The Blériot flew for ten minutes at about 500 feet once when it first was restored, now they fly it straight at 20 feet because it's so fragile. But it does fly. As does the sweeping red cape with ski wheels, the 1911 French Nieuport 2N, which once held the World's Speed Record at 78 mph. They fly the French Hanriot, which looks like a pug-nosed dragonfly, the length of a movie set, evoking the scenery it might once have been part of. Of course, there are the Sopwith Camel and lesser known Sopwith Pup and a beautiful Fokker triplane sitting in the hangar like a badly shuffled hand of cards. And then all the planes from the Lindbergh era: the 1929 Pitcairn Mailwing, from whose open cockpit Lindbergh jumped on a few occasions, when fog or snow made crashing a certainty; the 1929 Curtiss Fledgling, whose stabilizer and tail are B-shaped (unlike most planes' guitar-pick tails); the Great Lakes Trainer, whose fuselage has an odd curvature of the spine.

Such comparisons evoke the painter Paul Nash, who, as official war artist to the British Air Ministry during World War II, did a series of watercolor studies of planes, *Aerial Creatures*. He wrote tenderly about their dire, creatural beauty in "The Personality of Planes," a phenomenological essay published in, of all places, *Vogue* (March, 1942):

> I could see the fighter tearing across the spaces of the sky and the bomber ploughing through the clouds, or the mighty Sunderland, most animal of

all planes, charging along the coast with its great snout thrust out, defiant and terrible. . . . To watch the dark silhouette of a Wellington riding the evening clouds is to see almost the exact image of the great killer whale hunting in unknown seas.

Antoine de St. Exupéry found in planes a kind of zoology, too, and a humanism beyond grease and power. Whereas Nash became interested in war only when he "realized the machines were the real protagonists," St. Exupéry thought of planes as more seraphic, their liveliness softer-edged. There is something of the nineteenth-century explorer's vision of jungle creatures in Nash's and St. Exupéry's rapture with planes, the romance of the primitive at home in its element with naive, unselfconscious grace. These days, people describe planes as sassy, sleek, silk-muscled, mean, proud. To me, they resemble less humans or animals than a moment of energy caught and flash-frozen. On the ground, energy resting; in the air, unbridled flight. It's hard to talk about motion, energy, grace, power, and delicacy without referring to animals (*unbridled flight*). Our history as creators of complexly moving things is so brief, and our passion is somehow to reenact that Creation of which we find ourselves daily startled to be a part. So it's not enough to create something from metal that flies; it must soar like a gull, it must gallop like a horse, it must "take no prisoners," or be "forgiving" when it lands. It must be a *Warrior* or *Grizzly* or *Sabre*, a blunt instrument to rise aloft with and whip the forces of nature into shape. Nothing like a seedpod or constellation. Something brute, elemental, inexplicable. This isn't true of those called things like *Sundowner* or *Chaparral*, but mainly there are *Stallions, Vikings, Tigers, Vampires, Shrikes,* and other predators, the long list of which makes you start to wonder if we've ever fully accepted the fact that we're lucky enough to be at the top of our food chain. It's that hidden fear that prompts most horror films, I think: the monster that can track us down and eat us: the Killer Shrews, the Cat People, the Wolfen, the Alien, and all the other incarnations of our prehistoric terror. Loren Eiseley in *The Immense Journey* notes our human penchant for eating food at the temperature of freshly killed prey.

With this in mind, it's especially charming to look at planes from the beginning of aviation called such birthlike things as *Fly Babies, Cubs, Fledglings, Pups,* and marvel at the men and women brave enough to have barnstormed the nation or crossed water in what look like badly folded pieces of origami. If you believe in magic, then most anything will work—a magic carpet, a pair of wax wings, a canopy attached to a lawn chair. And some of them did work. Now that we know it isn't magic, private aviation has suffered from lack of design creativity. They're all much of a muchness—high-wing or low-wing, with minor changes in wing, nose, or tail. At Oshkosh, there's more variety among the homebuilts, but even they run to a few basic patterns. In the beginning, inventors tried fabulous and strange designs, planes held together by sunlight and termites, it seemed, most of which never flew, but a few of which launched us into seaplanes, helicopters, rockets, and jets, as well as the miscellany of full-contact, slow-flying, buzz-the-countryside planes swooping and floating over Old Rhinebeck.

23

WEEKS LATER, I bank steeply around a sandtrap off one wing tip, as Poleskie leans out the window at 150 mph, snapping pictures for an aerial guide to golfing in the Finger Lakes. "Bank!" his voice blows into the cockpit, and I tilt the twin-engined Apache up on edge like a painter's hands framing a perspective. "Straight!" he yells, gesturing with one hand in the cockpit, holding the camera with the other as he leans farther out between the fuselage and engine, and I level out, gain speed, bring the plane close to stall in a turn at 100 mph, bank around again, pivot and swing. Over the fairways and water hazards, the small rigid shadow of our airplane scoots flat for a moment, dark as a floating curse, then vanishes on knife edge as we pirouette once more over the baffled putters.

A dark cross on the earth, flat among the cornfields, is a grass landing strip used by parachutists. "Let's see if my friend's home," Poleskie says, buzzing the house. He circles round to check wind and runway, then swoops down and lands between two fields of clover. The owner is nowhere; Poleskie owes him an unused chute. But the stillness of the open hangars, which planes share with tractors and grain trucks, the improbable rustle of the wind sock, and the fields overshot by the heat vapor of late August is peace beyond memory. In the empty wooden clubhouse, Poleskie leans against a window, in whose corner flies buzz to break free, his hands and face dark as iris roots, from flying but mainly from repairing his new house, building a cold frame for Jeanne, learning to golf with his carpenter friend.

"It used to be just like this when I was young," he says softly. "A few pals and I would barnstorm from one aerobatic competition to the next all across the Midwest. We'd fly our biplanes into some small strip like this one, where we could practice above the cornfields and sleep in cheap motels. The local kids would come running from everywhere to watch us, their moms would bring us barbecued chickens for dinner, their dads take us into town, buy us drinks. All we ever wanted was a place to fly, a place to sleep. In the morning, we'd wake up and it would look just like this, exactly like this: planes standing in the flat fields, with the sun bright and the wind blowing. I guess it'll never be that way again." Suddenly aware of the Coke bottle in his hand, he crosses the room to put it neatly into a waste can. For a brave, steel-nerved man, he is remarkably shy and soulful, a Pole in the tradition of Chopin, but also of Polish fighter pilots in World War II, who flew snappy planes with unique precision and nerve. To close part of your life on purpose is not to stop missing it, especially when you find yourself improbably adult, no longer the brash, wild-eyed starving painter in a Soho loft, or the aerobat happy and poor under a wing in Ohio, but a respected artist/professor/pilot, with a wife and home, choosing a livable routine at life's meridian.

Off again, we photograph three more golf courses, the prettiest one attached to the insane asylum at Willard. Though the inmates no longer use it, the state keeps the greens trim and the fairways overlooking Lake Seneca neatly groomed. Some of the courses are hard to spot from the air, even when you know what you're searching for: an arrangement of lawn and tree that must have been thought into being. Steep turns around a small, poorly landscaped course in Virgil, while Poleskie photographs, and we are off to Cortland, Watkins Glen, and back to Ithaca for more film. It's a delicious way to pass a summer afternoon in upstate New York, floating over the miles of vineyard, which look like rows of tightly knotted hair, buzzing village golf courses, and searching out the planned landscapes from the accidental. For gas, we land in Tri-Cities Airport, near Oswego, and pay a man in a low office building that was the airport's terminal in the 1940s. Inside, nothing has changed. Not the soda fountain counter, not the glass canister of cigars, not the old weather equipment or dozens of small windows. A photograph hanging above the counter shows local businessmen boarding an airliner in 1949. They are walking out to the plane through a cyclone-gate fence, wearing baggy trousers, and two-toned shoes with tiny perforations across the top. Their hair is short as boot campers', and the war has only been over for four years. Behind the counter, a heavy man with a tire gauge sticking out of his shirt pocket and a Bunsen burner igniter sticking out of his pants pocket methodically fills out a charge-card blank. "Things sure have changed around here over the years," he says, pointing up at the photograph. "Look at the size of those trees." Poleskie and I smile at each other; the trees, so much larger now, are the only things that haven't changed. Along the Susquehanna, flowing the full length of the small airport, a line of gliders sits nose up in the sunlight. A small corporate jet lands in a rush, appearing in the left-most window pane and filling another dozen in turn until it rolls out of view. But inside the terminal it is still the late 1940s, you can hear the pop songs like "Some Enchanted Evening," hummed by people not yet used to associating planes with peacetime.

By late afternoon, when we finally return to Ithaca, to bed the plane down, because the scattered clouds that have appeared will cast shadows on the ground and make photographing trickier, I've been flying Poleskie's Apache for four hours. And it occurs to me that we landed six times. It all seemed so reasonable—putting down for film, gas, to find his friend, and such—I didn't realize I was receiving instruction in the tenderness of landing, how to gentle a plane to the ground.

I see it all again in my mind: with Poleskie working the throttle, I glide it around, uneasy at first with not being able to see over the left engine and wing to where the runway must be, in a minimum drag airspeed recklessly high for a Warrior. Everything is peachy until we close in on the threshold; 20 feet off the ground I panic, turning the ailerons, working my feet on the rudder, clawing the plane to death. *What the hell are you doing to this plane?* Poleskie says. *It wants to land; let it land.* His suntanned face is awash with contained amusement. *You're in a perfect glide straight in. Trust the plane; it knows how to land. Can't you feel it?* Yes, I feel it holding the air under its wings, the way a horse fumbles the bit in its teeth. I feel it settling, pushing its wide metal palm stiffly down to the runway. But, instinctively, I punch at the rudders when we start drifting off the center line, instinctively grab at the wheel when airspeed wavers. *Stop that!* Poleskie says gently, and reaches a hand over to my right wrist, holding it back with a cuff of his fingers, as if it were a fragile, fluttering bird, so that it can only make delicate nudges at the wheel. *The plane knows how to land; don't get in its way.* Then I start to laugh and relax, and life becomes so simple at last, as we float in with nothing more than my fingertips pressing, lifting, pressing, until the back wheels touch down, nose barely up but up enough, as the plane rolls out toward the first taxiway, as Poleskie adjusts the throttle. After the last landing of the day, I notice two figures far across the field in the control tower, standing against the window, with what seem to be arrows pointing from each ear. Puzzled, I look at Poleskie, who is grinning, then back at the figures. Of course. They're holding up binoculars. It's their elbows I can see. *They want to know who the hell's flying this airplane,* he says. *But you landed great. What's the big problem? The Warrior should be easier.* Will be easier, I say to myself in wish-magic, will be one engine easier tomorrow, if I just loosen up and not let anything harass me, if I calm myself down first, then the plane, if I try to remember the gentility with which airplanes float, if you let them, out of the blue toward the flat rigor of the earth. *Float*, I think, letting the notion wash over my mind. Fish, balloons, seedpods, parachutes, paper, humans, wood, insects, satellites, otters, water lilies. Float is part of what matter does, if you encourage it, what matter often does even if you ignore it.

24

THICK WITH RAIN, the sky is a foggy moor that begins
a thousand feet above ground. Brad and I are doing touch-
and-goes in the downpour, with the sound of rain on the
cabin like water on a steel sieve, climbing out through
rivulets streaking the windscreen (there are no wipers),
and turning left to follow a Cessna downwind. That is the
first mistake, going left when the corridor right of the
airport is empty and visibility is poor. *What's your plan?*
Brad asks. My plan is to follow the Cessna at a safe distance, and as I turn into a downwind leg well behind it,
I'm just in time to see it disappear into a pocket of sky,
little by little, as a dappled gray might into a fog. *Do
something*, Brad says. *Find out where it is, fast.*

"Ithaca tower, Twenty-two Juliett, left downwind for three-two. There was a Cessna in front of me that I've lost sight of. Can you tell me where it is?"

"Cessna is turning base now, Twenty-two Juliett. You're cleared to land number two behind the Cessna."

Because I'm busy talking to the tower, because I'm looking hard for the Cessna, because the rain is all around like a beautiful silver veil whose weave one is a part of, I let my airspeed zoom to 120 knots. *Look at your speed!* Brad says. *If you know a plane's in front of you somewhere in the fog, the last thing on earth you want to do is speed up.*

It is all good advice, he is absolutely right. I know that. But the tumult of his voice so alarms me that my thoughts jumble and bounce, and when I call the tower to tell them that I'm going to do a longer downwind, to give the Cessna time to land and me time to spot it, he slaps his knee in disbelief and sits back, shaking his head, then gives it up and searches the cloud-curded lake off to the right, glowing white and blurred with thick fog. At last he says, *You don't need to extend your downwind. Visibility's terrible. Just fly a normal pattern. You're nowhere near that Cessna.* His voice is so weak and disgusted, it's worse than yelling. And I no longer know what to do, how to do it, what to be, how to be it. No longer know which way will lead me out of the maze of defeat I'm in. If I think for myself, I think wrong. If I don't think, I'm wrong for not thinking. Not only can I not seem to act correctly, I can't even seem to act neutrally, try though I may.

"I quit," I say limply, and take my hand off the wheel. "I quit." This time I say it identically, but for myself, so that I will understand the miserable resolution I'm making, pressing it into my psyche until it stays there. "I quit." My left hand hangs in the air for a moment, like something severed. I don't know where to put it now, so I rest it on one knee. Brad will take the plane in safely. All I want to do is vanish somehow, into the metal, into the seat back, into the thick white air.

Fly the goddamn airplane! he snaps, and picks my hand up, shoves it back onto the wheel. *FLY THE AIRPLANE! I SAID, LAND THIS PLANE! LAND THIS GOD-DAMN PLANE. Fuel pump on. Come on, come on. Fly the plane.*

I flick a switch on the instrument panel.

Flaps!

I reach down between the seats and pull the long hard piece of licorice until it clicks 10 degrees of flaps into place. As we turn base, I say, "You've got the controls," and try not to cry, as I push my seat back, too far from the rudder pedals and instrument panel to use them, and return to the grim state I began in, forever and always to be a passenger. "I don't land airplanes anymore," I say, as if an explanation were necessary to the part of me watching in such sadness and disbelief. "I hate flying. This is where the inquisition stops."

For a week, Brad has been relatively quiet in the plane, chastened by my quitting resolutely, on final, in a fog, with airplanes entering and leaving the pattern invisibly all around us. But it feels only like a reprieve from shelling during a religious holiday. You know the strafing will continue sometime soon. It's been going on without mercy or letup for so long. Don't leave the house, or you may get caught in the open. Lie down, but don't close your eyes, or you may be asleep when the bombs start falling. Even though he sits silently in the seat to my right, I still hear the hurled abuse, the tantrums, and the ranting that made life a horror for so many hours. After a summer of my begging, he's finally stopped brutalizing me; but it's too late. The summer is over, and I feel cheated out of what could have been a lofty, gorgeous experience of airplanes, a romance with flight. I still don't know how to land, which is incidental to what troubles me more, how much I've come to associate flying with personal attack, how jumpy I am the moment I climb into the Warrior, my nerves all ascramble. I need to solo now so that I can try to retrieve some of the original enjoyment of flying, which I no longer remember, except for the miraculous days when I'm up with Poleskie, and stealthily he teaches me. Faustian, I've let my mania for knowledge lead me into a kind of trauma, too addicted to give up, a trauma it may take me a long time to unlearn, if that reverse education is even possible.

25

AT 8:15 A.M. the telephone rings, and I hurry to catch it before the house wakes up. Though I live close enough to the airport to hear changes in pitch when pilots cut their engines abeam the numbers, the weather can be alpine or rancid only two miles away, blustery and rain ready, with a low quilted ceiling, though the sun is deadening in my backyard. So the apparent calm outside may be a local delusion. Bob's voice is half-asleep, bored by summer.

"Weather's good," he says flatly. It's the tone of a pump boy saying my oil is okay. "See you at eight-forty-five. Bring your medical."

Despite the low, gray ceiling above the airport, for once everything is still. That's obvious even though the wind sock is down for repairs: its swivel-less frame is quiet as a picked-over carcass, and the weeds around the cyclone fence, where no mower can reach, are slumped over. Outside the hangar, 22 Juliett is ready for preflight, which I finish just as Bob arrives in his station wagon, wearing paint-splattered blue jeans, shirt, and peaked cap. Saturday morning chores. Up since six, he's still yawning as we climb aboard and taxi to 32. By afternoon, I'll be en route to Williamsburg, Virginia, to begin a stay as visiting writer-in-residence at the College of William and Mary, for nine months, and I don't want him to feel some sort of false climax is necessary to a summer full of frustration and expense.

"The other day, flying with Brad, when I was so teary-eyed and upset . . . it wasn't because I wanted desperately to solo, which is probably what he told you. I was afraid that I'd never learn how to land, that I'd come to the end of my ability to learn. I'd run out of hope. Soloing doesn't matter. Developing some confidence about landing matters."

"I know that," he says, brushing the thought away with one hand, as if it were a length of wood he was getting ready to paint, "which is why you're not going to solo today. All we're going to do is work on landings in calmer weather. There's a slight crosswind, but it's nothing compared to how gusty it's been for the last week or so." By *gusty* he means the 90 degree crosswinds sometimes at 15 knots. Seventeen knots is the recommended limit of the airplane, and it takes robust attention to land on the center line. But that's normal for Ithaca, and learn it you must if you don't want to be stymied by weather most days.

Cleared for takeoff, we are up smoothly, climbing straight, fighting no wind, bobbing across no invisible pockets, and turning left easily at just the right altitude. Plum clouds swarm 1,000 feet above, but no rain is falling, no turbulence buffeting the airplane around. Bob looks actually asleep now, catnapping as we sail downwind, and I feel as alone as I've ever felt in an airplane, quiet, and thrilled just to be in the sky on so calm a day, before I leave town for a new climate, locale, and routine. Ithaca can look like a winterscape even in the fall; the sky opaque as the glass roof of a cold frame, when the frost obscures even the hardiest seedlings. But I'm not thinking of that, or anything at all; I'm out for the simplest, most casual of strolls. Much of the town isn't even awake yet. On the radio, a Cessna announces itself like a species of bird in a swamp. The tower replies with instructions for approach and landing, then adds, "Twenty-two Juliett, you'll be number two after the Cessna."

A look clear round the pattern turns up no Cessna. "Ithaca Tower," I say, "twenty-two Juliett. I don't see that Cessna. Can you tell me where it is please?"

"Twenty-two Juliett, Cessna is turning right base."

"Looking." By now I know the full warrant and strain in that simple participle pilots use. *Looking* is desperation hanging on the latch; it means one is searching keenly for the plane supposed to be close at hand, roaming out of the fog perhaps, or closing in at 80 knots. To be *looking* is not to have *found*, but only to know that finding is possible. And there are ways of looking. A steady, panoramic scan from side to front to side window won't do, since it's too much like the blur it hopes to make sense of. Ground against ground, there is no picking out the tiny stiff figure of a Cessna, even though you may know where it should be. Perhaps it's the brief dark hedgerow line at the summit of a tawny field in the distance. No; too far. Perhaps it's the tan paperbaglike movement at ten o'clock. No, that's a pond with a fence in the background. I slow the plane up, fly a longer downwind leg, and continue looking.

"Twenty-two Juliett," the tower urges, "Cessna turning right base to final."

A white wing appears close to the end of the runway.

"Roger, Ithaca Tower. I've got that Cessna in sight now and will be number two." Picking up glide speed again, I bank toward the runway. Bob stirs a bit when I cut the engine and prepare to land. Too high, I add flaps, see the runway moving down my window, add more flaps, then line up square with the center line, and keep the airspeed glued to 80 knots.

"Amazing," I sigh.

"What is?" Bob asks.

"There's no wind to fight. It's so easy."

He smiles. "There's always a wind. Just less today. In fact, this is a nice day to finish painting the porch. Have to take the pups to the vet, too."

As the threshold of the runway, with its enormous white numbers, drifts closer, I ease the nose up to 70 knots, and float calmly down to the ground, easing the nose up higher and higher as we descend, landing at last like a word whispered onto the runway.

"Damn, that felt wonderful," I say, self-amazed. "Can I try that again?"

He laughs. "Sure, it's your nickel." Tilting down the peak of his cap, he leans back, and dozes as we take off again, now and then looking at the Cornell research ponds to the north. The second go-round, I land less nimbly than the first, but nose straight, on the back wheels, and with no pogo-sticking. I can't believe it: twice in a row I've done that alien thing called landing. No fuss. Just put it down so it stayed down.

"Let me have your medical," Bob says, and my heart cartwheels as I pull a tattered yellow card out of my wallet and hand it to him. It occurs to me that we are sitting in the middle of an active runway.

"Taxi over to the control tower," he says, "right to the base of it." Then he picks up the mike and asks the tower if they have any coffee left. It is all so archly low-key.

"Turn the plane around over there." He points lazily to a ramp hidden by the slight curve of the field. When I pivot round like a diva and apply the brakes, he climbs out, grinning.

"Listen," I put a hand on his paint-splattered leg, as he subtracts himself from the cockpit, "are you sure I can do this?" It's a stupid question. I've been able to do it for ages. It isn't a serious question, but some verbal token of my fear.

"Just do three touch-and-goes," he says, "that's all." Laughing, he closes the door securely behind him, presses it tight, checks the latch, then is gone behind the fuselage. I don't look back. The runway is on a rise straight ahead, and what happens now will not have anything to do with him.

"Ithaca Tower, twenty-two Juliett. Ready to taxi to three-two," I say as evenly as I can.

"Twenty-two Juliett, taxi to three-two," the tower answers immediately, but at the end of a held breath, as if it were waiting to speak.

It's just as well the tower is as far from the end of 32 as it is, I am thinking, as I slowly taxi up the ramp and then along the parallel taxiway, adjusting my gyro and collecting myself by thinking of nothing at all. My mind is a blank in the open barrel of the morning. Thought will frighten me. It's too late now to rehearse or reason or consider possibilities. What I need to do exclusively is act. At the edge of 32, I do a brief run-up and call the tower, which clears me for takeoff. Nothing more. Then I taxi into position, as I have a hundred times, between the 3 and the 2, pull the stick back to my chest, and push the throttle full open. Before I have time to think about what is happening, the runway rushes under me like a long gray pelt, the trees floating twice as fast at the outer edge of vision, the nose climbing until I press it smoothly back down. At 80 knots, the plane takes the best rate of climb and surges into the sky as if it were being hauled up. I tuck my long thick hair behind both ears, unbecomingly, though I know Bob and the tower people are watching me through binoculars. It doesn't matter. I don't even look at the tower. Grinning, I watch the altimeter hit 1,700 feet, then I bank left, climb to 2,000 feet, and cut the engine back, turn downwind, turn off the electric fuel pump, check the sky for planes, and call the tower.

I am up by myself, with the city and lake sprawling around me. It seems impossible. But I still have to get down. Abeam the numbers, I cut power and put on the fuel pump, wait until my airspeed drops to glide, then make a clean left-hand turn onto base. *Pay attention, I say to myself. You've got to do it right. There's no second chance, no one to fix things up. If you blow it, you're dead. Do it right! Pay attention.* Now all those weeks of demanding perfect patterns begins paying off. In the relative calm, I square off a 90 degree angle, and line up for final. Too high, I add flaps, then must add power to make up for it, but it doesn't matter, I am floating in quietly, right on target, dead center on the runway, bleeding off my airspeed as I touch down gently, straight, nose wheel off. I'm stunned. The airport is so silent. For a moment, I run my hand over my sweaty neck and try to make sense of what is happening. Something new. I start to grin, take off the flaps, give full throttle, and take off again.

I know Bob is in the tower, watching me, but I am not looking at the tower. I am too intent on flying everything right. Nothing matters but getting down safely, as I must, as I can. Haven't I just done it?

On the second and third approaches, I land less and less well, once without flaps, floating long down the runway, once with full flaps on only to discover that I'm dropping too fast and must do something quickly. Rather than remove them so close to the ground, I play it safe and come in with power until I sidle up to the end of the runway. My landings get progressively sloppier, too, but they are always on the right side of the ground, and I cannot stop grinning. Just to persuade myself I've really done it, I go round a fourth time, then land, panting loudly, and call the tower.

"Ithaca Tower, twenty-two Juliett. Thanks for keeping an eye on me. Do you know where I can pick up my passenger?"

"Twenty-two Juliett, taxi to the ramp," a voice replies formally. No congratulations. No sympathetic cheer. It is all so stoic and restrained, so man among men. The pilot's attitude again. It occurs to me, as I taxi back to Cayugair, that Bob is not in the cockpit with me, though I'd felt him fully present in his absence the entire flight. Not once had I glanced right into the empty seat. He was as real beside me as he had been on the first two circuits, a silent body, more a charm than a safeguard. How odd, I am thinking, the day comes when what one clings to so ferociously is just deadweight, when an instructor is just a signature on a card, not an umbilical cord.

I park the plane and run full-tilt into the office, where Bob is standing with the line boy, who puts his hand out for the ritual shake. Bob holds out a pair of scissors, to cut my shirttail, soloing ceremony all over America.

"Oh, no," I say, waving the scissors aside, "this is a good blouse, to hell with tradition," then notice that my hands are shaking like dust mops.

"You'll be a wreck all day," Bob says.

"Thank God that's over," I say weakly to the line boy and rest my cheek on the counter, as I've done so often in steepest dejection all summer. "Thank God that's over now, and I can start learning how to fly. . . If I can just stop grinning."

They laugh. My cheeks are wired to my ears. After thirty-five hours, finally, I have taken the plane in hand, landed. Only a week ago, I had quit for the third—or was it fourth?—time, because it was clear the sky was not some place I would ever comfortably be. And now I was back in the blue of possibility.

But where the hell is Brad, anyway? I assume he's too

ashamed to come and watch another instructor solo me, or perhaps he's simply too mean-spirited, or too bored. What a louse! I've spent more hours with him over the past few months than I have with my brother over the past fifteen years. I've helped him accumulate the flying hours would-be airline pilots crave. And I've enriched his bank balance. But he would never dream of saying good-bye or good luck. A very slimy character, indeed.

It was to Bob's credit that he insisted on trying to solo me, even up to my last morning in town. But I'm sure he knew too how embarrassing it would look if, after an entire summer, they could do nothing but send me out daunted and depressed after so many hours, so much expense.

"Thank you," I call to Bob, as he gets into his car and drives away. The owner, at his computer, doesn't even bother to come out to congratulate me.

Home again, the anticlimax is oppressive. Had I done it? Did I really take the bird round by myself, finally, after so many months of frustration and gloom? How could the tower be so inhuman? Not even a verbal wave, not the slimmest reply to my thanking them. How could the owner of Cayugair be so mercenary and uninvolved, care so little about the lives of the people who passed daily through his world? Two months of nonstop misery, frustration, war games, anger, self-denigration, heartbreaking, full-scale, all-out *trying*, with Brad screaming over and over that I was not *really* trying, didn't hate myself enough, and now there was no back patting even, no conspiratorial delight, no jubilation. They may take your money and time, but don't expect them to take your side.

When it happened, I thought I would be agush with sense impressions, the texture of the grass, the wire-whisk sound of the crickets, the feel of the sun through the windshield, the loneliness of the cabin. But nothing like that happened. Thought would have been a luxury, dangerous even; instead I was all impulse and attention. I was a single, narrow, livable purpose: land safely. Lift off smoothly. Land safely. No ruffles. No poetry. Pick it up, put it down. Make it dull. Make it normal. Let the grin, almost painful now, be all that's out of control, not an expression of thrill, but of cold relief.

Soloing is not the end of flying, but the real beginning of it, as I had said to the line boy. Staying on a horse takes quite a while to learn, but the real riding comes when falling off is no longer a threat, and you can concentrate on things like finesse. Bob's right: I'll never forget that Saturday morning when I soloed. But at the same time it seems terribly unreal. Tomorrow in a different state, at a different airport, I'll begin flying different planes, with new instructors and new instruments and new personalities to deal with and a new solo to work toward.

Was there a time when flying had seemed a wonderful, do-able summer adventure? At what point did it stop being fun and become something brutal—an ordeal not a challenge, an inquisition not a liberation? And what could I do about the fact that I no longer *liked* to fly. Flying was waking up shaking every morning, going to the airport and being screamed at and humiliated for an hour, broken up by things like failure and frustration. I want it to be like it was in the beginning, when I was in love with the sky, but all that has long since drained out of me. When finally I climb into my car and start a ten-hour drive that will take me to Williamsburg, I know that my career in flying is just about over. How could I possibly start again with Cessnas, from scratch, going through the impossible ordeal I've just been through? It's too tough. I'm too unable. Sure I soloed, but only on the calmest possible day, on one occasion, and perhaps that was just blind luck. I don't ever remember feeling so depressed, or so incompetent, or so resented, or so defeated, or so wished-away. Worst of all is losing my delirium for flight, losing the rapture I would feel just to be in the sky, something I wouldn't have thought anything could kill. I let it go too far, when I should have baled out, before doing serious damage to my sense of wonder. And now, having finally soloed, soloing no longer matters. What matters is this sickening conviction that I *cannot* learn to fly, that I will never learn, and, worst of all, that I have lost something irreplaceable —an attitude, a playful curiosity about flight, a necessary passion—that I'll never have again with that blend of innocence and zest. Why try at all? Why go through the motions? Isn't it braver just to admit defeat now and cry quits?

Hanging Out at the FBO

26

On the Virginia sectional chart, all the elevations begin with zero, except far west, where the Blue Ridge Mountains snag at the sky and give glider pilots a lift. Across the rest of the state, there are swamps, peat bogs even, and large rivers and bays and flat, sprawling farmlands for peanuts and corn. Unlike in New York State, the tallest thing for miles in Virginia will probably be a tree, and the sky seems more domelike by day, a blue planetarium, which of course is just what it is.

During the summer, I'd written to Oceana Naval Base, from which jumpy-headed F-15 pilots called things like "Killer" fly, asking if I could take lessons, and I received a blunt, amused no. But I also wrote to Colonial Aviation, a Cessna Pilot School based at the Williamsburg/James-town Airport, which my chart told me would be close to town, with a single runway half the size of Ithaca's and no control tower. It would be between two large rivers, the York and the James, and only forty-nine feet above sea level, marshy probably, perhaps foggy and damp. A letter from Colonial's flight instructor, Martin J. Van der Linde, spelled out the program and the airport's resources, at length, comprehensively, and with daunting precision, asking me to reply with an account of my training history. How could I? No history would begin to tap my reservations or discouragement or warring instincts. So I told him what I could by letter, as delicately and unemotionally as I could, and made an appointment to stop by the airport when I arrived in town.

I didn't realize that the *airport* would be two metal trailers, one hangar, and a runway, and three rows of airplanes sitting like shoe boxes on the tarmac.

A CESSNA PILOT CENTER sign stands high above one of the trailers, and inside are blond wood classroom tables and chairs, whose glossy varnish is worn in spots from the elbows of student flyers who have spent hours studying regulations, doing ground school, taking quizzes, bemoaning the flunked FAA exam they must retake. Blue-lined notepads from a pharmaceutical company, advertising Anaprox (a menstrual cramp medicine), sit neatly at intervals along the table. Across the middle of each pad is a candy-apple red pencil, lying perfect as an equator, with "Colonial Aviation, Williamsburg Airport" in gold lettering. On the drapes are colorful, antique, open-cockpit planes and airport signs. There are two dark wood desks, on one of which a color photograph of a sleek, high-performance glider has been taped. Posters of planes decorate the walls and doors. A small, pulpit-shaped counter stands next to one desk, under a telephone and large wall clock. There's a coffee machine and a bathroom, and offices at either end of the trailer, one with a simulator and a refrigerator. The walls and floors are all buff—buff paneling and buff linoleum. As narrow as the trailer is, it seems spacious, though perhaps that's just how schoolroomy it looks; a space can't be too narrow if it contains wide thoughts.

From the simulator room comes the instructor I'll be working with, a tall, young Dutchman with cheekbones high as a landing strip and eyes the blue of control areas on the Virginia sectional. There is something gangly about him, too much length to keep upright all at once. He speaks with a thick Dutch accent, as he takes my logbook and checks the entries, shaking his head.

"This is very strange," he says, "the order in which they have been teaching you." On the desk beside the logbook is a pair of aviator glasses, which I recognize as Ray Bans, the glasses worn by all the flyers in adventure novels. "Why so long to solo?" he says, without looking up. "And why not the full stall series and other such things very early, as they should be?" He shakes his head thoughtfully. "I don't know who these people are, but this is not right." He looks at me sympathetically, with so much passing through his thoughts, readable but unspoken, that I feel gloomier than ever. "The best thing is to give you a test, see how much ground school you need," he says, "and of course we'll go up to see how you fly."

When he asks again why it took so long to solo, in a tone of voice remarkable for its neutrality, I pour out my despair: how difficult it's been to learn, how crazy and frightened my instructor made me feel, how much doubt I have about ever being able to learn to fly.

"Terrible, terrible," he says.

"I know. Pigheaded and self-destructive probably, too." I pick up my purse and reach for the logbook.

"Not terrible *because* of you," he says, quietly angry, "terrible *for* you. This is not your problem." He waves a hand across the log lying open like the tally of prolonged torment it is. "This is *their* problem. Who can learn when they're being abused? We'll teach you in the right way now."

I follow his glance up to where the wall meets the ceiling, where ground is at its highest before the sky, and in separate frames, one after another, all around the trailer on every side, are swatches of shirttail from which small, silhouette Cessnas have been cut, and under each one the name and date of the student pilot who soloed. The fabrics are so whimsical—stripes, checks, Hawaiian prints— it's a good sign, students whose sense of humor is intact. There must be a hundred of them.

"Look, don't expect much," I warn, as we go out to the 150 trainer, and he begins at the beginning by teaching me how to preflight the strange, tadpole-shaped plane. "I don't fly very well."

He smiles. "Nobody's perfect. Anyway, I don't get much exercise; I need to be bounced around a little."

As it turns out, there are few bounces, but much confusion and bungling of the plane, which looks lighter and less cumbersome than the Warrior, but flies completely differently and requires one's full attention. Now I know why people say that it's such a good trainer: if you can learn to fly a little bronco like a 150, you can fly anything. Half of what I've learned about planemanship won't work on Cessnas. Instead of all-rudder turns, I need more coordinated ones. And there seem to be only two conditions of rudder: complete right rudder and a little less right rudder. Landing is a snap, I suppose because you are sitting right over the nose and can see the runway spread out before you until the touchdown. It's how much bucking and rolling and swerving around in the air the plane does, across the gusty skies of riverfront Virginia, that really surprises me. *Back to square one,* I think, as I taxi the plane to the ramp, and Martin spends fifteen minutes just teaching me how to turn into the parking space, then endless time in the shutdown of the engine, the securing of the plane, and even in the special set of knots with which one attaches both wings and the tail to the macadam, so a gust won't send it strolling into the grass. Everything is different. The culture of tending the plane is different, as well as the flying of it, and the beat-up radio is a nightmare of ghoulish croaks and moans.

But a week later, I am still coming back for more, going through the druidically detailed checklist one more time. When the run-up's finished, I scan the skies, then lift up the mike. "Williamsburg traffic, Cessna one-zero-six-five-four, departing runway one-three, right turn out, northwest bound," I say as I thrust the plane around on one spot by holding the brake in and using the throttle in bursts. Then the short runway is all in front of me, and the trees that mark the airport's perimeter and the marshlands just behind them. Tufts of grass poke up through the paving. And the sky is a single bright opulent blue haze. Wheel back, throttle full. The plane lunges down the runway, lifts up neatly in a single, upward whim at 55, and climbs out at 70, then 78. At 400 feet, I turn steeply right and follow the Colonial Parkway north to the Practice Area. Martin yanks the throttle back to idle, to test my presence of mind.

"You lost your engine," he says, and suddenly my brain excludes him from the cockpit. *Go into glide,* I say out loud, but to myself. *Find a field.... That one.*

"That brown one," I say, pointing to a wide, furrowed farm.

Martin shakes his head no. "Too rough—corn," he says. "The green fields are better."

"That green one." I put on 20 degrees of flaps, knowing that once the flaps are down it's little use putting them back up again so low. In the 150 trainer, flaps are a whopping 40 degrees—*barn doors* as even the manufacturer affectionately calls them—and curved like armadillo scales. They make the plane land steeply and at a very slow airspeed, but take you down swiftly. Remove them when you're low to the ground, and it will *decrease* the lift. So flap decision is a crucial part of flying the 150. With a field made, I run through the emergency checklist, trying to figure out what's caused the engine failure: Did I forget to change fuel tanks? It's happened to many. No. Oil? No. Primer? No. Mixture? No. Magnetos? I flip the switch clean to the left and back on again.

"Not off!" Martin cries, but it's too late, I've already flipped off and on again, and it's just our good luck that the ignition restarted.

"That was almost a real emergency," he says quietly. "All you want to check is if one of the magnetos is out.

If it is, you switch to the backup one. That's what they're for."

Spiraling closer to the field, I extend another 10 degrees of flaps, wait until I clear the telephone wires just ahead, then add the remaining 10 degrees of flaps. Pretend to turn off the fuel valve. Pretend to turn off the ignition. Pretend to turn off the master. Anything that could spark sloshed-around gas. Last of all, pretend to radio for help on a prescribed frequency: 121.5, if possible telling them which field you are in, the one to the right of a crossroads, with a thresher in the adjoining field, two miles northwest of the Williamsburg Airport, to the left of a red barn. This emergency we take clear down to 50 feet, then Martin waves me up, "Let's go!" and a steep fast climbout includes a left turn, just in case the engine should quit, as it might during practice, or anytime there are major changes in power setting. A climbing turn makes it easier to return to the field for a real emergency landing.

Five times more he pulls the throttle on me when I don't expect it, so I can practice picking the right field, judging distance to it, smoothing out the full list of last-second checks and procedures.

The haze is like a soap film through which we fly. For a few minutes, he teaches me how to do slips, to lose altitude fast if my flaps don't work, or I'm too high over a field during an emergency landing. If you cross-control in a slip, the nose rears up, and I can see how easy it would be to stall, straight into a spin, as well, since one rudder is held in completely to the wall and the opposite aileron turned away from it. In the murk, the sky looks cold as

gristle, a blue-yellow haze. Heading back to the airport, I
call Williamsburg Unicom: "Please advise which runway
is active." And a voice I know belongs to George, the airport manager who also pumps gas and once cleaned my
windshield inside and out, tells me to use 13, then something else I can't decipher. It sounds like someone crack-
ing ice at ear-splitting volume. Even Martin has trouble
fitting a message to the noise.

"I think he said there was a Cessna in the pattern," I
say, following the Colonial Parkway to where it curves
toward Norfolk, then turning toward the runway at 850
feet. "Or perhaps he was telling me about the right-hand
traffic pattern for noise abatement."

Martin shrugs. The radio sounds like sugar spilling onto
a drum. Downwind, I call Unicom again, to make sure,
and learn that no one but me is in the pattern. We swoop
below, and I set the plane down like a piece of fragile
pottery.

Then we taxi back to takeoff position and, to my horror,
he starts to climb out.

"Martin," I say, stretching the syllables of his name as
pathetically as any imminent orphan, "I've only been up
in this plane a couple of hours."

"I know. That's all right. You just take it round three
times." His face says: *I'm not asking you to fly an Apollo
to the moon, just go round the pattern.* I want him to reassure me that I can do that magical thing in this new,
awkward, squirrelly little plane, whose every lurch and
bumble scares me. At some point I have to stop asking
when I'm fit for release, though; I know that and say
nothing. But if he's wrong? I didn't fly low-wings very
well and, after only one week, I know even less about

high-wings. *Fate be kind,* I say silently, wonder if I should say something memorable to him in case I die, then cancel that thought as too pessimistic, and shut the door, watching him watch me through the window for a moment before he heads across the tarmac and into the FBO to stand by the radio and keep an eye on me. As soon as he's well past my propeller, I turn the plane round and line up at the threshold, announce my departure, and go. Waiting for him to cross the no-man's-land of the macadam would be excruciating. This way I am up and flying before I can think about it, and if he is watching I can't tell, because my eyes are glued to the instrument panel, not to the plane's attitude, as it should be, or to the sky which may be packed with other planes, just to the instrument panel, in a paralysis of nerve. At 400 feet, I bounce a wing up, pretend to look, then cut a shallow turn, then another, ending up downwind at about the right altitude, but scared. The rich haze doesn't help.

Williamsburg traffic, Cessna six-five-four, right downwind for one-three, I radio, then slow down abeam the numbers, and try to judge how high I may be for final approach. So this is soloing, I start to laugh nervously to myself, not after thirty-five hours in a plane you know scratch by scratch, but like this, when everything is at stake, everything is unknown, you have minimal control, the airport is unfamiliar, the radio is indecipherable and may be telling you anything (that you're on fire, that you've lost your landing gear), when the winds seem to be sinking and gusting you in rabbit punches, your airspeed dashes between zoom and stall, and with cool, complete objectivity you know that you are only fractionally more in control than you aren't. That's why, on the third pass round, when you see the runway only 200 feet below, you head for it madly, through wing-rocking gusts and radio jabber, checking everything, airspeed, throttle, flaps, wanting nothing but to stop your legs from shaking, to be safe again on the ground.

For a moment I glance up above the center line, lifting at me like a pointer, and what I see is impossible: a red and white Pitts Special biplane landing straight at me from the opposite direction! Whole seconds pass, and the radio says something indecipherable; then more seconds, and I am rushing the throttle full against the fire wall, punching in the carburetor heat for whatever poor extra power I can grab, and throwing off my flaps at reckless speed, as I bank steeply right toward the river. *Cessna 654, go around, don't land,* the radio is saying, Martin's voice is saying, as I fly through, and the Pitts Special lands underneath me.

What shall I do? I wonder. Fly out over the river and collect myself, before reentering the pattern? What if the Pitts is still on the runway? Where did he come from, and why didn't I see him? How could I have been so careless? What shall I do, with my adrenalin pumping and my nerves in a twist? The obvious answer is to land as quickly and carefully as possible, and so I turn back into the pattern, announce myself downwind, and set up for final. This time there is no plane charging out of the haze, and when I land my hands and legs are trembling. The Pitts is nowhere in sight, and that's a mystery, since it can't have been more than two or three minutes since the near-collision.

Martin is on the tarmac, waiting, when I taxi back, looking like a tall metal soldier in gray pants and white sweater, a hand on each hip. He seems placed there. Then he moves, and the toyland vision disappears.

"Boy, you guys sure do like to solo people in style," I say, climbing out of the cockpit. "Do you always arrange that kind of excitement?"

"We didn't want you to find it too boring," he says, and picks up the end of a tie-down rope, feeding it methodically through the steel loop on the wing. His hand passes the rope through and through again, pressing, folding. "You handled that well," he says without looking up.

"I'm sorry about not seeing the biplane. I was so preoccupied with just getting round."

Past the propeller, I see George walking quickly toward us, obviously incensed, and it starts to dawn on me that perhaps something unusual has taken place.

"It was for *him* to see *you*," Martin says angrily. "First of all, he was higher, so you had right of way. Second of all, he didn't make radio contact. Third, he landed downwind, so he probably didn't bother checking the wind sock. Fourth, he disregarded the right-hand traffic pattern. And if he flies a Pitts around here, he's experienced enough to know better about all of those things." His face is a sheet of protectiveness. It's not that rules were broken, but that his student was endangered. George adjusts and readjusts his glasses, shifts from foot to foot, too pent-up to stand still.

"I've already started drafting up a letter to the FAA," he says. "Jesus, when a student's up there soloing yet. And wait till . . . "

Martin silences him with a gesture that says *Let's talk about it over there, out of her hearing,* and they walk

171

slowly toward the FBO trailer, from which other con-cerned faces begin to emerge, as I continue tying down and securing the plane. Seconds pass during which I can't remember if I've just landed or am getting ready to go up. *Ridiculous*, I whisper, picking up the clipboard on which my Hobbs time has been noted, and head toward the trailer, stopping underneath the wing of a plane to watch the men still standing by the fence across the way, their faces animated as they talk. I know they are deciding how best to handle a bully who just threatened one of their children, their student pilot, and something very ancient in me feels a rush of intense, unshakable well-being.

27

I OFTEN WONDER what flight instructors are thinking, as they wait for the preflight to be finished, the complex, methodical *looking* that begins at one wheel, with one cotter pin, and continues in a long advancing retreating-advancing walk around the plane, as you check every screw, every scratch. Is that collection of white grazes in the bleached maroon paint where it was yesterday? Or is it new, a stress to be reported? Your hand slides along the bug-encrusted leading edge of the wing. Not searching really, but being open to the appearance of something out of the ordinary. The ordinary is what you want, business as usual in the odd life of this metal someone has taught to fly. Ordinary weather, ordinary performance of the plane, an ordinary man for an instructor, no tyrant, no toddler, no lothario, no daredevil, just a good-natured man with keen reflexes and a determination to teach you. But your instructor has done preflight by himself every time he has flown. This laboriously as a student, and now with a galloping, trained eye that knows the 100 points on the checklist clipboard too well to need to keep picking the list up between points, then running a hand over the flap, or stepping up high onto the nose rung to check the gas, and returning to the list again, reined back by caution. Nothing can be more boring than watching this fits-and-starts walk around the plane when he could be in the air already, but he says nothing. To do nothing is his job at this point. It is more important that you are thorough. *Never rush a preflight. Never change the order of the checklist.* You are paying him not just with money, but with the long lead of your desire, the snaffle sound that wakes you up in the morning and decoys you out of bed because the sky is a blue smear fit for flying, because the sky is *flyable*, and that is too miraculous and impossible a thought not to become part of. You pay him for these moments of teaching you what is, and how to be, ordinary, when all you have ever been is freakish, when all you have ever known is a human condition extraordinary, unexpectedly lush, full of surprise. With the hazy blue hours of your fall, you pay him, with your enthusiasm, which you will never have again in the same ratio of intensity and zest, pay him with your youth, which you would always regret if you wasted it in an empty addiction, something that used you up and gave you nothing. On hands large enough to straddle two octaves, the nails are trimmed well below the tips of his fingers. His cheekbones are squared off high, so that his face seems to have plateaus, inclines, and shadows. It is a face made serious by control, and by the aviator's glasses that deepen his eyes to the color of a summer field. What pilots prefer across their eyes is the flat, lush paradise of emergency—a growing field of new wheat: calm, still, fully open to one's descent, a soft place to settle, if one must, belly down.

Meticulous and precise about everything—a lesson in navigation or the arrangement of papers on his desk or the carefully observed servicing of his car—he is devoutly thorough, methodical, organized, a man most comfortable with the deft arrangement of details. He is not yet a wise man, but he will be, because even now he is a kind man, with a puppyish sense of play and a mercifully long fuse, whose severest reprimand is a look of vacant disappointment or a stern tease. Like other young flight instructors, he is a man waiting for his future to unfold into something better, but in the meantime he is happy to drink Mr. Pibb on the sofa in the FBO, from which we all watch the runway through thirty feet of plate-glass window, happy to chat with George and Mike and Tom about nothing, about everything. If the chat is never probing or philosophical, it is also never mean, insidious, or malicious.

He is just beginning to be bored by the adventure that first thrilled him, flying gliders in Europe and then powered planes here, coming to the United States to learn to fly where flying is cheap and the sky is a borderless expanse for 3,000 miles. A trifle shy, he jokes easily with friends, and in a job that keeps him brushing elbow and thigh with students in a cramped cockpit, he shows no trace of self-consciousness. Even when, as recently, he had to stand by as a woman in a white cocktail dress clambered up onto the wing to continue her checklist, despite heels, petticoat, and nylons, before flying off to a meeting.

But what is he thinking during the arranged tedium of the preflight, when he must not show any impatience, when he follows me round a pace or two behind, munching potato chips or a candy bar instead of lunch, looking where my eyes look, where my hands make the tough hollow metal move through an angle, when he is waiting in the broil of sun on black macadam, too tall to stand under the relative shade of the high wing, waiting for me to finish the complex novelty he takes for granted. I will make it new for him. He will make it old for me. I will find in it the strangeness he once found and some things perhaps he will never find, or wish to. I smile at him through the bug-jellied plane windows, on the other side of which he waits to climb into his seat beside me when at last the lesson can begin.

I complete my checklist. "Yep, it's a plane, all right," I say and climb aboard.

28

EARLY ON A BRIGHT, WARM DAY in mid-September, when
the sky is the color of Wedgwood blue, broken by a few
cumulus puffs and the staccato skywardness of every light
airplane owner for miles, I phone the airport. Martin
and Tom are both out, so I phone the FBO next.

"How's the wind today?" For a moment, it seems like
an odd question to begin a conversation with on a balmy
morning in historic Virginia. Although, perhaps it is the
perfect question, one a general might have asked his aide
before a Saturday morning battle not far from the airport
and its nearby strategy of rivers and island hideouts.

"Wind's calm," Mike says. The alternate FBO manager, he's a little more reserved than George and stockier,

with a trim mustache and short neatly kept black hair. "Tom doesn't come in on Saturday," he continues. "He'll be out on some golf course, probably . . . and Martin left this morning on a cross-country to Norfolk. He should be back right soon."

"Winds are calm, you say?" It's a question that only a student pilot would repeat with such tentative sincerity.

"Sure are."

"Great. See you in a few minutes."

All I need to hear is that the clear sky is also calm enough for me to do what I've been itching to for so long, take a plane up by myself, without an instructor to cajole or lead the way. Not that I want to stray from the false security of the traffic pattern, where you are always gliding distance from the runway, even though nasty things can happen and often do. Half a mile away, to James River, seems never-never land, the Practice Area five miles away, a spot of myth and rumor. All I want for the time being is to lift the bird up softly, thread by thread, into the invisible weave of the sky, and then cozy it back down again, doing touch-and-goes by myself, somehow to develop a *sense* for the plane that still threatens to lurch away from me at every climb and whose turns I never seem to coordinate just right. Demoralized about landings for so long, I want to persuade myself that I can bring it down to earth, ladderless, without mishap, without losing control, without losing nerve.

The airport is postcard-perfect: royal-blue sky, bright sun, not a leaf trembling on the lush, dark-green perimeter of trees. Cessnas are everywhere, some flying in tandem (a word too sonorous and suggestive for the blunt Latin it comes from: "at length"). An occasional Aztec or Baron or other low-winged plane appears downwind, scooting in to land, some touching down as fast as my trainer cruises. Two planes in a row jump a bit at the treeline just beyond the end of the runway, where a cleared fairway boils the air whenever there's a crosswind. Today, it's just a little "squirrelly," as the flyers say, but nothing like the treacherous wind shear Poleskie found at Sky Park when we went to Old Rhinebeck.

At eleven-thirty, a green-and-white Cessna 172 enters the pattern: Martin returning with a student who, after 300 hours, is learning to read the sky by IFR. *I got tired of flying into places and being unable to leave because of the weather,* he will tell me later, but at the moment he is landing from an horizon-to-horizon sky, with the earth popping up like a storybook underneath him, and a crosswind giving him an unexpected bit of trouble. A gleaming little silver Ercoupe taxis out to 13, and I can hear its pilot checking his radio, *Williamsburg Unicom, do you hear Ercoupe 715?* With his head poking up through a plexiglass dome, the pilot can see all around him in the squat, tiny trainer, whose rear fuselage points straight back like an Irish setter's tail.

By now, Martin and his student have taxied over to the gas pump, and as Martin gets out, I begin to pester him about letting me go up alone. He makes a melodramatic check of the wind with a finger. He consults both wind socks (one is blowing straight out, the other hanging limp).

"Have you called Flight Service Station for the weather?"

"You're kidding. It's beautiful. Look—blue skies, no birds of prey circling at the end of the runway." I'm amazed to find myself whining.

"Only if you check the Flight Service Station first," he says, fighting back a smile.

"Right." I dial the number printed across the base of the black wall phone, and when a man answers at Patrick Henry International Airport, at Newport News, Virginia, I tell him that I'm a student pilot in Williamsburg, who needs to know the current state of my weather, as well as the forecast. *10,000 broken, 25,000 scattered, visibility unlimited, winds under 10 knots,* he says. Perfect flying weather. Because I'm a student pilot, he translates the forecast from zulu time to what's local. When I hang up, Martin checks the weather report sheet I've filled out in a messy scrawl, then shakes his head.

"The visibility isn't unlimited," he says soberly. "I couldn't see California."

"Could you see your hand in front of your face?" I ask brightly.

"Yes."

"Then you were within legal minimums. Can I fly?"

"Do you know how a plane flies?" he asks.

"I can spell the word *lift.*"

"That's good enough," he says, and adds something else, but I've already grabbed the clipboard and key for 654 and am rushing out the door to start my preflight.

It's only at the plane, which looks suddenly wrong in every way, that I have second thoughts about what I've gotten myself into, and proceed with the longest preflight in history. Everything looks unfamiliar, the cotter pins, the elevator trim, the rusted bolts on the fuselage, the cracked wing tip. But everything is also as it should be, I know. And it's only when I climb aboard and run through my checklist to turn the plane on, enriching the mixture, pushing the carburetor to cold, turning on the master switch, pulling the throttle out all but a quarter inch, and yelling CLEAR PROP! that I realize exactly how nervous I must be. It's no use trying to start the ignition with the key still in my pocket. *Settle down,* a voice whispers from somewhere underneath one of my vertebrae. A long time has passed since Martin first saw me scampering out to preflight the plane, and perhaps that's why he's now taxiing a Cessna 172 around the ramp to park it off my left wing tip, a casual, unobtrusive way of nonetheless seeing what I'm up to. I bring my throttle hand to a nonexistent cap in a mock salute, then taxi past him to the runway I know is being used, or is *active,* as they say. Turning into the wind, at the threshold of 13, I do my run-up, and hear the engine grind and splutter so hoarsely I become seriously worried. That isn't normal. Or is it? Do I play it safe and taxi back for Martin to listen, and risk looking like an idiot when he tells me I'm hearing ghosts, or do I take off a plane I think may be unsafe? After a laughably long run-up, I decide the engine is probably normal; I hadn't listened to it closely before. Then I tell Williamsburg traffic—all of it, anyone eavesdropping on the airways—that I'm a Cessna departing runway 13 and staying in the pattern.

"Watch out for the Pitts," a voice says over the radio, and I laugh back, "I'll do that."

Kiss the world good-bye, I think, and press the throttle against the fire wall, while holding the nose wheel gently off the ground, at just the angle I hope to be climbing out at. Seconds later, I reach airspeed, and the plane follows its nose upward, lifting off in the silkiest, gentlest climb I could wish for. But too soon I am at 400 feet and trying to coordinate nose and wings in a decent turn, as the turn-and-bank ball falls far right. *Jesus, I'm skidding at 400 feet*, I think, and shallow out into a messy, wide arc that takes me a mile toward the river, on a wide downwind. Now my airspeed is too high, and I'm 150 feet above traffic altitude. I cut the power, pull on the carburetor heat, and slow up to 80. Then call the tower, in a husky rush, *Williamsburg tow* . . . no, no tower, it's an uncontrolled field . . . *Williamsburg traffic, Cessna 10654 right downwind for 13, touch and go*. Abeam the numbers and the perfect round run-up bay at the end of 13, I cut the power back to 1,700 rpms, and slow up to 70 mph, adding 20 degrees of flaps. I had meant to add only 10 degrees. The runway seems far away, so I turn straight toward it, adding more flaps and cutting the power, then bringing in more power, as I line up with the center stripe, cutting the power again. Over the trees, the airspeed plunges to 60, and it's in that slower-than-sensible attitude I float in, flaring to a gentle, nose-up landing almost halfway down the runway. But only half remains, and it occurs to me that the electric flaps will take their own sweet time to raise. I won't be able to yank them up or down as I could in the Warrior. I bang the flap switch up, punch the carburetor heat off, palm the throttle clean open, and begin taking off, turning my head as I approach lift-off speed and the end of the runway, to see the last angle of flaps disappearing into the wing.

In the 400 feet between takeoff and first turn, there is a moment of peace, so I check my wristwatch. Only five minutes have passed. How can that be possible? A gust changes my airspeed, and I try to turn more smartly onto a downwind leg, slow to 80, lift the mike to announce my whereabouts. A Cessna Cardinal begins a full conversation with the Unicom operator. When they finish, I lift the mike, try to slow abeam the numbers, begin my descent, and talk at the same time.

"George, is that Cardinal entering the pattern?" I ask with anxious informality.

"Williamsburg Unicom," a voice replies.

Of all the times to remind me that I summoned the demon incorrectly. "Cessna six-five-four," I say, gabbling, "right downwind for one-three. Please advise if that Cardinal is a factor."

"Cardinal is still five miles on approach, six-five-four," Unicom answers. I start to laugh, as no doubt the men inside, watching me through the sun-crazed windows are laughing, and end the conversation: "Six-five-four."

After two more go-rounds, only fifteen minutes have passed. It seems impossible. Though I've mastered the timing right for touch-and-goes—the knack of using up as little of the little runway as possible, and taking off, full throttle, as the flaps are still sliding back up into their housing—my approaches are terrible. Each turn to final, I am all over the sky, lacing it up, rearing through it, bouncing and sliding. It can't be the wind alone making my airspeed so wavery and fitful, all around 70, but not locked onto it. The hands are the flags of the nervous system, and as keyed up as mine is, my hands must be inadvertently trembling, fretting the wheel. Turn to final. Let down 40 degrees of flaps; I feel the plane balloon because I've forgotten to hold its nose down while the flaps go on. Coming over the trees, on a fine, steady descent, I see the runway in front of me, but something is wrong. My hand hasn't moved on the wheel, I'm positive it hasn't, but my airspeed has changed swiftly from 70 to 50. *Jesus*, I whisper, *40 is stalling speed.* Before I have time to correct, the plane lurches into a 45 degree bank to the right, all at once, as if a hand had grabbed the wing tip and yanked it down. I could fall now like a letter opener, on edge, slide a wing deep into the marsh underneath me. My ribs hurt from the tight, loud drumming of my heart, nothing like thought happens, but my foot has already solved the problem, pushing in the opposite rudder pedal, as I level off, force the nose down for speed, and add power to make the runway. Down at last, I hit the flaps-up switch, and taxi to the ramp, still shaking, and decide to stop for the day, while I'm still in one piece. *How could I have messed up that badly? Some solo flight,* I think, as I open the window and let a whoosh of prop-swept air cool me down, and wind my way back toward the FBO trailer and long line of tethered Cessnas. Across the airport, I see Martin and the FBO guys all standing outside the office, applauding with large open-palmed motions, so I can't mistake them. On the radio, and over the loudspeaker, Unicom says, "Nice flying six-five-four." My mouth falls open, and I feel a rush of such intense affection for these flyers who have looked after and protected me, even defended me when necessary, and who encourage me with such generosity. In Ithaca, soloing was an empty climax to months of excruciating trial, degradation, and frustration. The tower was aloof as an Old Testament god, my instructor was unexcited, the FBO boss didn't care. Flying was not something sharably human and delightful, a jump from one energy state to another. It was a taboo-laden ritual by which they defined their seriousness and proved how manly they were, how solid, how in control.

Freeze this moment, I think, *this moment of pure, terse jubilation,* so that you will remember it when you are older, sofa-flying your memories through all the gusty emotions of being young. Not disabled perhaps, but with a quieter, less-visible degeneration of self, when you will need to remember this moment of deep-down, starry, self-amazing thrill.

Martin leaves the others as I taxi back to my stall and try to figure out how to wedge the plane into it. Patiently, he waits until I pivot, gun the engine, and struggle, then finally sweep round, pick up the checklist and turn the engine off, step by step. Together, we drag the plane backward into place and tie its wings and tail. I am grinning so hard you could slide a cassette into my mouth, and he is grinning, too, because he knows that I have just crossed a barrier I'd thought impossible only weeks before. A month ago, I was a groundling. Today I drove to the airport, rented a plane, and took it up by myself. *I did it,* I say with urgent surprise, as we walk back to the trailer. He nods exaggeratedly, eyes wide: positively, absolutely, hats-off, gentlemen.

29

Even in the impossible muck of a cold, drizzly October morning, an airport is a magical place. Richard Bach is right to be excited everytime he sees the word *Airport* on a highway sign. An airport is where *planes* are, and planes are what carry you deep into the infinite. Some of them tuck their feet up when they fly—RG the specs say, for "retractable gear"—and some fly with their feet hanging down, the way wasps and mosquitoes do. But they are all strange, mythic-looking, magical bits of screw and rivet that float on nothing. They are all transporter beams to invisible planets; they are all stagecoaches bucking and galloping across our vertical frontier.

In a field at the edge of the runway, an old silver

Ercoupe sits moldering until the next war. On its nose, someone has tethered a full-length, realistic rubber snake (to scare nesting birds away), so it looks more like a scene from jungle combat than a casual tie-down at a small Virginian airport. Beside the Ercoupe an orange and white Cessna 152 II has its nose plugged up with blocks of styrofoam and yarn streamers, to thwart nesting birds. An orange Citabria is roped down a few yards farther back, lest, wind-buffeted, it begins aerobatics all by itself.

Today will be my fifth solo flight, but the first time that I'll be straying from the pattern. Yesterday, I braved a wider circuit, to the James River and the pancreas-shaped marsh island that signals a turn for the airport to local flyers. Today, Martin has assigned me to fly the perimeter of the Practice Area, which he traces with one long finger on a sectional.

"So, you will fly to the bridge about seven miles west of the airport, and follow the five lakes here north to West Point," he says, letting his stiff, steady finger trace a fourteen-mile course through a blue Rorschach on the chart, to where an open blue parachute next to a magenta circle warns about the skydiving across the York River. "From there, you follow the river past the Harcum VOR until you're southeast of Williamsburg, then cut across to the airport here." He touches the magenta circle in whose center is one short white line, our small runway, and as he lifts his finger from it, I realize for the first time how much like a goat's eye the runway symbol looks, deep red with a barred pupil. "Another thing," Martin says, "I want you to practice steep turns and also minimum controllable airspeed while you're out there." His voice is so resolutely confident there is no disagreeing or need to disagree. It's only when I'm outside, preflighting 654, that I realize that I'm off on my first cross-country, even if for logbook purposes I'm still flying "local," anything within a twenty-five-mile radius.

Limp, the wind sock says runway 31 is active, or at least was active whenever there was last wind.

"Williamsburg Unicom, Cessna six-five-four," I call, as I taxi from my berth toward the runway.

"Six-five-four, Williamsburg Unicom," George's voice answers—George, who is going back to college four nights a week to study criminology, and who is a marriage counselor in addition to working at the airport; George, with whom I shoot the breeze, along with Martin, so many afternoons in the FBO that I feel at ease just hearing his voice over the radio, a friendly timbre along the airways.

"George, is three-one active today?"

"Well, there really isn't any wind. But the needle in here says one-three."

"Okay." I pirouette at the intersection, and taxi to the threshold of 13.

"Have a nice flight, now," the radio says.

And I answer, "Right, see you in a bit," do my full run-up, and announce my intentions to any planes in the area, but also to whoever is at the Unicom mike (if anything goes wrong, I'd just as soon they remember where I said I was headed): "Williamsburg traffic, Cessna six-five-four departing runway one-three, right turn out, northwest bound."

The runway is all in front of me, open, rushable, waiting, and when I push the throttle against the fire wall and tilt the nose to where I want it to be on takeoff, I am bridging the ground and sky so smoothly I barely notice the lift-off, when bouncing speed turns to float and the runway plunges away below you as in a dream. At 400 feet, I turn left and head for the highway skirting the river, which I know leads to my first checkpoint, the bridge. I begin to sing to myself, but the engine clamor is too loud to hear oneself sing, and it's eerie forcing air through your lips, knowing you are singing but hearing absolutely nothing. In a few minutes, the bridge appears, just where it's supposed to be, but haze has begun to settle under 2,000 feet, where I should be flying for safety's sake, because from 2,000 feet at 70 mph I could glide six miles in a 150 Cessna, time enough to find *someplace* landable. Instead I decide in favor of visibility, and stay at 1,500 feet, while scouting the mounting autumn of the fields below for places to land. And there aren't many of them; most of the terrain is marsh and settlement and stands of tall, scrubby trees, and rivers whose surface is no easy runway. Right turn, due north, following the mazy, intestinal lakes below, whose limits I can't define from so low an altitude in such poor visibility. A rustling at my left; I notice the window is loose and vibrating. Fiddling with the handle doesn't secure it any, and I'm afraid to open and shut the window again, at 100 mph, even though I don't recall its shimmying like that before. But then solo flight makes everything seem eerie; all the bolts and wire sheaths look wrong in the engine, all the cracks and crazes on the fuselage look new, the engine sounds wrong, the gauges seem to be reading in Swahili, and nothing can seem more perilous than a loose window. I smile and take a good long look down below for the first time. *This is flight*, I am thinking; *you are flying over the countryside, those rivers, those houses, that highway, all by yourself; you are making in-*

*visible tracks across the county, you are FLYING BY
YOURSELF, you are FLYING.* All the maddening hours,
the bumps and circuits, the ground school, all of it is for
this scary glide under the rain clouds, all of it is leading
to this first time when you leave instructor and traffic
pattern at home, and cross the first street into a new
neighborhood. "Time for a longer leash now," Tom Johnson, the owner of Colonial Aviation, had said matter-of-
factly. "Go see if the Practice Area is still there today."

At the top of the lakes, I head north and begin to look
for West Point, a town jutting out into the York River.
Nothing. I climb to 2,000 feet and see a peninsula full of
houses and smoke-spewing factories. But between me and
it are dozens of wispy clouds. In fact the clouds have begun to pour over and around me. *Jesus,* I say quietly, and
clumsily jerk back the throttle to descend fast. The rate-
of-descent dial says I am dropping at 1,000 feet a minute; I've been taught not to drop faster than 500. My airspeed has jumped from 100 to 120, and my adrenalin
starts to make me feel hot and shuddery. I bring the power
back in and try to dodge the clouds instead, while descending to 1,500 feet, then 1,300, when a mass of blue
clouds, trailing ropes of rain, stretches overhead. *VFR
minimum, 500 feet below the clouds, and 2,000 feet free
of the clouds all around me at my altitude.* Now I know
why they call it *minimum.* At 1,000 feet, while clouds
blow over me like bursts from an atomizer, I follow the
York River to the Harcum VOR cone, a clear landmark
on a marshy outcropping. The next checkpoint is about
seven miles farther along—high tension wires and a major
highway—where I turn back toward the airport, to complete my aerial shoebox. It won't come a moment too

soon, I think, and wonder if perhaps I shouldn't just turn back toward the airport now, since the overcast is so low and gloomy and the sky seems to be deteriorating every second. Flight Service Station had said it would be okay until 2 P.M., when rain would move in. It's noon now; suppose they miscalculated by two hours? Suppose that cobalt blue goop straight ahead and above me thickens opaquely and descends? For five miles, I fly looking almost solidly over my left shoulder, to make sure of the area I would turn back to if I became suddenly enveloped in cloud. The airport at West Point, that's where I'd head. I check the chart again, looking for the turning spot back toward Williamsburg, then at the ground rolling indistinctly below. No high tension wires. No highway at all. Perhaps I am simply too low to see it. Then, in the distance: what looks like a bridge I know must be the one over the York River, ten miles too far south. Turning abruptly east, I notice a runway at the exact tip of my left wing. An airport? The chart doesn't show any where I think I am. I tune in the Harcum VOR as fast as possible, to see where in fact I am. 160 FROM, it reads, and I trace the radial to a small red circle around a capital R on the chart. A restricted airport. Military, probably. And just north of Williamsburg. Now that I'm home, and know where home is, I climb back to 1,800 feet, and fly over the city toward where I know Jamestown Island must be. The airport appears, cozy and calm, and I steer wide of its pattern and north to a practice spot just a mile off the runway. Four steep turns, two right, two left. Five minutes of slow flight. *Right, that's it,* I say formally, to no one but my willingness, and head back to the airport, announcing myself over Jamestown Island, entering the

pattern in the usual way at the right altitude and feeling
deliciously exhilarated and relieved all at once, as I turn
final, float in to land, drifting halfway down the runway,
then pulling roughly to a stop while the nose-wheel shim-
mies and jerks as it always does in this quirky, but de-
pendable trainer.

What an odyssey, I'm thinking, as I taxi back to the
trailer, and tie down, jotting my Hobbs time on the ap-
propriate chart. I have been up for exactly one hour.
And probably it was supposed to take me just that long.
It's the not knowing of parameters that's so scary, the not
knowing of what is normal, expected, hoped for. Behind
the Venetian blinds, at his office window, where one as-
sumes that Tom is doing paperwork or schmoozing with
Kay, Peg, Tex, or any of the others who stop by just to
visit for a moment, ribbing each other and making flying
jokes (Example: a sign hanging on his door, which says
"Flight Instructors Never Sweat—but when they do, it's
only on the right side of their face"), Tom was probably
checking his watch as I taxied out. Had I been half an
hour longer, he would probably have had someone make
casual contact with me over Unicom. Perhaps as casually
as C.T. did when I was entering the downwind at last
for 13. "Cessna six-five-four, do you copy seven-seven
Yankee?" a voice said unexpectedly over the radio. For a
moment, it startled me, and then I said, quickly running
through what I might be doing wrong, "Yes, seven Yankee, go ahead." "Say is Martin up there with you?" he
asked. "Why, no, I'm up here by my lonesome today,"
I answered. "Well, this is C. T., Martin's pal, we met the
other day, remember? Say hello to him for me when you
see him." "Right, I'll do that," I said, laughing at how

alarmless and mundane the exchange was, and how I'd let it send me farther downwind than I meant to go before throttling back and turning base.

In the Colonial Aviation trailer, Tom and Martin are all smiles.

"How was your flight?" someone asks, and I tell them about it, step by step, minute by frightening minute, just as if I had come from a strafing run in the Congo.

30

"STALLS AND STEEP TURNS?" It seems like an odd question to ask a Dutchman on so graphically blue and still an afternoon. Painters of shadowed absences, caged motion, and prowling light; explorers and scientists and poets. Amsterdam in the seventeenth century was a crossroads for people on the move through space—over oceans, over land, over time.

"Let's go to Patrick Henry," he says, his face tinged with prankishness, "and visit the control tower and Flight Service Station."

"The control tower!" I cry, unable to trim my excitement. "Martin, let's go visit the Control Tower!"

I want to meet the disembodied voices that fill my cockpit with liquid gravel stirred by command and permission, the aerial traffic cops who hold up the airport-sized palm of one hand or wave a plane through an intersection on the ground. I want to see the airport as they see it, from their glass eyrie, their widow's walk high above the hubbub of the ground, almost in the traffic pattern itself, a permanent piece of the changing clamor of the airways.

In ten minutes, we are left downwind for runway 2 at Patrick Henry, having told the tower that we are a Cessna 150, student pilot, at 1,500 feet, cognizant of the prerecorded airport advisory, whose code word today and at this hour is "Tango," and that we are making a full-stop landing. Not who we are or why we are or how long we are, only *what* and *where*. Life reduces quickly to these code words and locations. "Have Tango," I tell them, and smile at the accidental felicity. I have *Tango*ed across the sky from Williamsburg to Newport News, in the *Uniform* of a plane, with the *Victory* of flight, drunk on the sky as on *Whiskey*; *X-Ray* my ribs and watch my *Yankee* heart drumming like a *Zulu*. After landing, I taxi to the ramp and take an invisible stall marked only by a white cross on the ground, flanked by ropes ready to bind down each wing tip, as if to become part of some technological crucifixion.

In a small room, with many cramped desks and the green glow of small computers, and curiously out-of-date-looking switchboards and dials one might expect to find in a large, but deteriorating grand hotel, is the weather center for most of eastern Virginia, the Flight Service Station. An old-fashioned flyswatter hangs next to a barometer on one dingy wall.

"I'm the one who pesters you so often from Williamsburg," I apologize, shaking hands with a stout, middle-aged man who leaves his desk to give me a detailed tour of the place. "Thanks for being so patient when I call, explaining the fronts, translating Zula time. . . . Of course, telling me that when Mickey's big hand is on the four and little hand is on the six . . ." His eyebrows raise as he laughs, and the men in surrounding desks start to chuckle. I look at each face and try to attach a voice to it. Then try on him some of my other student-pilot humor—about how in Ithaca, for instance, when I first called Flight Service Station, and they closed the briefing by asking for my airplane's number ("What's your sign?" they had asked), I'd nervously answered, "Libra."

All around the room, machines are busy charting and counting. Magenta swirls burn into tissue paper-maps. One man hand-tints a printout to make IFR and VFR areas clearer. A machine measures in slice-of-pie dots exactly how broken or clear the skies are over Denver and Roanoke and Seattle. At each station, a computer scans the country in code, a chunk of which Martin walks me through—the winds aloft at 3,000, 6,000, 9,000, 12,000, 18,000, 24,000, 30,000, 34,000, and 39,000 feet. Which direction the winds are coming from over twenty cities, how fast they're blowing at each altitude, and what the temperature is. Then we decode general forecasts for Virginia and notes that individual pilots have radioed in about unusual conditions.

ICG . . . NONE. FRZLVL AON SFC OH WV SLPG TO 30–50 VA AND TO 115 SC. FRZLVL LFTG TO 50 OH WV BY 18Z

Translation:

> Icing . . . None. Freezing level at or near
> the surface over Ohio, West Virginia, sloping to
> 3,000–5,000 feet over Virginia, and to 11,500 feet
> over South Carolina. Freezing level lifting to 5,000
> feet over Ohio, West Virginia by 1:00 P.M. EST.

Which means that, if there is precipitation in Ohio, it
will probably be snow or sleet, and one would be better
out of it. A pilot has radioed in reports of severe updrafts
on the lee side of the Blue Ridge mountains. Good to
know about and plan extra altitude in the crossing. For
now, I'm just learning how to read this weather pidgin;
in time, I'll actually use it, when I decide whether a flight
to the Midwest is go or no-go on a particular day.

From FSS, we climb the steps to the observation deck
of the airport terminal. Through a locked glass door, the
control tower is visible. Martin lifts a wall phone and
speaks with one of two figures who come to our side of
their glass room. For a moment, two ladies seem to be
watering plants in a hothouse.

"I'm a flight instructor," he is saying without fuss, "and
I have a student with me; I'd like to bring her up there,
if that's all right."

A buzzer opens the door, and we walk across a rooftop
to a steel door, which another buzzer opens, then up a
spiral metal staircase, narrow enough for a submarine tur-
ret, through another buzzer door, finally emerging in the
glass prow, where two men stand talking casually into
microphones. The first thing one notices is the absence

of static background noise, just their voices, pristine, human, ordinary, speaking with inflected purpose, but relaxedly, as over a hand of bridge. The younger, slimmer man has his shoes off and is eating a bowl of honeydew melon balls, which he has salted heavily. The other, in thick, photosensitive glasses, looks like he'd be more at home driving a New York City cab. He has pinprick skin cancers on one cheek, below the sunglass line. The younger man wears no sunglasses at all. Despite the gray plastic curtains covering half of each window like bifocals, glare is a whole note playing loudly through the room, and there is no direction safe from its echo off chrome or plastic. Using the mike like a tag team, they greet us and land planes, chatting effusively. It's clear at once how delighted they are to have company. For an hour, they show us how everything works: the light gun that flashes signals to planes whose radios have failed, the radar scope, the weather dials, the flight plan recorders. At one side of the room sit an oven, refrigerator, and stove. There are no plants, no paintings but the ones changing through each pane of glass; but it does look like a small loft in Soho. It's not at all what I expected. Martin and the two controllers tell aviation jokes and chat about the changes at Patrick Henry Airport now that the big airlines have pulled out their heavy passenger jets. As we're talking, a Cessna requests permission to begin at the end of one runway and takeoff and land repeatedly the length of it. The controller shrugs and clears him. Three planes appear in the pattern at the same time, from different directions, and the other man separates them, gives them number of order to land, and tells them about the planes in the pattern, and about the Cessna galloping down one runway. When we leave at last, they repeatedly invite us back to visit. It must get lonely up there, limited to the predictable Simon Sez conversations with all the people who pass through their lives each day. Whatever I expected to find—a sober voice crouched over a World War Two radio microphone, his tie knotted and perfectly centered, his eyelids tight with fatigue as he solemnly lands planes—I didn't expect a laid-back Southern guy with his shoes off eating melon balls. Back in 654 again, I taxi to the runway threshold and tell them I'm ready for takeoff. "Good-bye, Diane," the voice says. "Come back and see us."

In some ways, Martin has been proud to show me off. I think he gets a kick out of walking into Flight Service or a control tower, with a strange, exotic bird on the leash of his instruction, which he winds up and sets on the counter, knowing that out of its mouth will pour bizarre and unexpected things.

Twilight is falling, as we fly back to Williamsburg low enough to see the roller coaster at Busch Gardens, lighted with a ghoulish green neon, snaking through the marsh.

"Want to be a glider?" Martin asks.

I do, and relinquish the wheel. He climbs up a thousand feet, cuts the engine and does glider aerobatic turns, silently toward the James River. The sun now is a hot yellow vitamin disappearing into red batik at the horizon. Twilight is never so lavender as at 2,000 feet, when the air is visible and large, like separate crushed petals in a potpourri. I take back control of the plane, hold the stick like a beer stein handle in my left hand and adjust the power with my right, grinning at Martin, whose face is veiled by lavender glow. When the runway lights appear in front of us, we fall to them greedily, rear wheels first, wings arched high, frozen at mid-flap.

31

Taking the clipboard for 654, I swig the last of my coffee and prepare to go to the bathroom for a final time before flying. Vibration and a full bladder don't mix. And it's very bad form to land at a neighboring airport just to use the toilet.

"Where you headed?" Tom asks, with the astute casualness I've come to associate with him.

"Oh, I thought I'd go see if the Practice Area has moved any during the night," I say. "You know how mobile they are."

"Variation," Martin says, without looking up from his paperwork, and we all start to laugh at what is a very esoteric and funny aviation joke. *Variation* is the gradual shifting of magnetic north, thanks to the irregular shape of the Earth, which is why pilots have to take into account changing isogonic lines on maps when they plan cross-country trips.

"Take a sectional with you," Martin says. "We haven't done cross-country planning yet." *True Virgins Make Dull Company*, he jots down on a notepad, the acronym for how to compute your compass heading (True heading $+/-$ Variation$=$Magnetic heading $+/-$ Deviation$=$ Compass heading), says nothing, but shoves it into my eyeshot, though out of Tom's.

"I thought you flyers used a trail of bread crumbs," I say, while scrawling *yawn* under the True Virgins slogan. "I'll practice some stalls."

Martin purses his lips and shakes his head sternly.

"Right, that's what I meant, the one thing I *won't* practice is stalls. Wouldn't do a stall if you paid me."

"Do you always roll out of bed as spunky as this?" Tom asks.

"I resent that. I've been up for *hours* already, performing acts of mercy and heroism . . . but I've got a question for you. If my calculations are correct, that's the third coffee machine you've broken in two months."

Tom laughs, running a hand over his bare head as he nods. I feign high seriousness and stare him straight in his retired-Air-Force-colonel eyes. "Are you instrument-rated for coffee machines?" I ask.

"Only over thirty thousand feet," Martin says.

"Okay, *Gruppenführer*, what shall I do today?"

It occurs to me that Martin's father was held in a Nazi concentration camp in the Netherlands during the war, but he doesn't seem to mind the tease.

"You just do what you did the other day: minimum controllable airspeed, steep turns, circle the Practice Area, then come back and do short and soft-field landings and takeoffs." He salutes me with a raised Mr. Pibb can, as I go out to the airplane, run through my checklist, and taxi out.

In a moment I am up, listening hard to the engine, and noticing for the first time the farms off the right wing tip, glidably close if the engine fails. I never noticed them before. The engine sounds gravelly and wrong, as it always does on takeoff, and at 300 feet I ignore its wheezing bark, the sound of a giraffe choking on an abacus, flip one wing up to see no one is in the way, and then bank smartly toward the James River, whose bank I'll follow first to where the ferry carries fifty cars across it at one clip, then to the Practice Area, the farther bridge, West Point, Harcum VOR, and other landmarks. Over the ferry dock, jutting out like a tail into the brownish water, I do four steep turns, my invisible tutu twirling, then climb to 2,000 feet, from which I can see West Point clearly. Visibility is impeccable.

On the way to West Point, I do steep turns about every cow or piece of livestock I can find. S-turns around a farmer, eights across a jeep. Near the river, I slow to minimum controllable airspeed, rear up close to stall, am tempted to go ahead and feel that rapturous shudder and sideways plunge, but think better of it. Now the York River is sheep-pupil blue, stretching long toward the south and Norfolk and Virginia Beach, over whose sands the Blue Angels (the U.S. Navy's jet aerobatic team) practice. I dial in the Harcum VOR and track to it, then spin around the countryside, whistling and watching highways, farms, and fields underneath me. Lost again—wasn't I supposed to be at the unnamed restricted military airstrip by now?—I tune in the Harcum VOR, radial 190 degrees, remembering that Martin had told me if ever I was lost to look for that radial, on which Williamsburg lies. To my shock, the needle centers. *Christ, you're dumb,* I think, as the restricted airstrip appears, and I know just where I am, headed straight for home base. Time check. I've only been up for half an hour. What to do now? Fort Eustis is close by but off-limits to civilians. West Point airport is nearby and pretty, but I haven't been cleared by Tom or Martin to touch down anywhere. I can solo as long as I stay off the ground and in my own backyard. I could sneak off to Patrick Henry and visit the control tower again or, better yet, do touch-and-goes on each of their runways, then buzz the ranch I saw off the end of runway 2, complete with grazing horses and a full course of well-laid-out jumps. Very tempting. But Martin would fret. I would fret if I were he and my student wasn't back after more than an explicable amount of time. First he would summon me by Unicom, then probably come up looking in a school plane. Pretty embarrassing to have to be fetched home. I could fly over Colonial Williamsburg and check out the hoopskirts and breeches and restoration work. But it's off-limits to low-flying planes (noise abatement). Gliderlike, I bank left, then right, looping toward and away from the river, then chug back to the Practice Area the locals call Fred's Farm: a single crossroads with four symmetrical fields we use for ground reference maneuvers and pretend forced landings. Poor

Fred must get tired of Cessnas running rings round him. More steep turns, round and round, until I start to get dizzy, and my right leg aches from all the rudderwork. Then I turn back for the airport, descending gradually en route, to hit traffic pattern altitude over Jamestown Island. I lift up the mike and tell Unicom where I am. No reply. It was not a question, just a scrap of information for them to file, that I'll soon be in the pattern. The altimeter looks wrong. I thought I was at 1,000 feet. Is it really saying 1,900 feet? Am I going to enter the pattern 1,000 feet high, with the runway tiny as a domino far below me and people wondering what the hell I'm doing? No. It must be right. I'm just getting tired. *Fly the pattern, Diane.* I do a short-field landing and take off once more, land again close to a full stall, but not quite. It's good enough. My reflexes are shot, and I decide to pack it in for the day.

The rest of my energy bleeds away as I flex the plane's nose wheel off the ground and, leaning on the tail surface, dolly it into place between two planes. A thousand pounds empty takes a little muscling. Afterward, I tie it down with strange, meandering knots which Tex, watching from his Toyota Celica nearby, laughs out loud about, before driving off to the health spa. Martin appears from the FBO with yet another Mr. Pibb growing warm in one hand, nods appraisingly as he sees my tie-down knots. It's weird, he's thinking, but acceptable. Anyway, he can read the familiar expression on my face.

I am grinning too hard to be able to ungrin, and he is smiling widely because he has seen that so often before: the raw thrill about flying I feel, which I can't shake down or disguise or make well-mannered, which pours over my face like a dam burst. "I can fly," I say to him in a conspiratorial whisper so no one will hear, separating each word because they can't possibly stand for the sheet lightning of what I mean. "*I can fly.*" He smiles and nods his head. "I don't mean that I can fly well, or for very long without getting tired, or with any real gift, but for the first time I'm closer to flying than to *not* flying. I went up today, and I wasn't scared; after a while I was even a little bored. Imagine, I was bored! It was wonderful!" He laughs at how thrilled I am to be bored, knowing just what I mean, that at last I'm starting to feel at ease in an airplane: he had felt the same thrill only a few years ago.

As I slide the steel toggle of the control lock into its canal in the steering column, and reach for the Pitot tube cover, to hood it like a falcon until the next flight, I look up at him soberly. Something occurs to me for the first time.

"You're going to teach me to fly."

For a rare moment, there are no jokes, no horseplay, no banter, no deflected emotion. His eyes close as he nods his head solemnly. It is a pact between us. There has never been any question about it. Knowing what I've been through, he is as hungry for me to learn as I am hungry to learn. His face is a portrait of the verb *to promise*.

And then the moment passes. Stretching his arms along the leading edge of the high wing, he leans forward, sees my eyes teary with emotion, turns to the nonexistent crowds of judges, and says loudly, "I didn't do it! She just happened to run into the baseball bat I was holding."

"I'm too tired to fall down," I say, picking up the

clipboard, and we head back to the trailer so I can pay $39 for an hour and six minutes aloft, and fill out my logbook under the heading "Pilot in command." A breeze is just starting to pick up the wind sock, and in the distance a wide range of lens-shaped clouds begins moving in.

32

Love is something like the sky, that begins and ends with the earth and makes everything else one-dimensional by comparison. Look down over the ocean, which you have been part of, in scuba gear, floating long as a chromosome in its cell. Look down at the flat gray shudder, which looks nothing like it does during early morning at Virginia Beach, when sun dazzle on the water makes the waves glow like molten metal, the waves burning like tungsten in the 10 a.m. light. A blond girl of six, in a pastel maillot with a tiger printed on it, climbs over the redwood fence surrounding the hotel swimming pool. She pauses at the top, straddling the highest board, her slender, perfect rump stuck out for all to marvel at. For a moment, she pauses to decide which early-morning seaside pleasure to enjoy, riding the top rail in the rodeo of her girlhood, then climbs down the other side and pads across the grass like a cat, bounces down the sandy cement steps to the beach, and sprints, hair flying, straight into the green quartz of a breaking wave. She turns around and smiles, as if observed, flicks her hair self-consciously, doesn't know yet how to be alone with poise.

An insanely blue sky hangs over the beach, as the hot day deepens. The sky is smeared with high white cirrus nebulas and an array of wind-widened contrails, some indistinguishable from the blowing clouds. Where one contrail crosses another, you can see which plane was higher, which closer. All the contrails lead to Oceana NAS; you could follow the billowy white streamers home. A small Cessna banks and climbs over the beach, then an old postwar military plane (a four-engine Convair), from whose termitelike tail once poured jeeps and equipment, doing low, lazy circuits over the beach. An army helicopter appears from behind a hotel block and begins patrolling the shoreline for sharks or distant bathers or nice bikinis.

The clouds that are sheep-ripped tufts of cotton, the clouds that are white ducks on bleached lawns in sunlit catherine wheels of glare, the clouds that are an Appaloosa's spots, the clouds that are soft lumpy curds of cottage cheese, the clouds that are cotton candy tugged apart by the hands of eager children, the clouds that are star nurseries in the constellation Orion, the clouds that are white fleshy scars over translucent flesh, the clouds that are whipped cream smeared with a knife.

Sand is only size, not composition, I must remind myself. Dunes form when an obstruction breaks the wind, and then the dune becomes an obstruction itself. As the wind blows across it, some grains lift into the air, gravity tugs them down again, and they may knock others aloft. The leaping grains may move larger grains when they strike one another; bouncing grains form small ripples on the larger dune's surface. On the windward side of the dune, sand moves up and falls over out of the wind at last, down the other side, stable, and in time the dune will move in the direction of the prevailing wind.

Poets have always been interested in size and composition, in sand and space. Indo-European, the reconstructed language from which many of our modern languages spring, includes a word for poet, *wek-wom-teks*, a priestly person who was a *wek-wom* (weaver) of *teks* (words). We know a little about the concepts he or she applied to the world from the words that have come down to us. For example, there is a word which means "to retreat in awe" and a verb for "speaking with the deity." The *wek-wom-teks* also had a delicate, powerful, startlingly inclusive word that meant that everything was in its place in both the heavens and earth, from which has evolved our modern word "holy." They were keenly aware of the sheer abundance of life, the interrelatedness of all things that centuries later Darwin would refer to as "panmixis" (the everythingness of everything, which reminds you of the everythingness of everything else). If their mysticism was professional, it was also avid and nomadic. They oriented themselves by standing with their backs to the sun (for whose various intensities and times they had dozens of words) and were attentive observers of the moon and stars, as well. You can almost work out where they might have lived from the pieces of their vocabulary that are missing: no word for a large body of water, no tropical trees or jungle-living animals. Many words for snow and ice and wolf and Baltic trees. And a very ancient word, *pleu*, an outcry or exclamation, almost a gasp, probably accompanied by a hand pointing toward a bird or butterfly, which meant, *it flies*.

33

Pass into mastery, as with driving a car, say, and you discover yourself, as I did yesterday, in the wrong lane of a three-lane highway, into which cars are merging from either side, bumper to bumper at 60 mph, some gunning ahead of you, some drifting blindly out of their lanes. You brake, swerve, speed up, or correct through an arpeggio of approximations and reflexes delicate enough to be an artisan's labor, without once thinking about the intricacy of what you're doing. Instead, you are jackrabbiting the car radio for catchy tunes, thinking about the Cessna 172, the safest airplane ever made, you think. Why it's so reliable isn't exactly clear. Have its owners mainly gone through the safe, planned Cessna schools? Is its simple construction a plus? Is it because most people who buy the plane think of it as a workhorse—a car that flies, not a sports car? But in any case you are not thinking of driving at all. Pass into mastery, and you become a passenger again, for the first time able to see the landscape below you, without riveting your eyes to the instrument panel. What you lose is novelty, the human craving to revel in perception. When you master something, you lose all the qualities that first attracted you to it. I don't know this yet, as one knows the cheese shop on Prince George Street will open tomorrow with its long counter of hard delicacies drawn from the bodies of ungulates. I know it only from the poignant bemusement my enthusiasm provokes in long-term flyers.

I can see it in Tex, who enjoys his Citabria most with someone else aboard in whom to see reflected his original thrill. For Poleskie there is the impatience of accomplishment and the fun of having a pal in the air who can share his inner language. For Martin, the amused satisfaction of setting fire to my discovery of flight. For all of them, some early warning system of life's perishability, lost now except in surprising predicaments, in challenging weather or planes. Tiring of the Cessnas, Poleskie went into aerobatics in a Citabria, tiring of that into the center ring of lion taming in a Pitts Special, tiring of that into a twin-engined Apache, whose challenge now is paling. Next he'll want an Aerostar or Shrike Commander. *It can never be satisfied, the mind, never,* as Wallace Stevens says in his poem, "The Well Dressed Man with a Beard," never satisfied by charm or reason, fact or cunning, love or passion. The mind that quests to be fit, to be seemly, fears death second of all; first it fears becoming as plural as all it surveys. The mind fastens onto challenge like some train that will carry it direct from the tedium of downtown Newark to the dramatic samovars of Paris, fastens onto challenge even though it knows that novelty means change, which is intolerable under any other circumstance, change which means death.

In time, when all the sweets of passion fade, there will be this, a small primer in the schooldays of my wonder, when time was tillable ground and the world always in season. And I will remember what the shell-shocking moment is, the miraculous leap from the earth to the sky that, like childbirth pain, boot camp, or some other trauma, flyers forget swiftly. It is too horrible, waking all through the night with anxiety dreams about crashing and burning, as I did last night. Each dream is similar: on takeoff, the engine quits at only 200 feet, too low to turn around, and then the scenario varies—I crash into ground, swamp, water, or treetop. What to do sends my heart pumping long enough to wake me up, sweating, finding the radiant hands on the clock touching 6 A.M., then 6:15, 6:30, 6:45, until finally I get up. When I tell Martin of my nightmares, he smiles indulgently. By now, he has forgotten what it was like to be this smitten with flight, this new to its dangers, this far short of mastery, this deeply in love with a Universe in which things can *fly*.

At eleven one day, when I have flight time scheduled, Tom Johnson summons Martin from bed, and that disquiets me. Surely Martin wasn't going to let me go up by myself without his being round the airport at all? I'm both encouraged and upset. He knows I will be all right, that I can fly well enough to return safely to earth. But he doesn't know what I know, how my heart staggers when I go up alone, how my eyes barely leave the instrument panel, so that I could be in a bumper car or on a racetrack, for all I know of where I am over the ground, that *sky* is not where I am. Trying to fly, I am holding the rails of a walker in a crippled embrace, dragging myself downwind in lurches, too high, too low, too close, too fast, and landing in ponderous smacks or gust-stunned, mad corrections back over the runway down to which I drop like a piece of meat onto a scale. He can't know that, because when I fly with him I am at ease, I am protected, and though my flying is inexpert, it's calm as a lesson plan. It's when I am on my own and the intimate terror of where I am hits me that I lose control, not altogether, but in small subtractions of faith. The Cessna 150 responds to every twinge of the wind; even on calm days, there is no taking it for granted. No act is ever final, even when you decide to act, no revision ever safe or clear or useful except until the next minute revision. It is like this with many things, with everything, I am thinking, with driving a car on a crowded superhighway, with jumping a horse, with scuba diving, with falling in love. You think you need only the courage to act decisively, to commit yourself once, but that is sheer cowardice masked as laziness. You can never stop deciding, never stop correcting, never lose control for long. Loss of control is what you crave, of course; otherwise sex wouldn't boil you out of your flesh with such willingness. Loss of control is part of what appeals to you about flying and why in time it will arouse you less and less, as it does these other flyers, for whom it takes a pretty woman or a neurotic plane or an unexpected danger to thrill them as originally just being in the sky did. Tap the original spectacle of life, when waking is adventure, and you are home and free.

34

"MELVILLE," MARTIN SAYS, as I search the sectional chart with a glance like a long gulp of water, and then switch my eyes to the instrument panel, to make sure everything is as it should be. Already, though, he has one hand on the wheel, nudging it down. I have climbed 200 feet while I wasn't looking. Then I hurl my eyes down to the ground below, throw them like a fishing net into the pouring landscape, searching for a grass strip at Melville, Virginia. Now it has been so long since I looked at the chart I've forgotten what I'm looking for and hold the chart up again. It should be somewhere straight across from Williamsburg Airport, across the James River, just before we get to the ferry landing, rising over the plane's nose now like a beckoning finger. *You know it can't be this far north,* Martin says. *Use your chart better. Look for the roads, the obstacles.* On the chart two teepees mean 400 foot towers. But as I search, the plane noses up another hundred feet. *Fly the airplane first,* he says. Settling the plane down, I begin a wide circle around the area, combing the fall foliage for two antennas.

"There!" Two red and white radio towers stand close together like goal posts. But the landing strip, where can that be?

"Okay," Martin says, "now where is Melville in relation to the towers and the roads? Look at your chart." He is speaking so evenly, so patiently, though of course he has had the airport in sight for some time, has been to it often, does not find it a figure lost in the ground of a fall landscape. I search the chart, a rigging of lines and land masses. The airport is somewhere between the towers and the road. But where? *You can see the wind sock,* Martin urges. Round and round I circle, making an uneven hoop around the towers. I bank steeply away, bank back, scout under my wing, lift the blocks of land apart, and ask them the question.

"Is that the strip?" I ask, pointing to a line some miles off.

"Road," he says, in a voice that is shaking its head no. "You're on a left downwind for the strip right now."

Below me the autumn corn is standing dry in the fields, the ears picked but the stalks not yet cut for fodder. Occasional farm buildings and roads divide the farmlands. Between two sections of corn, a dusty fairway is edged by white pigeons standing at twenty-foot intervals. Pigeons?

"There, Martin! I see it, right next to me!"

"Ah. All right, now do everything as normal for a short-field, soft-field landing."

In a few minutes, I am on final, heading straight for the field, at whose threshold is a nasty line of tall trees and wires. You have to fly high enough not to snare your wheels on them, but low enough to be able to get down swiftly to the field.

"Keep your airspeed up!" Martin cautions, for I am pulling the nose up, by instinct, to get clear of the trees. I know better, bring in power, sail yards above the trees, then cut power and drop in over the rolling, broken, pitted grass strip.

"Fly the terrain," he says. "Up where it goes up, down where it goes down."

A hillock rises high in front of me, and I pull the nose up to ride high over its crest.

"No," Martin says, "fly the plane to the ground in the usual way."

But I have already dropped down hard on the soft dirt, holding the nose off as long as possible, then jogging unsteadily to a stop. In front of me a tall curtain of trees is what I'll be aiming for at takeoff. A green sea that won't part around me if I try to enter it.

My thoughts are on my face. "You won't need that much runway," Martin says. "Just aim for the trees anyway, and as soon as the plane can fly, get it off the ground, keep it low to pick up speed, and climb out steeply. You know how to do it. You'll be looking at the trees, aiming for them, but you'll be well clear of them." Don't trust your instincts, his voice is saying, trust your learning. Forget the positive reality of raw sight. Didn't your sight deceive you only minutes ago, when the landing strip was unfindable in the turning autumn of the fields? Observation is not enough. Instinct is not enough. Trust experience. Trust knowledge. Have the courage to act contrary to what all the rushing details of the here and now say must be right. Be available to the moment, be ripe for revision, but trust something deeper and more complex. Trust the accumulating experience of each day aloft, trust insight, forget the solid green wall you must aim for, as if you could insinuate yourself through its processes of moisture and light, because you know what lift does to a winged thing at speed, which follows its slope upward. Aim for the green waterfall.

Holding the stick hard against my chest, as if I were pressing a weight, I jog back to the end of the grass strip and slowly turn around. Pivoting in the usual way would dig in the wheels. Then a quick check of the cabin. Full power. Hold the nose up high until the plane can just lift off, not climb, not fly, but lift off the ground. Then press the nose back down again, to gain flying speed, low over the grass and bald dirt. At 55 mph, the plane rises up as if on a ray of light, having found its best angle of climb, and in seconds the wall of trees is straight ahead, then underneath, then far behind. *See?* Martin says. *Plenty of room over the trees.* I file the information in the folder of my memory, which is bulging, not from great reams of knowledge, but from these small, bit-by-bit parts of a puzzle, whose final picture I will probably never see or need to. It's enough how snugly the pieces fit, when they do, enough to see emerging the edge of a tree, a stripe of sky, something human, flesh-colored, a wrist perhaps or a knee. *Round again,* Martin says, gesturing idly with one finger that, from our vantage point, is as long as the downwind leg for the grass strip. Tomorrow, when we fly again, I will not do this well. Martin will have brought my log-book and medical along to solo me in 437, a Cessna 152, the plane I must advance to before real cross-country work. But it will not be so smooth and well-planned a landing. Although I'll have 4,000 feet, plenty of time to choose a good field, I'll choose a poor one, which has three tall towers around it, set up to land downwind, and misjudge gliding distance, so that, despite all my altitude, I come in too short to make it. Returning to the airport, I will make too wide a traffic pattern, with the airport far enough away that I can't see it past the trees, then land in a good attitude, but too high over the ground, and drop in. He will carry the logbook and medical back inside the trailer with him, saying nothing, saying, *Next time*, when I comment on it at last. There is so much to know. How can one ever know it all? There are so many steps and stages and understandings and revisions and extenuating circumstances and shifts of perspective and almost unob-servable changes in attitude and direction, and then there are the thermals and the gusts and the unpredictable weather works we scry from the advice of office-bound men and women whose numerical hieroglyphics we must deci-pher. And vaguer skills, blended like tobaccos or coffees, to achieve some mental aroma right for a plan or decision. How can one ever know it all? And to know less than all is to be relegated to the ground, when the sky is the color your memory records as *sky blue*, as if it were a perfect state of itself, a flawless definition, when the air is calm and visibility telescopic, and there is nothing on Earth as close to magic as winging up to where the hawks find the perfect center of a thermal, just where you find it.

35

As I DRIVE DOWN A GENTLY WINDING ROAD, the airport appears in the distance as a valley full of planes and wind socks, one hangar, and two trailers. Smoke from the FBO chimney makes the wind socks superfluous. And at the far end of one runway, earth movers are churning up such a cloud of dust to build a taxiway and new hangars that you could judge wind direction from their stir as well. I've already gathered some of my winter kindling from the heaps of brush and trees they've cleared. Supposedly, a motel and restaurant will be part of the final development, too, not on the airport exactly, but set back in the woods a little, on the edge of a small picture-book lake, which at the moment is overrun by seepage and loon. Then the airport will be different, busier and less clubby, and I won't remember what it was like to sit at one end of the side-by-side sofas in front of the plate-glass window, having lunch with the mechanics, or climbing into the cockpit of a Cheyenne turbojet with Martin, to play charter pilot while its real pilot has a candy bar and a cup of coffee in the FBO, or prowling round a plush King Air jet until a small voice from within calls, "It's all right, you can come in and look." Or rummaging through the many sizes of cotter pins in the shop storeroom, then climbing into the exposed hull of a Piper Lance, to feel the depth of its seat pile and try my feet on the rudder pedals, or like yesterday morning, arriving with a copy of *The Great International Paper Airplane Book*, because there is a plane design in it which does not look flyable, which seems to have no airfoil at all, but which apparently flew so well that NASA began researching its structure. Martin and I built it out of paper and Elmer's Glue All, and then I talked him into climbing onto the FBO roof to launch it in the 5 knot breeze. What a strange, beautiful design: a triangular straw, with a big loop at one end and a smaller loop at the other. So simple, so clean, so unplane-looking, so aerodynamic. *But how does it fly?* we kept asking, as we baffled everyone with its transits across the room or over the tarmac. "Cigarette holder?" Tom Johnson had guessed when I presented it to him as a mystery present. Then I launched it, and his face was a map of surprise—*Damn, if it isn't a plane!*

All that frivolous prowling and playing and ferreting into the way things work and teasing and romping and idle hours of hanging out at the FBO will all change. What's so delicious about the airport now is that it's un-

busy enough to let each day there fill up like water finding
its level in a well. People are always gathering and dispers-
ing and gathering again—around a plane someone is wash-
ing or on the sofas at the FBO or at the gas pump or in
front of the shop or at one of the Luscombes, Citabrias, or
other planes tied down to cemented car tires in the grass
that borders the macadam. Small eddies of conversation
pooling, drifting away, gather again elsewhere, in a gentle, unspoken tropism. If George and Martin and I are
on the ramp, we will drift together. To see one another,
to be in eyeshot, is already to begin moving together with
no purpose in mind, no phrase on our lips, just a friend-
ship whose idleness draws us. "Nice day for Widgeons,"
I'll say if drizzle is in the air, and they'll laugh generously
at my reference to seaplanes, as I will laugh generously at
their jokes. And, if it's sunny, we'll marvel at the cloud
types for a moment or the heat mirage blazing at the
end of 13 or the array of corporate jets in the front row
or the helicopter that just landed in a hush to let some
VIP dash to a waiting limousine. Then Martin will say,
"Lunchtime," and go in for a Milky Way, George will
mind the counter, close enough to the Unicom to answer
all callers, and I will chance fate by drinking a Tab but
also eating a Three Musketeers, as we wait for the day to
deliver up its bounty: the visitors in from Texas in Moon-
eys; the airline litigation lawyer in his rebuilt 1941
WACO, a two-place, open-cockpit biplane, in the front of
which his secretary sits in furs; the F-15 jet pilot who flies
gliders and aerobatic planes for a hobby; Tex with his
pooch, a high-strung little gray terrier, whose whole body
wags when it's excited; or perhaps a hot-rod Aerostar, landing badly enough to need to have its wings replaced, as one

recently did. The owner had been cool, or crazy, enough
to climb out, take his golf clubs from the baggage compart-
ment, and say, "Well, that's about all the damage I can do
for one day," and go off to the golf course while the mechanics fretted about how to put the twisted plane back
together. Perhaps the day will produce an escapee from the
mental hospital nearby, rolling his eyes and requesting a
charter flight to Connecticut. Or perhaps it will turn up
the two fish spotters, who often bring their plane in for
servicing and repairs, before heading out to read shadows
over the Chesapeake Bay. Old-timers come in occasionally
and reminisce about their one accident in twenty years,
when they were dragged out of the plane's carcass, a carcass themselves. But mainly the regulars are middle-aged,
with just enough money to own a plane and just enough
zest to want one. Because of the size of the airport and its
locale, it seems to attract a wider miscellany of people than
most airports—fewer dentists and lawyers, more army people from Fort Eustis, and the occasional eccentric like me
or the petite girl taking lessons, whose job is to tend sheep
in Colonial Williamsburg, who sometimes arrives at the
airport in full shepherdess outfit with crook.

No one ever buys any of the knickknacks for sale in the
FBO, but the counters overflow with flying doodads like
patches and bumper stickers and model-plane kits and
airplane-design wrapping paper. And then there are the
cake-decorating paraphernalia on sale—all sizes of plastic
babies, little monkeys and bells and beer cans even, and
flags—and fireworks and books about cooking and baking.
There are airplane mobiles twirling near the coffee machine. Ladies and men's overnight kits. Inflatable animals.
Fluffy toys with faces. Postcards. Magazines. Ray Ban

sunglasses. And a superfluity of buyable objects that seem not to fit into any category: something small, brown, and perhaps standuppable; something flat, tan, and perhaps useful for cleaning; something flexible, yellow, soft, and perhaps givable to a child. Two large waste cans behind the sofas are marked CANS ONLY and NO CANS. There is also a junk-food machine, which we raid like Holocaust victims, a soda machine stocked mainly with Martin's transfusion of Mr. Pibb, and a video game I find too abstract to bother with but whose outcries of distress or triumph one often hears when pilots of jets unwind over an imaginary battle zone. In the FBO, flying knows no sex or race. A "bad pilot" is someone who bungles the laws of flight and airplane handling; the tag that identifies man or woman, or race or national origin, comes late in the conversation, as an added detail, if at all. But perhaps that has to do with the blended backgrounds of the regulars: Mike, who married the Korean headmistress of an orphanage near where he was stationed in Korea; Tex, who is married to a Japanese woman he met in the service; George, laid back and quiet, whose wife is a marital counselor as he is; Martin, who grew up near Amsterdam, in a conservative but cosmopolitan atmosphere; and the assorted mechanics, most of whom were flying planes before they were big enough to see over the instrument panel of their dad's crop duster or rebuilt World War II trainer.

One game we play tirelessly all day: which plane is the best, easiest to maneuver, has spawned the fewest accidents, requires the least servicing? Some are rabid Cessnaphiles, others Piperaddicts; and Martin and I usually smirk at each other when the two factions square off for a good long debate that will become as detailed as talk of vacuum pumps and moment arms, but be prompted, as we know deep down, by something quite irrational and unarguable, like blind preference, like beauty. Anyway, Martin prefers gliders to powered planes. Not me, but, out of curiosity, I spent a lesson flying over to Garner, a private airport half an hour away by air, where a soaring club operates. I liked the sense of being encapsuled in the plexiglass nose of the plane, the open metal scaffolding under the seat, the impossibly long wings that make you feel like what Martin always refers to as "B 1 rds." (A variation on that is his "Gu elevens.") Watching B 1 rds work the air currents round Garner, before I put on a similarly snug, light-as-bird-bone costume, to begin to sense like a bird, is a thrill burned deep into my memory. The sight of the biplane that would tow us pivoting in front of my nose, then the tow line suddenly tightening, a man running alongside the glider to hold its wings off the grass as we built up speed for takeoff, the sense of being *towed* at speed through the air, while weaving and bobbing and trying to read the changing course of the tow plane. The small piece of yarn fixed to the glider's nose is a brilliant piece of inventive simplicity (when the yarn is straight back, the plane is perfectly coordinated; when it blows left, use right rudder; when it blows right, use left rudder). Pulling the bright red release knob on the panel, watching the tow plane dive left, trailing its umbilical, and the rushing sound of the wind through the fabric giving way to a soft, airy silence. *Take the controls*, the pilot, sitting behind me, had said, and it was so easy, so smooth; right aileron, right rudder, one coordinated turn, but a turn at only 35 miles an hour, soundlessly, gracefully, 3,000 feet up, and then a left turn as if the plane were sighing around a point, while the sunlight peppered my hands and face, and I waited for the familiar sounds to take over, the radio squawking like a herd of porpoises, the engine churning and grating, the whine of the flaps, sounds that would never show up. Then I settled down to the still, even surf of the wind and the almost audible sunlight and the slowness over the earth that is peace without parallel, and the realization that there can be no go-around in a glider (you must land perfectly each time), and the odd sensation of diving straight down to the runway through a notch in the trees, straight down onto the single wooden ski under the plane's belly, as we skidded across the grass clear down to the end of the runway. And especially, at day's end, the putting away of the gliders, into a small hangar, wedging and maneuvering them, until they sat with their heads nestled against each other's wing, so birdlike, as we covered their cage and left them in blackness. But I still prefer powered flight, as do the others at the FBO, even if I sometimes wake up in the morning with the room turning at just the same speed it turned in the glider and know that I have been soaring again in my sleep.

The Split Infinity of Sky and Night

36

THE AIRPLANES ARE TIED DOWN, as if they would otherwise escape. There is the almost audible heat of the sun reflected off the macadam. And the only sound is of the American flag being snapped and rippled by the wind, and the occasional electronic buzzing of crickets. No birds, no humans. Some of the planes are hooded against heat on the instrument panel, and look like falcons waiting for release after prey. Two wind socks: the standard elephant trunk and a delicate long Chinese dragon on a pole. When night falls, the bright blue taxi lights will come on, and the green lights that mark the beginning of the runway and the red lights that warn of the runway's finish, and the amber lights that peg out the black alleyways where motion is safe. An airport looks most like a wharf after nightfall, with carefully lighted docks, canals, and steerages. The green and white rotating beacon atop a tower, the same beacon one finds at nearly every airport at night, is silent comfort to all flyers. Above the clouds perhaps or weather-bound or just out for a lengthy tour of the countryside, you return later than you planned, dusk has already fallen, and you begin to scout the lavender twilight for some sign of your airport, almost invisible now in the surging shadows. Then you pick out a flashing green-and-white beacon in the distance and can sit deep into your seat again and point the ship for home.

When night has thickly fallen, we fly to the radar room at Norfolk Airport, where men and women sit at luminous green screens, in a womb-dark room overhung with other video displays, where they touch panels of softly glowing colored numbers, honeycombs of red, yellow green. Rolling a black rubber ball in place, one woman moves a W across a lighted screen. When it touches a scintillation, numbers appear: the airplane's code, altitude, direction. Remove the genie, and the airplane returns to a stitch of light again. Magic. How I would like to be able to do that with the heavens: move a cursor up to a star I'm curious about, and wait for its vital signs to appear below it in the mute black. I've always been a sucker for new ways in which to conjure the unknown. Now I sit at the console, and seize anonymous planes in my forceps and drag them into view. Planes like mine, without a trans-ponder, are mere twinkles; others are boxes and lines. Two apparently converging at breakneck speed are really 1,000 feet apart traveling in opposite directions. But it is time to move on, to where the Approach man and the Departure man sit side by side, like two views of the same process, each speaking softly into a headset, while following printout changes on the shimmery green screens vertical in front of them. A sweeping yellow line spreads a thin smear of electrons round and round each screen. In the coffee room, controllers are watching TV and drinking coffee, cup after cup, drifting in regularly from their dimly lighted grottos of eye-deadening green.

There is no way to make sense of the two rooms side-by-side: the overlit TV room in which the world is simple as an urn of coffee and a dinette set, and the Star Wars video Valhalla of the radar room. How does one pass from one culture to the other, from the locale made of styrofoam and yesterday's sports section to the abstract urgency of a Cessna 172, "out of nine for seven," as he says to confirm his descent from 9,000 toward 7,000 feet, a pilot who will disappear from the screen in a moment, the firefly of his plane subtracted from the green meadow of the radar, disappear from radar sight and radio contact, as if he were an hallucination, as if he never was a forty-five-year-old engineer from Roanoke, with a second wife and three children, en route to Norfolk for a meeting about foundation stresses. He will disappear from the screen like a small flame being snuffed out, as his life will be one day, his small light simply vanish.

"Norfolk Departure, Cessna four-three-seven is with you," I say softly into my mike, as we fly toward the James River Bridge. The night deepens, and there is no way to tell the difference between the black waters below and the black waters above.

"Cessna four-three-seven, are you intending to fly up the James River?" Departure asks.

I smile. His radar has me firmly fixed. "Yes, that's right. I'm just coming up on the James River Bridge now." But I am thinking how poignantly we say this to Departure, *I am with you*, I cannot travel through the blackness without you, I am holding onto your sleeve through this mike, with this slender voice.

"Okay, four-three-seven. Say when you have Williamsburg runway in sight."

"Roger, when I have Williamsburg runway in sight. Four-three-seven."

He will be following us the thirty miles clear to Williamsburg, keeping an eye on us over land and water, though his screen shows nothing of the fabulous gem-studded vista spread out below us: the Norfolk shipyards, the light-festooned bridges, the neon sprawl of housing tracts and Main streets and highways. In the measured world below lie unmapped constellations: a winged camel, a milkman, a bee-clustered hive. We will never name them any more than the lighted veils on the skyline or the gold membranes, as city lights float under us the tracery of a fluorescent sea creature on a moonless reef, its backbone a tilted highway glittering to the horizon, neon hubs its organs, and in between the webbed tinsel of suburbia. Even at 2,000 feet, lights below dot the blackness as if by rule, fill our ever-arranging eyes with sparkling motifs, a parole of order vast, doping, and certain.

Red lights in the cockpit. I cradle the wheel's two uplifted arms, as unerring numbers count backward toward zero. Their message is not new. Drifting mindful somewhere between the cities and the moon, I watch the panel numbers flicker, as if I could unravel them and name their starry sum, as if I could speak the patois of sheer light.

37

Last night, I asked a poet friend what plane his father flew, his father who was lost over France during a war fought by machines, not men. A Flying Fortress was their god: four engines that kept no one from the fiery plunge and, worst of all, the resolute unambiguous sound every pilot knows, of airspeed rocketing, the loud whoosh that never ends. How could I not ask in what plane his father died, when planes are now so much a part of my eschatology? We have all gone down with lesser drama in the night, a deadly descent unlike death or descent. We have all tuned our ears for that telltale whoosh, not because we could stop it, but because we could not let it go by unnoticed, one of the ghostlike moments of undefiable delicacy that begin and end life, that we cling to, that we lunge for. The last whoosh of air, when even that sound is miraculous, surprising, indelible. We all know what it's like to spin fast toward the ground, and not be able to pull up before the inevitable becomes evitable as we pierce the tight, blue fabric of the sky in small acts of self-immolation. At night, sometimes, I dream of crashing. It is only a pilot's dream. There is nothing to be learned from it. I wake over and over in the night with a fear as old as that of falling from a tree. But it will pass. In the night, I am dreaming of the jungles, in which animals fly, not wooden or metal things; animals who trust the invisible to hold them up along the length of their bodies, with their fur and scales and feathers and small, fallible engine.

38

On the cowlick-shaped dunes of the Outer Banks, near Kitty Hawk, North Carolina, I am standing in the blustery cold November wind right where Orville and Wilbur Wright did, eighty years ago, on a day that would change the culture of our planet. On December 17, 1903, the two brothers rose early, as they often did, in part out of intellectual eagerness, in part because the slat house in which they lived let in blowing sand and ferocious cold, so that in their diaries they record being at the stage where five blankets and two quilts and all their clothes still won't keep them warm enough to sleep. Wilbur cooked eggs, coffee, and biscuits for breakfast, after Orville swept the night's sand from the tables, and started a fire in the stove.

Soon the men from the nearby life-saving station came, as they did each day, to help with the experiments. And by ten-thirty, they had launched us into the age of powered flight.

These men, with little formal education, were nonetheless meticulous and inspired observers and mathematicians. You need only look at their drafting tools, on display in the local museum, and at the tables of figures for propeller design and wind-tunnel experiments with airfoils, to understand the precision and doggedness of their minds. It was not at Kitty Hawk but at nearby Kill Devil Hills that they flew, after first researching beaches all over the country for a felicitous combination of wind, sand, and sun.

Although a tactfully imagined museum and monument mark the scene of their flights, the fullness of what is not here is chilling. There is no longer the flat, sandy beach on which they flew, with the ocean a blue razor line in the distance. Now there is a lawn, hat-shaped gallery, obelisk on the hill, and a U.S. highway blandly called "158 bypass." And endless wooden cottages on stilts on the dunes, standing like a flock of leggy seabirds. The sound of the surf is often joined by the aerial surf of F-15's en route to their base at Virginia Beach, or the small growl of the Cessna 172 tour plane giving scenic rides from the local airport. There are none of the seven men who, even among themselves and hard at messy, physical work, wore ties and stiff collars and bowler hats, as respectable Victorian men did. Hold up a photograph of their 1903 camp—two bleak sand-scoured barracks, a fragile and rather clumsy-looking contraption, and two brothers with a single optimism between them—and then consider the sprawly vacation strip in the present, which they unknowingly spawned: Wright Shores, Orville Beach, First Flight Inn, etc. An unintentionally ironic sign at the city limit says, "No Vehicles on the Beach."

But for someone who knows what took place here in 1903 (only two years before Einstein's theory of special relativity), the barracks, iron launching rail, and markers are holy relics. It's not unusual to see people sitting quietly in the glowing solitude of their wonder or teary-eyed as they walk the simple distance of the morning's first flight. In the museum is a miscellany of artifacts: a piece of cloth which they used to cover the wings, sewn on their mother's sewing machine (Neil Armstrong took a swatch of it with him to the moon); most of the propeller of the original plane; ingeniously adapted bicycle fittings; Orville's drafting tools in a gray and tan case darkened from handling; an extraordinary photographic history of daily life in the 1903 camp (because Orville was an amateur photographer). Some souvenir hunter has broken the pinkie finger off the reclining model of Orville Wright that flies the reconstructed *Wright Flyer* in the replica room. All around the walls, a gallery of oil portraits depicts the history of aviation through personalities—inventors, fighter pilots, astronauts, aviatrixes, record setters—watched over by the twin portraits of the Wright Brothers themselves. Wilbur's portrait looks a bit sterner than Orville's, but that isn't surprising when you remember that he had his teeth knocked out in an ice-skating accident in his teens, which, absurdly, is almost certainly what made him decide to switch from a public life of being a minister, as he had planned, to the private life of a scientist.

Orville lived until 1948 (Wilbur died thirty-six years

earlier of typhoid fever), and so attended the dedication of the Wright Memorial in 1932. He probably walked the first flight markers, as we do, clocking the twelve seconds of the 120-foot flight, 30 miles per hour into a 21 mph headwind. Orville lived to sit in the cockpit of a four-engine Lockheed Constellation, the most famous airliner of its time; he knew about jets and rocketry and aerial combat in World War II, and in fact had discussed with Wilbur the possible military application of their invention at the time of the first flight. But reconnaissance was all they shortsightedly predicted, not bombs and dogfights, or the Concorde that flies at the speed the Earth rotates, and space shuttles that do precision dead-stick glides in from outer space—and certainly not within only eighty years.

Orville's name is more familiar, but as the letters and notebooks reveal, it was Wilbur who was the real aeronautical dynamo (though both were avid inventors of everything from printing techniques to inflatable bicycle tires). A photograph of Wilbur, taken in Europe in 1909, shows him standing with a group of men in front of a *Wright Flyer*. He is holding his right hand stiffly, thumb extended, to demonstrate an aerial maneuver. It's a heartbreaking shot. It's precisely what you see pilots do all over the world, as well as little kids: use one hand as a plane as they recount a hair-raising flight. Only he was the first; he made such things possible.

As difficult as it is to find the truth about the oddly ascetic, interwoven personalities of the two men under all the layers and cosmetics of myth, it is easy to imagine them into this landscape. The iron skid and the barracks (in which even the canned goods have authentic labels) are just as they were, as they are in old photographs. The wind is blowing from the northeast, as it did on the morning of December 17, at about 20 mph, the same speed. Look upwind, toward the dune on which the wing-shaped obelisk now stands, and you can see them, hear the wind in the struts of their biplane, hear the men from the lifesaving station calling to Orville, because Wilbur had told them for heaven's sake to clap and yell encouragement, so Orville wouldn't be too nervous, see Wilbur running madly beside the plane, which his grinning brother is *flying*. Instinctively, I check my watch, clock the twelve seconds.

A young couple with a toddler is launching a mechanical bird in the stiff breeze. An ironic sight, since the Wright Brothers' real success was in inventing a plane aerodynamically sound enough for a pilot to maneuver without acrobatic skill (many of their predecessors died trying to flap cumbersome wings or contort the body into airworthy angles and balances). In the background is the short paved runway of First Flight, an airport where private pilots may tie down for twenty-four hours, to make a pilgrimage. Aeronautical charts of the area mark an obstruction to the north of First Flight Airport, a teepee with a dot in it, as all obstructions of that sort (radio towers mainly) are usually marked. But this obstacle is the Wright Brothers' Memorial itself, and nothing could be more apt. The memorial obelisk is a single wing atop the highest hill in the area, with roads winding up to it, so that the eye is drawn from the sand below in a narrowing spiral toward the sky. At night, the moon passes behind it, over a rippling orange sunset and the mad purple rigging of wind-blown clouds, and the mental eye moves from earthly flight to space flight, as it is meant to, and back again to the homely lives of men driven by the affectionate curiosity of naturalists, who painstakingly studied the glide and bank of birds, and said, "Possible."

39

AT PORTSMOUTH, VIRGINIA, AIRPORT, Martin and I lie down in the grass beside the airplane, to wait for the mechanics to fix its radio. Martin rests his head on a rolled-up flight jacket, and I rest mine on a wedge-shaped brown purse, listening to the men tinkering and tamping, as we watch the clouds form shapes that resemble nothing and laugh when we see between the shadows under the wing, into the cabin, behind the removed avionics, a simple bicycle chain that controls the ailerons. The day is so still; it is like a postage stamp of a foreign country. We are the tiny figures caught at midskate on its frozen canal. It is before the time when minutes were measurable or life inexplicable or anything fit for the open bondage of a day but the lazy contemplation of grass and sky. You could use the airplane's wing as a sundial, just as a cowboy I know uses his horse as one. Martin is talking about his brother back in Holland and his best friend Frank, with whom he glided and sky-dived, and his mother's cooking and the house outside Amsterdam, in a small town called Weesp, in which he spent his childhood building model planes. It is nearly Christmas, and for once he will not be going home to spend it with his family. I tease him that it's growing up always in full view of turning windmills, those slow, graceful propellers, that drove him to aviation. And then we lie silently again, watching the sky with such tenderness and serenity. The silk chutes, in which we float safely from the imminent explosion of our lives, billow around us, and we slow to where time and descent no longer matter. He would not call it mysticism, or anything by name, except to say how peaceful the day is, how restful the lying out in the grass, in this wide alien country, whose skies are his home.

40

THE SUNLIGHT-FRIZZLED RESERVOIR, bright as a marquee. The sunlight burning flecks of glass in the macadam highway. The sunlight that looks like water on the glossy green leaves of the magnolias which, unlike their deciduous northern cousins, do not drop their leaves in the fall. Only their VOR-shaped cones, which pilgrim squirrels gnaw on like cobs of corn. *Even the small mammals are colonials*, I think, as I drive toward the airport for my first solo cross-country, noticing, as if for the first time, the way sunlight transfixes the planet, through a complex lexicon of physical laws. All echoing that hot mass of jelly so many light miles away. We are all burning from its distant fire. I notice the sunlight because I am afraid that I may die in a few hours, and something about the blue sky or the holly hedges, whose prickly leaves roll to three-cornered hats when dry, or the palm-warmed amber of my lover's flesh even, is not the last thing that springs to mind, not the token I hold with my eyes as one might hold a pebble from Troy or a trilobite fossil or a bit of cloth from the Wright Brothers' plane.

Sunlight is the marvel my eyes lift up and palp, as if in the touching I could etch it forever on that part of my brain that sums life, that spanks life awake in the memory. *Hold the thought of sunlight in your mind, the sunlight that drips hallucination from rime ice in the winter, the sunlight that makes a six-foot barracuda at dockside, lolling in a voracious slant, look like a gleaming nail driven into the water, the sunlight that feels peppery on bare leg, the sunlight that makes rainbow sun dogs between the high clouds as you fly away from Richmond Airport, saying to Departure Control what you cannot yet say without a poignancy so vivid your eyes begin to tear: "Departure, I am with you. . . . Departure, changing frequency for a moment. . . . Departure, I am back with you again."* Departure, we are always with you. We are born with you, we carry you in our cells. We choose to forget that, or there would be no dealing with the UPS man or sorting out the laundry or falling in love. In our twenties, we feel immortal, life is all in front of us, like a runway. But by our early thirties that changes, and Departure is with us; we are aware that we have been on its radar all along, a small silent light moving slowly toward the edge of being. It's a cumbersome truth, difficult to slip into in the morning, when time is the muffled electronic bleep-bleep . . . bleep-bleep . . . bleep-bleep of a quartz alarm clock, you've the delicious quicksand of a new book to wade into, soon you will be flying, and you feel such tenderness for the man half-asleep beside you. It's the sudden saying of it, out of the clear blue on a fun flight to a new airport, full of romp and banter that does it, saying *Departure, I am with you,* that reminds you what you had almost successfully forgotten and feels like steel wool rubbing over the heart.

So I am thinking of sunlight and death as I drive to the airport, how one is the cancellation of the other, but I cannot say which better cancels which. The sky is open and blue, broken clouds loom low enough to worry about, some dark and battered, some wind-ripped into nebulas. Winds aloft must be brisk, and I'll have to fly reasonably low, so there will be no long perspective.

Tex, Martin, and a young soldier taking lessons are waiting in the Colonial trailer, together with an older man come to rent the Cutlass RG. They're full of jokes and ribbing, but all I want is for them to vanish so I can fumble my circular slide rule in unobserved nervousness and hit the aerial road before my nerves quit on me. I'm all twitch and bother. Concerned, Tex takes me aside and reminds me to look for the smokestack atop the pulp mill at Franklin, a sure checkpoint you can see for many miles away, and not to be surprised by the reported intense gustiness along the route. Finally he offers to fly escort, doing polite loops around my plane in his Citabria, but there is no use trying to shake down my growling dread. When someone begins anecdotes about first cross-countries, I seize the chance to file my flight plan, without their fish-bowling me, and that is that: I'm in the computer, I'm duty bound to leave. "How's the restaurant at Emporia?" I ask. They guffaw. "Better take a pilot's lunch," Tex says.

"Know what that is?" I don't. "A candy bar and a Coke . . . if the Coke machine works." I decide on a Mars bar from the FBO, make a few morbid jokes with the guys, and pre-flight the Cessna 152, which stands dripping gas from the overflow tube. On its panel, the indicators read low. "Martin," I call across the tarmac as he climbs into a plane for a lesson, "I thought four-three-seven was full. The indicators read less." He smiles. "Indicators are wrong—look at the tanks. It was filled this morning." One tank is full clear up to the cap, the other less, but I can feel gas with one finger. Better top it up before I go, I decide, and get ready to taxi it round to the pump. On second thought, I climb back up and look at the less-full tank again. I can see the gas sloshing against the cap. By now, Tex, looking uncharacteristically solemn, strolls over, taking everything in. "How full has it got to be?" he says wryly. "It's dripping gas from the overfill." This time I see the gas well up to the top, sloshing about from the induced wave of my climbing onto the wing. What jitters. Had I taxied the plane to the gas pump and waited for the lineman to get out his ladder, climb up with the hose, and be set to pour, only to discover the plane was full, I would never have heard the end of it. "I'll be all right," I reassure Tex, who hasn't asked, hop into the plane, and start it up.

When run-up is complete, I breathe deeply, like a woman in labor, and take off into a 10-knot crosswind that sends me lurching and sailing close to the ground. But once the plane is truly, smoothly aloft, I bank onto my course, and try to balance the flight plan and chart on my lap. The pencil I fit behind the window-sill bevel, which traps it securely and keeps it close at hand. Before I cross the James River, I activate my flight plan with the

Flight Service Station based at Newport News, then look for Melville, the grass strip, and my first checkpoint. But that is like looking for a sand crab on the beach. When I know for certain that I *should* have been there, I jot it down anyway, as a checkpoint reached, relieved then when I see three towers out of my right window, the towers I remember were just south of Melville. But suppose I hadn't known about Melville's three towers? I didn't actually see the airport. Does it count as a checkpoint? Not in my internal records anyway. The next checkpoint is another private strip, Wells, and I can't find it anywhere. The sky is falling, the clouds down to 1,800 feet, so even though my flight plan called for 2,500 feet, I hurry down to 1,400, then 1,000 at one point, and back up to 1,500 when the clouds permit. The clouds are bluing overhead, gusts rack me, and I start to laugh.

Wasn't there a time when, flying the Allegheny Commuter in and out of Philipsburg, Pennsylvania, I would get airsick from the rocking-horse rigors of the air pockets? Now it doesn't bother me. I have that in common with my mother, the ability to erase discomfort with curiosity. When she had been to China twice and seen a pack of totalitarian regimes and the archaeological in-spots and cremations along the Ganges and the bat-curded caves of New Zealand and every landform the planet offers (glacier, mesa, volcano, savanna, pampas, salt flat, et al.), she decided one day to sail to the small island off Tahiti which Michener called Bali Hai. While everyone else on the swell-leaping boat got seasick, she clung to its prow, thinking how merry-go-round horses bob rhythmically as she was doing, and eagerly searched the horizon for a first glimpse of Bali Hai.

Aren't I supposed to be flying at 95 knots? My airspeed indicator is reading in the yellow arc, the caution range, then falling back to 90, 80, up again to 110. Gusts. With a strong wind in front of me, my ground speed is only 78 mph, car speed. And I'm deeply grateful for the extra time it gives me to find checkpoints. Melville doesn't really count as being found, Wells is completely lost, and now I search for Ivor, a settlement bisected by a large road and a power line. Yes, that appears, also the two lakes just before I get to Franklin. And, sweet mercy, I see a smokestack in the distance, which must be Franklin. But suppose I didn't know about the smokestack? My VOR work is perfect, the needle smartly centered, then recentered whenever it drifts. But suppose the VOR weren't working, or were off, as it had been by 16 degrees that time I flew the Warrior with Brad from Teterboro to Ithaca? He had known the route by heart anyway, but suppose I had been alone in the plane, looking for checkpoints like this and not finding them, not knowing, as Brad and I didn't until we landed, that the VOR was off enough to be a menace? By the time I see the city of Franklin drawing up close on the left, I am angry with myself for not being able to read the land better, read the chart better, make sense of the foreshortened fields and infrequent highways. Virginia is mainly trees and farms and marshes, I note. That and naval bases. I can see how one could fall in love with the faithfulness of the VOR, can appreciate how desperately pilots must cling to it at night especially, that single radical line pointing home, straight as two hands held palm to palm, in an Indian salaam, in prayer.

When Franklin slides by to my left and the VOR

needle starts to quiver, I search for a shiny white cone below in a field, shaped like the Sombrero galaxy and about twenty feet high. On the instrument panel, a small sign changes: TO becomes FROM, and I know I must have flown over the cone at that moment, but I can't find it anywhere in the rolling fields, and now I must assume a new heading pronto. I crane my neck one last time to find the VOR cone. Nothing. Too steeply, I bank onto a new heading, one that parallels a highway my chart says will lead me to the airport at Emporia. Runway 15 is active, the Emporia Unicom tells me. Still holding my VOR radial, still following the highway, still working with my altitude, I grab a hand-drawn layout of the Emporia runways from my bag, and work out where 15 will be. Just in front of me is a clearing. According to my flight plan, I should be at Emporia in two minutes, so that must be it. The road is right, the radial is right, the time is right. Descending gently, I announce to Emporia traffic that I am approaching runway 33. A moment later, I see the numbers at the runway's threshold. Actually, I am on final for 15, that is at the opposite end of the runway. I'd misimagined how the airport was set out. *Oops*, I say out loud, and fly all around the A-shaped display on the ground, checking things out, making sure this time, and entering a normal downwind for 15, touching down without much turbulence and rolling toward the ramp. Had I asked about a restaurant? The runways are tufted with weeds, there is an old gas pump and two small buildings that look like a motorcycle gang's clubhouses. Only two airplanes are tied down: a Warrior and a crop duster.

In the FBO, I find a stocky, curly-haired man in a black Harley-Davidson T-shirt, who stamps my logbook almost too delicately with the desperate sounding "Arrived at Emporia O.K." I phone the local Flight Service Station for weather. Outside, the cloud deck is low and gloomy, and FSS tells me it's going to rain and thunder as early as 4 P.M. It's 2:30 now, and the wind coming through the FBO window is strong enough to whip three airplane mobiles into tight spins.

So I file a flight plan, taxi the length of the runway, and take off briskly over weed and cracked pavement, this time starting out under 1,000 feet and waiting until I can climb up to 2,000 farther along. The checkpoints come fast, with the 20-knot wind behind me, and a ground speed of 110 mph. The two lakes I hoped to find are unidentifiable among so many similar-sized lakes. Using tangents of the Franklin VOR, I know when I cross each spoke of its wheel. If necessary, I could pinpoint my position by tuning in a VOR at right angles to my course; where the two VORs intersect I would be exactly. The spoke trick works, but it somehow feels like cheating. Aren't I supposed to be able to *read the land?* Wakefield appears on schedule, because it is a town with an odd-shaped lake south of it and a major highway running through it in a recognizable way. And after that there is no problem: just head for the James River. When you get there, turn either left or right, depending. I can see the river from twenty miles off and start to relax a little, now that I'm back in my neighborhood.

Ahead of schedule when I land, I'm glad to be back in one piece. I made great time, so I couldn't have been off course at any point. But my nerves feel shot, and I'm so discouraged and depressed. There is no way I'll be able to fly to Elizabeth City, a longer haul, with no familiar checkpoints, on my next solo cross-country. At home, alone, I start to cry, in drab little sniffles at first and then sound-lessly intense, until my eyes grow hot. Crying both from the pent-up fright of the day and from my anger with my-self for being so out of control. Wasn't it just luck that took me safely to Emporia? My airspeed control had been miserable, so too my altitude control. All right, probably that's true for most students, only they don't make a big deal of it, they don't confess it to their instructors. I phone Martin, in tears, and spill out my upset, how discouraged I feel, how incompetent, how weak, how badly I flew, how I found almost none of my checkpoints, how deeply, pain-fully *scared* I was. "I'll never make it, I'll never be a flyer," I moan, and he tries to reassure me. Late at night, I am still miserable and weepy, and it really isn't until the next morning, over breakfast, that I begin to understand.

My VOR navigation was flawless, which is why I flew the route so well and promptly. The moment the needle wavered, I was settling it back into line again, not having to think through intercept angles but understanding in-stinctively how to judge and revise. Somehow, somewhere, I'd finally learned how to steer by VOR. But to me, num-bers aren't real. They never have been; I still can't add and subtract. I trust them, as I trust the VOR, as an agreed-upon truth, as I trust the chair beneath me. I trust physics without necessarily understanding it, otherwise there would be no crossing the street or asking for a half pound of freshly sliced cream cheese. But the numbers aren't real to me; the invisible radials are nothing like looking out the window at the land below and feeling *lost*, feeling *out of control*, not knowing where the lo-cal village of Yale is or Drewryville or Wells. Melville doesn't count, because if I hadn't flown to it before

I wouldn't have known about its towers. Ditto the smokestack of Franklin. So, in truth, there were only three of the ten checkpoints I did find: Ivor, Emporia, and Wakefield. Not enough to give a sense of being able to decode the landscape. So, despite the fact that I flew the route reasonably well, I had done it all by radio navigation, invisibly, while frantically searching with my eyes for what would satisfy and comfort them. *You thin-skinned sensitive*, I think, as I pour another cup of coffee. In flying, it's the arrival, not the getting there, that matters to most people. Hence the logbook stamps "Arrived at Emporia O.K.," "Arrived at Williamsburg O.K." Only you would worry about *how* you found your way.

It's no use telling Martin any of this, no use trying to explain to normal people what it's like being such a blood-and-guts perfectionist that, even after what appears a homerun success, you feel driven duty bound to confess the breadth of your failure. Life is mainly full of people trying to disguise their shortcomings, and here you are openly exposing yours. Why? Because you know you must first expose your wound if you hope to be healed? Or because only an acceptance that includes the shortcomings, that knows all the rough spots, pitfalls, failures, and bad grace, only an acceptance undeceived by all the disguises, will count somehow as a checkpoint to depend on in the desolate, fog-rimmed landscape of self-esteem. These are clumsy weights to carry on a short haul in a light plane, and are better left in the Pleistocene of one's psyche, where they belong. I know that now. And also the best cure. Take a chart, climb into an airplane, and lose yourself without getting lost.

41

THE WAY IS CLEAR: follow the river; look for the "dead fleet" anchored in its shallows like so many bathtub toys; look for Smithfield; look for Portsmouth Airport, where you once flew with Martin in a 172 (the gas station next to the hangars sells inflatable planes—Spitfires, Zeros, Wildcats, and Kittyhawks—for $1.86). Look for Lake Drummond, then for a large highway that leads straight to your destination. It is so easy to get to Elizabeth City, a hundred miles as the Cessna flies in a light headwind, even though their VOR, which was supposed to lead you there and roll you in on an invisible string like a wayward kite, is down for repairs, something you learn of only after you're airborne. But how could that matter when the

256

coastline stretches before you, and then all of your check-points, and at last the odd dog-legged highway pointing to an airport in a bay.

Five miles from Elizabeth City, I radio their control tower to say what and where I am, and ask which runway to use. Twice I must ask for an altimeter reading, since mine is apparently off by as much as a hundred feet, and in any case the radio static is so bad most sounds lose their clarity. A sentence is fathomable, even when some of its words are garbled, but not so a set of numbers, spoken lightly, in a drawl.

"Cessna four-three-seven," the tower asks when I have its runways in sight, "say your intention, please."

My intention is not to be confused by the layout of the runways as, unfortunately, I am, flying straight to the air-port's heart instead of paralleling the correct runway, whichever it may be. Between juggling a schematic of the runways, looking at the aeronautical chart, and figuring out what's where on my directional gyro, I reassure the controller that I am with him in spirit and doing my best to enter a "left downwind for runway one," one of the lines below me and off my left wing. A twin-engine leaps into the sky from one of the lines, and I set up for that runway, seeing its number on the threshold a few moments later. But this is so unlike the parabolic panic of my flight to Emporia. The sky is unsullied by clouds, though a haze level at 3,000 feet makes it preferable to fly lower.

When I return by way of the Cofield VOR, about thirty miles from Elizabeth City, I find it nimbly among the twists of the Chowan River, a shining white clown's cap in a field. Circle it once, steeply, in celebration, then head home on the correct heading. An hour later, Jamestown Island drifts into view, with Williamsburg Airport one minute beyond it, though quite invisible until you are smack on top of it. Site on the water tower, turn at the bend in the river, wait for the runway to appear out of the north. The sun is down by now, but the sky is still bright; with the sunset behind me, haze is minimal. None of the runway lights are on when I land, grinning and well pleased with myself. Martin, George, and one of the mechanics are all outside waiting for me. "You're one minute early," Tom Johnson says at last when I enter Colonial's trailer. "Poor planning." He laughs. How could I be the same person crying after a short hop to Emporia?

The next trip is to Shannon Airport, a hundred miles northwest, by way of Richmond. My preflight planning is all aces, but at Richmond a maze of revised routes and nervous guesses begins, thanks to the whim of an air traffic controller, who decides not to let me fly directly to the airport as I've planned. First he cross-examines me about where I am *exactly*, though I've told him I am roughly ten miles southeast and that I have no DME with which to measure the distance more precisely. Waiting until I can locate the airport at New Kent off my right wing and see Richmond's Byrd Field in the distance, he demands an immediate course change and, when I'm slow in figuring one out, vectors me swiftly out of his hair. Now all my checkpoints are wrong; there are no salient landmarks wherever I am, and I'm obliged to keep to the path he's given me until I vanish from his radar, or he gets tired of tracking me. I'm afraid to risk angling off on my own to intercept my original course somewhere north of the city. When Richmond radar says good-bye to me, I look down at where he's dropped me off: splotchy buff hills with dark craters. "Oh, great," I say out loud, to the ghost of whatever benighted student controller got me into this mess, "I'm over a restricted military area, whose craters look recent, *and I'm low.*" Small planes sometimes get shot by missiles; hence all the warnings on the aeronautical charts, which outline the restricted areas in what looks like aerial barbed wire. But at least it's a landmark, bold as a big blue VERBOTEN on my chart, and I can see that if I just head north to the first river, the Potomac, then turn left, I ought to be abeam Shannon Airport at some point . . . yes, the point where a VOR radial from Brooke will read "240° FROM." Tom had made me swear I would call Shannon Unicom when I had the airport in sight and ask about the winds, gusting stiffly right across their paved runway when I set out from Williamsburg. *If that makes a headwind on the grass strip, land there,* he had said. *But otherwise, don't you dare try to land. Just circle the airport and come home.*

Shannon appears beside the river, beyond a factory, before the town of Fredericksburg, right where my VOR needle says it should be. What a sweet little airport, banked by trees and railroad, with one paved runway and a grass strip leading away from it at a right angle. Over and over, I radio its Unicom for a wind advisory, as I circle the airport, but get no response. The wind sock is out stiff as a trumpeting elephant, and there's a direct crosswind for the paved runway, so I know that if the winds are soft enough I'll be landing on grass for the first time. Still the Unicom doesn't answer. Circling the airport, lower this time, I scout the grass for holes or obstructions, check how short the field looks, especially with that stand of tall trees right at the end of it, and try to gauge from the wind sock just how rough the winds are. The grass looks as beautifully groomed as a croquet pitch. Next pass, I set up to land, as I've practiced so often on Williamsburg's macadam—a short-field, soft-field landing. Bring it in slowly over the cornfields, add full flaps, hold it off to settle at as slow a speed as possible, keep the nose wheel off the ground. My wheels touch on the lip of the paved runway and slide onto the grass, where I come to a stop amazingly fast, with perhaps a thousand feet to spare before the trees. From the air, though, the strip had looked ominously short; I'd forgotten how little room trainers need to land. Jogging over the turf, I hold the plane's wheel well back; the winds buffet me as I turn, and I feel like an escapee from *Alice in Wonderland,* a queen's lawn sport pursued by a deck of cards.

A bank owns Shannon Airport, as well as the museum of planes commemorated by color pictures lining the walls of the FBO. "Caution, microwave in use," it says over the door to what looks like a country diner, with curved counter and small tables and chairs crammed into one end of the FBO. A country and western singer sings over steel guitar chords. I can hear cutlery clink and the sizzle of my cheeseburger and fries. "Betty, you got something I can catch a drip with?" a bleached-blond, blue-jeaned Unicom woman calls with a twang. In a moment what must be Betty, the counter lady, returns from her pullman kitchen with a pan.

"First solo cross-country?" a stocky man says with achieved casualness.

I start to laugh, as I sit down at a table with a mug of

coffee, whose lip is so thick I can barely drink from it. "That obvious?"

"No, no, no, you did fine. There's just one little thing . . . I'm sorry, my name's Judd Frazer, I'm a flight instructor in New Jersey. . . ."

"How do you do, Judd Frazer," I say and shake his hand, wondering if he can tell that mine is shaking still from the excitement of landing.

". . . one thing. It isn't such a good idea to land as short as that—off the runway, I mean—and then roll onto it. See it doesn't matter now when it's warm and the grass is soft. But suppose there were a frost and the grass heaved up just an inch or so. You'd catch your wheels shifting from the cement to the grass, and I'll lay you odds it'd be your wheels that would stay right there."

"He's right," says a lean, middle-aged man in a gray jumpsuit, as he leaves his perch on a counter stool and brings his cup of coffee over to my table. Before I leave, three flight instructors from around the country, whose lives happen to be intersecting in Shannon, all say hello to one another and offer me appraisals and advice. They caution me about the winds I'll meet flying back to Williamsburg, they advise me what to look for en route if I lose my heading. Then I push aside the uneaten plate of greasy french fries, file my flight plan, and climb back into my plane.

It is exactly as I have practiced it, taking off on the grass strip, and what a wonder to wrestle the plane off the ground the moment it can fly, then push its nose back low to pick up speed, zoom straight at the onrushing militia of trees, and climb all at once as soon as I have climbing speed. Up steeply, I circle the airport once and hear an incoming plane trying to make radio contact with the Unicom, as I had earlier. None of his calls are answered, so I speak to him directly, tell him which runway is active. He thanks me, and then a moment later, a high-pitched, frantic woman's voice enters the conversation to tell him that I've given him the opposite runway number by mistake and by all means *not* to land as I've advised him. Stupid doesn't touch how dreadful I feel. *Quel jerk,* I say to myself, as I make tracks for Williamsburg, by an alternate route, miffed at the mistakes I've made.

Later, when I tie down and go inside Colonial's trailer, Tom says, "Welcome to Williamsburg. Have a good flight?"

"I don't want to talk about it," I say as I head for the cabinet where my paperwork is kept. Tom gets up quickly, smiling, and says, "Sure you do."

I've saved a vial of glitter for my *long cross-country,* which must include three 100-mile legs or approximately three-and-a-half hours in the air, flying by VOR navigation and sheer nail-biting pilotage. I figure I'll want to leave a small discreet dune of something symbolic and iridescent at one of the airports, something that will fly shimmery in all directions when a breeze hits. So I tuck the vial into my flight bag when no one's looking. Martin checks my flight plan, makes me verbally rehearse the route, lends me his headset to make the radio work more comfortable, preflights the plane once by himself, then watches as I preflight it again, and waves as I taxi nervously out to the runway. Soon he'll be inside calling the local Flight Service Station we activate our flight plans with, to make sure I landed safely at my first stop and am off again on the next leg, the one I am honor bound to fly seat-of-the-pants, not by VOR navigation, over confusingly ordinary terrain.

It's a long haul from Rocky Mount Wilson to Charlottesville, but that's the route I'm supposed to fly by eyeshot, and after fifteen minutes of positively, absolutely not knowing where I am over the repeating farmlands and orderless woods, I decide the wisest thing to do is admit to myself that I am lost, and head for the nearest VOR cone I can find. Lawrenceville is the closest, but when I tune it in, I discover that instead of being west of it, I am due east, though I've no idea how far. What I can do is fly toward the VOR site and wait until the box on my instrument panel shifts from TO to FROM. Miles and miles pour underneath me, while I frantically search the land for some tidbit that will tell me where on Earth I may be. Nothing. The same corn rows and farmhouses. Then the box rolls from TO to FROM, though I see no VOR cone anywhere. No matter. The trick now will be to leave the VOR site on a heading that will lead me directly to one of my original checkpoints, a small airport northwest of Lawrenceville. The landscape is still a mystery, and then Lunenburg County Airport appears, with all the right landmarks surrounding it. I circle it once and leave on the originally planned heading, realizing now that I neglected to get an update on the winds aloft, which have obviously shifted direction and grown rapid.

Soon mountains begin to appear off my left wing, some of them visibly higher than I am and all of them looking close. The chart says they are where the Blue Ridge range begins, and the highways I see converging ahead of me will lead to Charlottesville, a town tucked among the mountains. Sure enough, I see a mountain pass straight ahead of me, with a super highway threading it, and as I approach it's like peeking through a keyhole at the city of Charlottesville, sprawling and silent. The airport (Albemarle County) sits on a plateau northeast of Charlottesville, but all I can see is the fascinating, flat city below, broken by waterways, rimmed by quarries.

"Charlottesville Tower, Cessna four-three-seven," I call as I scoot through the pass in my tiny, high-winged marvel. A woman's voice answers, and we exchange information, gently, in a conspiratorial whisper. Martin's headset makes radio work like telephoning instead of shouting. He'll be amused by the lipstick I've left on the boom mike, the snatched filaments of my thick hair trapped in one of the joints. I make a mental note to clean it well.

"Four-three-seven, Charlottesville. Report three mile base."

"Roger. You say three mile base. Four-three-seven."

On final, I float low over the trees, and it swiftly dawns on me that I am not at Williamsburg at sea level, but over land 600 feet higher, doing a traffic pattern at 400 feet, instead of 800! Still a mile from touchdown, I climb to make sure I'll be at a safe height for the airport plateau, then drop down to a normal final when I'm closer. On the ground, I speak to another frequency as I taxi, and a patient voice reminds me of something else I forgot: that I am overdue on my flight plan, since I got lost for a good half an hour at Lawrenceville. Martin and Tom will be worried. The FAA will be getting set to send out their detectives.

"I imagine you tried to extend your arrival time in the

air and had . . . ah . . . difficulty," the ground man says chivalrously.

"Yes, yes, that's correct," I say quickly.

"Right then, I will record that you made an attempt to change your arrival time, but couldn't make radio contact."

Sweet mercies, I think, thank God for gentlemen.

"Yes, sir, thank you very much sir."

I'm hoping to find Frank Jongepier at Charlottesville, a Dutch pilot Martin grew up with and roomed with during his training at Greensboro, North Carolina. I know little about Frank, except what Martin tells us, that he's handsome in a swashbuckling, Errol Flynn way, is more sober about life than Martin, even melancholy sometimes, and is a first-class pilot who's avid to fly DC-3s. He and Martin are the same age and applied for jobs together, with their shiny new credentials, down in Greensboro. Frank landed a fine job as charter pilot at Waring Aviation, just an hour's hop across the state from Williamsburg. Martin sends his students on cross-countries to Charlottesville as a kind of calling card, and sometimes he and Frank recognize each other's voices in the air, greet one another by wavelength though miles apart.

But Frank is up flying one of the hulking B-18s in the Waring fleet, on a milk-run from Charlottesville to Dulles. In any case, the day is growing shorter, and I'm already overdue. A quick cup of coffee, and I jump back into my plane, taxi the long roll to where the runway begins, and take off toward an observation knoll just northeast of the airport, a strange teepee of Earth called Piney Mount, which rises 1,182 feet above sea level.

Finding Richmond is easy; soon I can see it in the distance, and I ask Approach Control if I may fly directly over the VOR cone to take my bearing for the last leg home. There's something comforting about the moment when you tell the tower where you are, "approximately five miles northwest of the airport," and they pick you up on radar, exactly where you thought you were, though now you are a scintillation of yellow on a screen, now you are a gold nugget against the background of the sky.

When the airport glides under me, everything seems to be in the wrong place. There is no other way to explain how gently confused one can be in the air, or how swiftly that confusion becomes rigid disorientation. In Williamsburg, I'd planned a heading for this leg; it now looks wrong. After a few minutes of following it anyway, I spot the James River crawling darkly off my right wing, and I fly straight to it, because I know it will lead me home, and I am saturated with exhaustion. A dank, sweet, vapory smell in the cockpit; I turn the heat off, open an air vent wide. But the fumes may not be bothering me at all, anyway not as much as the effect of spending four hours straight in a cramped cockpit, in which I dare not let my mind wander for even a moment.

Over the Chickahominy River, about seven miles from home, I feel my spine relaxing against the seatback for the first time, and I radio Williamsburg that I'm in their backyard. The sun has just set, which means I'll have a slim hour until nightfall, but already I can see the water tower off the end of runway 13. And two figures outside the FBO, as I land; one of them lifts a soda can to drink, the other salutes me with the peak of his cap. They vanish as I chug round the ramp, pivot beautifully on point, and tie the plane down. Exhausted, thrilled, I stumble into the Colonial trailer.

"Welcome to Williamsburg," Tom says from his desk in the adjoining room. Martin is trying to stifle a grin behind a Mr. Pibb can.

"Sorry I'm late. The lights were all against me."

"No problem," Tom says. "Tough trip?"

I pour myself a cup of coffee. "Why do you ask?" Out of his sight, I do a little tap dance of joy and mouth to Martin: *I made it! I made it!*

"Oh, nothing," Tom says, walking over to the door, and looking out its window to the plane which, for the first time in five months, I have parked in the wrong place.

42

WING BY YOURSELF across the skies of America, and no day that follows can be unremarkable. You were where the birds balance on the thermals, slightly rocking their stretched wings just as you do your high-winged Cessna. It's the same movement, the same delicate sampling, the same tightrope walker's cunning I've seen in the Wright Brothers' notebook entries on birds, and in the tilt and glide of hawks that loll around the airport. And I've done it myself.

Sprawling across one of the varnished tables at Colonial, a Cessna final exam book open in front of me, I stop to ask Martin what is really on my mind. Not *moment arms* or *Coriolis effect*.

"How do birds fly?"

He lifts his elbows up high and flaps like a Tweety-Bird in a tornado. I laugh. Then he checks the change in his pocket, which I know means he's going to buy a Mars bar or a Mr. Pibb in the FBO, and as he gets up from his desk, says, "Finish the exam, and I'll tell you." Pausing in the doorway to zip his flying jacket, he says in a charged whisper what he knows will drive my curiosity haywire: "They have doors in their wings."

"Martin!" I cry, pushing my chair away from the table. "Doors?"

"No!" He wags a long finger at me. "First the exam. Then all the good stuff about the birds."

I pout as if I were inventing one for the first time: a poignant, melodramatic, heartbreaking *pout*. He laughs, slides his hands into his pockets, and pretends to fall out the door. I return to questions about radio frequencies and VOR navigation.

But later I learn that, when a bird's wings are up, door-like flaps in each feather open, so that air can pour through them. When it pushes its wings down the doors close against the air. That's how a bird hovers. We agree that two trips are essential: one to the library to find scanning electron microscope photographs of the bird-feather doors in action, and one this Sunday to the Air and Space Museum in Washington, to look at their aviary of winged creatures, like the X-15, Lindbergh's *Spirit of St. Louis*, or the gull-winged Corsair.

But my final exam is terrible. A 63! Without at least an 80, Martin can't give me the go-ahead to sit the FAA written exam, which I must pass to get my private pilot's license. This time my pout is genuine, though just as graphic.

"I'm surprised you did that well," he reassures me, "without any regular ground school or anything. But from now on, you must study every single day." His voice is stern with a Dutch accent, as if he were remembering the school-marms of his youth. *"Every single day.* I want you to pass your FAA exam next Tuesday."

"Ouch," I say.

He smiles. "You will. I'll help you get ready. Mean-while, do this workbook." He drops a Cessna book onto my waiting hands. Riffling through it, I can see that my work will be cut out for me: graphs, formulas, expressions in an English so jargonized it reads like trade-route pidgin.

By sunset the next day, I'm overwhelmed by the work-book, only a third of which I've slashed and burned my way through, but drive over to Colonial anyway to meet Martin as planned. Tom is usually long gone by now, but his car is still in the lot, across from Martin's, and I can see the cozy light in his office window as I drive up.

I find Tom at his desk, in a trailer thick with smoke, two packs of cigarettes open in front of him, as he looks down at a chart of North Carolina. A cigarette trembles in one hand, while the other hand presses a telephone to his ear. He is trying to smile normally at me when I come in, but it is like putting the wrong change into a slot: nothing fits. When he says, "Hello," there is no register to his voice. His eyes fall back to the chart without really looking at it, and in between phrases on the phone, he pauses, waits a moment to collect himself, and continues, methodically inquiring, getting phone numbers, hanging up, and phon-ing again, all without looking at me.

Shaking, I go to the schedule and discover that the Cherokee 140 Martin had flown to North Carolina with two newspapermen was due back over an hour ago.

"Are they all right?" I ask, sitting down beside Tom's chair.

Without looking up, he shakes his head. "No, I don't think so," he says, his voice a dry reed.

The skin suddenly feels too small all over my body.

"Is Martin all right?"

"The sheriff's report says that there were two fatalities, one man in critical condition in the hospital."

Even Tom, after 14,000 hours of flying, much of it in wartime when many young flyers died, even Tom can only bring himself to say fatalities. Even Tom, the colonel who must rally under pressure, cannot keep his hands from trembling, over the map, against the phone, trembling against the truth that he already knows in his heart, that a young man he's loved, instructed, and been a father to in some ways, was in a nose-in crash. After 14,000 hours, you know what that kind of accident means, that no one walks away.

"Is Martin the man in the hospital? Call the hospital," I plead.

Jean, the owner of the airport, runs in to tell Tom that a hospital in North Carolina is trying to reach Martin's parents, to say their son is in the operating room and critical. Then Tom calls the doctors, hears the worst. We watch his face turning over slowly in pain as he listens to a doctor's report of the injuries. "No," I hear him say, "I'm his representative in the States, in place of his family."

And a waiting by telephones, in separate houses, begins that ends at 9 P.M., when Tom calls, unable to say it at first.

"Is Martin alive?" I ask a piece of electronics in my hand. And it answers, "I'm sorry."

Nothing is like the horror of having to understand that someone is dead, when the mind will not accept it as negotiable information, when the mind will not believe that someone twenty-four years old can die, when the mind cannot even depict with full horror how mangled one feels at such a moment, how helpless, how superfluous, how random, how vacant. Life suddenly has a hole in it. All night, I lie awake shaking and shivering, with the electric blanket up full, and two sets of pajamas on. Near dawn I begin to realize that I must be in shock, still to be so cold and shaking under all that heat.

Investigators crawl over the wrecked plane for some time, but reach no verdict about the series of events that led that plane to that field. Because there is no accepting it, by word or understanding, we hold a funeral for Martin Van der Linde, whom we love, even though there will be a funeral for him in the Netherlands, too. The casket is open, and he is "made ready" for us to see him because it is essential that we fully understand that he has died, really died, is not simply off on a cross-country trip from which he will return, sprightly and rub-plucking at his eyes the way he did when he was tired. His parents send as their emissary Bert Verduyn, who heads the organization that first trained Martin in the Netherlands and sends many Dutch students to the States for their ratings.

Bert surprises us all by arriving in command of the legal maze a death sets free, but also with such intuitive compassion for those who are grieving. It is Bert who wraps an arm around my shoulders and leads me to the room where Martin is, forcing me to look at him, though I shake with horror, and my eyes keep opening and closing as if they were a camera behind whose shutters I could hide the truth. Forces me to look because it is necessary for the living to make some formal arrangement with death, and he knows it. It is Bert and I who go through Martin's belongings in the small room he rented in a woodsy house near the airport. And it is Bert who must fly back to Holland, with Martin in a casket behind him in the cargo hold, only to rebegin the days of grief and mourning on the other side, with Martin's family and Dutch friends.

From Charlottesville, Virginia, Frank Jongepier, Martin's best friend, arrives, canceling his duties as a heavily worked commuter pilot to lend a hand for a few days. Sky diver, glider pilot, and now first officer in Waring Aviation's fleet of B-18s and other planes, pilot of corporate jets, and flight instructor, Frank is a man of constant action, who has spent his life taking command of things. It must have been especially hard for him to be helpless when the news came of his friend's death and there was no lever he could throw, no storm he could outwit, no course he could plot, no act of courage or heroism he could endure, nothing whatsoever he could do, though his life is charged with *doing*, with solving and protecting. For Frank honor is particularly merciful. He could not save his friend, but he can act vigilantly for the survivors, to help them back into the cockpit of their lives. And that is something, to fight the death flak on some level and win.

Together, Bert and Frank assume the extraordinary responsibility of looking after the bereaved, as well as Martin's body, affairs, and belongings. It is their duty, it is their grim privilege, it is their familial obligation to him, as a Dutchman and as a friend, to look after everything about him and everyone his life has touched. The way they comfort all of us on his behalf, the way they act from an inner absolute of what being humane is in the face of death, is something indelible. It will linger in my memory as the compassion human beings can rise to, as a definition for what used to be referred to as *acting honorably*.

In emotional disarray we all meet, with a single grief among us, and in a strange way that welds us together. Nothing like pretense is possible when death happens. The costumes melt. Life's trivia seem impossibly trivial, and things order themselves according to importance, with death and its rituals and managing one's personal grief at the top, and everything else, like work or even pinning up the fallen pieces of one's public version, second. I understand now why death rituals have formed over the centuries. To be alone when you first meet death would be excruciating. Or even when death is a familiar, I suppose. We evolve as a species whose will to live is paramount, and yet we also evolve as a species that dies. There is no way to reconcile that brutal collision.

Frank calls me regularly, as Bert does, as they do others, to reassure us that we have gained a wider family, not lost the hub of it. They chivvy me into getting back into a plane again, because I'm too shaken to fly. They call to be a shoulder to cry on, to nag us, to help us get our lives back to normal. It is such quiet and unrecorded altruism, given the tumult of their own lives, but compassionate duty is their privilege, and I'm beginning to understand how, in both senses, it is also their honor.

I had wanted to give Martin a present, to thank him for teaching me to fly at last: a piece of metal, like a wing, a key-ring fob perhaps. On one side would be the RAF's dog Latin, *illigitimis non carborundum est*, "Don't let the bastards grind you down," and on the other this line from the New York City poet Frank O'Hara: "grace to be born and live." As Wallace Stevens said, perception is itself a form of grace, the voluptuousness of looking is life's greatest bounty. "I'll have to ask my local neighborhood poet," Martin used to say to me in the third person. I called him "fighter pilot" or "flyboy" as a form of address. And, once, when I returned from the Bahamas, I found that he had borrowed my car Christmas day to drive down to Greensboro, where he and Frank once boarded with a woman named Jewell, who lived near the airport. He had washed my car, changed the oil filter, scrubbed it down inside, and left in the copilot's seat a soft white Snoopy doll dressed in a flying jacket, goggles, helmet, and red scarf. "A fighter pilot to do your radio work for you on your long cross-country," he had said. And I remember how on the day of that cross-country he checked everything through first—the plane, the fuel—then waited on the tarmac as I preflighted and took off, and later phoned the Flight Service Station with whom I would be activating my flight plan, to make sure I made it to each destination. I remember how, on my medium-length cross-country, to

Shannon via Richmond, I returned to learn by accident that he had been monitoring my radio frequency the whole way, to make sure the blustery winds wouldn't give me any trouble, to make sure I didn't get lost.

I remember how he would call up about some appointment or other, and his form of salutation would be "Boo!" We were always playing, always romping among the planes and the hangar and the FBO. Once, after hours, we drove down the runway in his Brougham, to see if it would lift off at rotation speed. We climbed into a score of planes: King Airs, Lances, Commanders, Vikings. Any new plane that appeared we scrambled around rivet by rivet or, when he had the keys or permission, climbed aboard. Any open plane, cowling, or door was an invitation we couldn't resist. We were everywhere around the airport, throwing snowballs, learning to fly, making paper planes that had radical wing designs, playing the video game, or shooting the breeze at the FBO. Certain games were part of our daily routine, like the clothespins, for instance. As I recall, it began one day when I clipped a clothespin onto the back of the collar of his flight jacket. Sweeping a hand over his hair, he found the clothespin by accident, just as he was set to go outside to give a lesson. The expression on my face told him everything. And that started the craziest, sweetest clothespin war of sabotage and inventiveness. I would find my car's aerial a vertebrae of clothespins. He would open his briefcase between lessons, reach for his gloves, and find a clothespin in every finger. I would go to teach my writing seminar at the college and have to explain somehow why I had a clothespin clipped to the back of my hair. I don't think it was as good as my filling his Ray Ban sunglass case with a Mars bar (packaged in Holland, with a black Dutch wrapper) that fit it exactly, so that he had to think fast when he opened the case casually before a lesson, and his puzzled student saw the Mars bar instead of his Ray Bans. I can't imagine what he told him. But when Bert and I went through his belongings after the funeral, all the papers and posters and corduroy pants (whose hems had all been let down) and Pink Floyd tapes and flying memorabilia, we found the wrapper from that Mars bar, kept because it was Dutch I think, or perhaps as a memento of the crazy games we played.

I remember how many tarmacs we landed on and window-shopped around. Any cross-country lesson with me had to include time to explore all the local planes for concealed felicities. But he liked that, too, he was so in love with flying and so in love with language, whose witty possibilities he was discovering at colossal speed. We were a good team for mischief. "Don't you get into any mischief at Patrick Henry," he would warn me with mock sobriety, before I took off to get into as much as I possibly could, asking the air traffic controllers for all sorts of special patterns and approaches. Once, after I heard the tower three times refer to me as "the Cessna on a short, high final," I requested permission to land and pull off at the first taxiway and pause for a moment to think about what I might be doing wrong.

"Ah, four-three-seven, you request permission to do *what*?" the tower had said.

"Four-three-seven would like permission to think for a moment, at the first taxiway."

Silence.

"I'm a student pilot," I added, and then the tower's response was immediate:

"Four-three-seven is cleared to the first taxiway to stand by."

I half expected to hear the tower telling the incoming Allegheny jet that there was no reported traffic, but to watch out for the Cessna 152 "thinking" on the ramp.

"Mischief" was my word; every week some new witticism would rub off on him so thoroughly I'd hear it a dozen times a day: an unusual word or phrase, or one said with a skewed meaning or inflection. Whenever I heard his echo, I'd stop saying the word and replace it with some equally eccentric one which, in no time, he'd be unconsciously using, too. It was a kind of mirror game we both began to recognize and enjoy. We were all mannerisms. We were all pranks. We were a secret society of children plane-maniacs. We talked about trivial things mainly, but occasionally about things that mattered, too, even emotions hard for him to talk about on the displaced threshold of his maturity.

Martin takes his last flight today, across the deaf, ambiguous Atlantic, to lie in a box too short to be a fuselage. As long as the Earth orbits the Sun, he will be flying. He was such a tall man; how shall I think of him now and forever lengthwise? I still expect him to jump out from behind a door and yell *lekker püh!* a playful Dutch taunt. He was so homesick. Holland was a state of mind for him, the complex intimacy of neighborhood life, where he could drop in on Frank's parents and stay a week without ever feeling out of place or secondary. The tiny room he grew up in, with its bed and desk pulling out from the walls; everything had its place, and you could almost touch one wall from the other. But he loved how obsessively compact it was, as he loved eating the kale and mashed potatoes and smoked sausage that he often made for dinner. First he would shape it into a neat, even mesa, then pour a meticulous layer of applesauce over the top of it, spread it even smoother with a knife, divide the concoction into lines, and eat the meal symmetrically, one side at a time. No one was more compulsive than he, who even gilded his car's engine one day and ironed his socks, until his roommates caught him at it and laughed so hard it occurred to him that it might be just a tiny bit odd. But that obsessiveness made him a wonderful teacher and a glorious friend, because he was obsessive with people, too.

"Little flyer," he used to call me with protective tenderness sometimes. And there was no way to conceal his sympathetic joy when he would see me get the okay to fly on a windy day and run hell for leather out to the plane to preflight it. Even when I was little, thrill would make me run like that. *Stop running!* was the litany of my childhood. *Stop running!* But not from him. I would turn, panting, as I began my preflight, and sometimes see him across the macadam, leaning against the steps to Colonial's trailer, with a Mr. Pibb in one hand, not smiling exactly, but with delight a long caravan moving across his face. Flight was all he believed in, and it was enough. For him it was the All I believe in.

His friends remember him in working terms, a little formal in manner and very thorough about every task, or that on that last fatal trip, ironically, he acquired 1,502 hours, just enough for the air-transport-pilot rating he had come to this country for. They remember the shy, quiet, plane-obsessed boy who left Holland three years ago. But not me. I remember a young man standing on the stairwell between impetuosity and maturity, still puppyish and innocent but also discovering life rapidly, the mind, the senses, language, his own ambition, with relish and gusto, with the same obsessiveness, in fact, that he brought to everything. It was as if he had stumbled on an array of gorgeous secrets that had been kept from him all these years. I remember him in a state of transition: emotionally alert, with a newly vigilant concern for people, becoming an extraordinary man.

Had Frank died and not him, someone he loved and admired, he would have kept flying. There was a sense he had, as I do, that the World is a fairground open only for one season, and you must enter it hungry and full of awe, eager for the rides that will thrill and teach you, though some may be dangerous. Anyway, flying was his way of branding the Universe with his presence, his form of ecstasy, his refusal to wait below while the sky turns and turns its indecipherable blue. Flying framed his life, as it frames his death. It was crucial to his intense liveliness to be that close to danger, to be above human society and on his own in the Universe, and then return, made new by the simplest voyage to Patrick Henry or Norfolk. Each flight defined him and brought him back in rearing awareness to all the things not-flight that he loved on the ground.

43

WHEN, A MONTH LATER, I still have not flown, no one asks why. By now the airport's routine is almost back to normal, but there are pieces of illogic as obvious as they are stubborn. Example: how can I feel the same innocence about flying when an airplane killed my friend? Example: if my flight instructor, with 1,500 hours, can crash, what chance have I? Example: wouldn't it be in some way disloyal to a friend to relish flying when it was his undoing? These are survivors' questions. They go along with the daily migraines I've had since the accident and Tom's ferocious case of shingles and George's increased nervousness and the general state of bodily unrest we all suffer silently. Lance, who also works the Unicom, began taking flying lessons right after the crash; it was his way of fighting back, I suppose. A new young flight instructor sits at Martin's desk and performs his duties. Various part-time older flyers pitch in with the lessons. We all joke heartily as ever, though there's a deliberate, almost desperate tinge to it, as if we were acting out the normalcy we'd like to feel, and will. Run the throttle forward, point your nose up to where it would be if you were flying, and wait for the flying that will absolutely come. Not just yet, but soon, provided you hold the right attitude.

The weather's been lousy; winter is Williamsburg's rainy season. But mainly I've just been too sad and too spooked to fly. One morning, Frank phones to order me back up in a tone of brotherly no-back-talk: "You will hang up this telephone, right now, and call Tom to schedule a flight this afternoon—not maybe, not tomorrow, not you'll try to, but definitely, *right now*." At the airport, Tom is ready to take me up, as he has been for days, and when we climb into the Cessna 152 to get on the go, he jokes about how cramped the cockpit is and casually settles his left arm around the back of my seat, keeps it there as a reassuring cushion for the entire lesson. And he works me ruggedly: the full stall series, steep turns, turns about a point, landings of various sorts. Speaking quietly all the time, he works me like a cutting horse through one maneuver after another, and there is no time to think about anything but mastery. Between grins, I tell him that I am sweating in places I didn't think people could sweat, and he laughs. After 14,000 hours in the air, he is a born teacher, and he is a master pilot. Somehow we've been up for an hour and a half, though it only seems like a few minutes, and I am a sheet of cold thrill again, grinning as

I sweep into a steep turn one way, roll out, then sweep back steeply the other.

"How does it feel?" he asks, asking everything.

"Great," I say and mean it. "I love to fly."

Now the arm around my seat back lightly presses my shoulders for a moment. "Good, that's real good," he says and smiles with relief.

A few days later, I am up by myself, after much nervous pacing and fretting and topping up of the gas tanks that are already full ("Took three gallons," George says, as he puts the hose away. "But don't you worry none; whatever you feel comfortable with is what matters."). Up to do stalls in the haze at 3,000 feet. Alone, with my nose high and a wing ready to drop, I scare myself so badly that it's an effort to stay up. But at least I'm not plunging close to spin entry, as I used to when I practiced stalls, and at least my truly rusty and disgraceful landings are salvageable. On the last one (because I am laughing too hard to go round the pattern again), I land like a rubber ball, bounce up fifteen feet, and am in a mess of no airspeed and too much height. Palming the throttle, I pick the plane up like a wet dog, fly it down the runway until I get it stabilized, then land again, this time right across from the FBO, with only a few hundred feet of runway remaining. My thighs are shaking tensely as I park the plane and tie it down. It was an awkward, scary, and giftless flight, but truces often are; the main thing is climbing back up into the sky. Tomorrow, I'll do better, I think, walking back to the trailer, and then laugh as I relive that last uniquely wretched landing, which was almost a thing of beauty it was so grotesque.

283

44

MY HAND HAS DEVELOPED so many new wrinkles, a spray of wispy creases and channels. It used to be simple: heart line, life line, brain line, wealth. Now each deep line has a hundred extenuating ones: basins, rivulets, and notches. In a few spots, there are actual X's, to mark the treasure of some indefinable moment. In other spots, the fleshy outer edge of my left hand, for instance, the lines become loopy as a weather map, full of small highs and lows, sudden storms, and areas where the ceiling is ground fog. And the veins are clearer now than ever, deep blue, rising thickly along the top of my hand, as they do all over the pale length of my body. Once, just after flying, I had blood taken during an exam, and the needle bruised the soft knoll of my arm just below the elbow into a sunset of colors large as a bar of soap. Blood stood up on the skin afterward, trickled out for long minutes before my blood pressure fell close enough to normal for the bleeding to stop. By flying, I make the blood want to leave my body.

I am waiting for Frank to call, though it is late, sleep time in Williamsburg, and I've spent a pent-up, mind-blunting day reading fiscal review sheets for an Arts Council meeting, then preparing student poems for an up-coming class. He is somewhere in the sky above Virginia, winging to Dulles and back again, flying the night shift. I am on his mind in the blackness he flies by heading, by compass cued not to true north but to a quarry of nickel askew deep in Canada, *magnetic north*. I am on his mind. He promised to teach me how to fly an Archer, a low-winged Piper, this week sometime and will be phoning to say when. It is already late. But I am on his mind. He promised to take me up in a plane I'm smitten with, not because it's *sleek* or *snarky* or *sassy* or *sexy*, but safe, faster than a Warrior or small Cessna, roomier than they are, and reliable as a sound horse. It has elegant lines and might just suit me.

I am thinking of his hand, how it lies along the neck of the quadrant throttle, which he moves by thumb, how all the other fingers cup the panel, a caution, lest the hand ever slip, how he looks to be shaking hands with the power and will teach me to do the same. It's a handshake be-tween us, which only the panel completes, which we could not accomplish hand-to-hand. I am thinking of his other hand, whose three fingers hold the stick like a bird's wing, delicate. I am thinking of his feet on the rudder pedals, as in a go-cart. I am not thinking of his heart or of the silent thundering blackness of the sky in which his mind may be roaming. Or anything but his thumb, caressing the throttle neck, feeling for its pulse.

I imagine what it must be like, right now, in the bordello light of that cockpit, where red is thick as smoke in the air. Only his passengers live by white light, framed by the lighted windows, as if they were in a dining car in a painting by Hopper. Frank lives deeper, in the tunnels of the night, by echo-location, by sonar. He glides pterodactyl-slow over the sandstorm of light that he knows is a city of 2 million people, writing letters, making love, buying loaves of bread, operating on ball-and-socket joints with thread-fine instruments. Around his uniform, dark as a night sky, his face and hands float like the constellations they are, his face assaying the bits of flicker on the panel, his hands feeling the plane's inner rhythms against his own pulse. He is listening to the rhythmic pant of the engines, for any sign of icing, any stammer or moan. Without listening, he is listening. Between the radio chatter, between the steady blips of the radar weaving him into its web of electronic cunning, there are silences vital as a power plant, serene but emphatic, in which his mind walks on a long tether, and he sifts the day's doings of a planet far below. In one such silence, he remembers that I am thinking of his hand, thinking in the easterly darkness 5,000 feet below, and so he slides it silently along the panel to where he knows I imagine it, lying against the quadrant, caressing the throttle neck, feeling softly for the pulse.

45

If anyone had said to me a year ago that I would soon blithely be spouting facts about the compression stroke of a piston engine, the rules concerning LADY and RAPPA MOAS, how winds swivel around low and high pressure systems, the effect of frost on an airfoil, how shifting the center of gravity may change an airplane's ability to recover from a stall, what a litany of colored lights flashed from a control tower gun means, how wake turbulence is created, and especially how to compute fuel consumption, rate-of-climb, gravity moment envelope, and takeoff distance necessary to clear a fifty-foot obstacle under varying weather conditions, loads, and elevations, not to mention all the weather lore, and navigational lingo, transponder codes, radio work, and laws governing who has right-of-way in the sky, I would have thought that person mad.

A new young instructor at Colonial asks me random questions from a private-pilot exam study book: 800 questions about regulations, graphs, charts, and physics, sixty of which will be on tomorrow's FAA written exam in Richmond. After the fifth question about squall lines, oxygen use, and flight through military practice areas, I begin to laugh. His thick mustache twitches, and he smiles sympathetically but doesn't sense how ridiculously alien I feel, like something washed up on the beach of aviation.

"A Ph. D. oughtn't to have any trouble with the exam; don't worry," he says.

And I laugh even harder. *What am I doing here?* runs a ticker tape across my vision. For the past week solid I've been boning up, learning how to use a circular slide rule, and make sense of chicken-scratch graphs in which ice cubes too tiny to rest a fingernail edge on are two or ten or one half of something, and lines sag across the empty boxes where I expect to find letters, not the abstract emptiness of space and numbers. But I do read them now. Learning to read a graph is a major accomplishment, right up there with learning to land.

"Ahem," Glenn says in an are-you-listening tone, "if you make a night flight, with passengers along, what are you supposed to have done within the past ninety days?"

"Three takeoffs and landings, to a full stop, in an airplane of the same category and class," I parrot.

"You're leaving an airport on Eastern Standard Time at seventeen-thirty; it takes you two hours to fly to an airport on Central Standard Time; what time is it in Greenwich Mean Time when you arrive? . . . . And while you're at it," he throws in, "what's angle of incidence?"

The angle of incidence is where time meets motion head-on in a field, but also the impossible high-wire beauty of the sky, which I have been trying to make sense of for almost a year now. The angle of incidence is the white picket fence around the house I live in in Williamsburg, on which the sky is impaled, the fence against which young lovers lean to hold hands in the still Southern evenings, whose skies are like crêpe paper, the fence which joggers come to know as a white blur. I sit typing at my study window, which looks out onto the restored colonial area. At night, I am lighted up like a miracle play if I neglect to pull the shades, and a town full of tourists and students can see me hard at work from far down Prince George Street. The angle of incidence is my view from the window: partly sky, partly the appraisable nodding of a tall tree, whose branches tell me if there will be a crosswind at the airport, partly the long, long hedges of holly, partly the cobblestone streets and the TV aerials and the eighteenth-century store signs, and the pigeons wheeling in a helix around a restaurant owner who now is standing on the sidewalk and hurling bread crusts into the air, partly the magnolia trees whose huge brandy-snifter flowers will make all the town heavy with scent in a month, and the tiny high-winged airplane appearing in the blue at the left of my window, fixing the whole scene with its devastating appearance—graceful, sudden—then vanishing silently beyond the right-hand frame.

46

THE WINDS OF APRIL have been stuttering and moaning
like ghouls freed by Pandora: gusting out of the southwest
at 30 knots one day, and the next swiveling round to
blow even harder from the north. There are hundreds of
demeanors of wind we humans fear, worship, or just like
to identify. The *simoom* of Arabia, the *haboob* of the
Sudan, the snowy *koshava* of Yugoslavia, the tooting
vento coado of Portugal, the bookish *noreaster* of New
England, the *etesian* relished on steamy afternoons in
Greece, the *tramontana*, which gives Italy an Alpine
twinge, the *kona* of Hawaii that's like a hot whip, the
tehuantepecer of Mexico sweeping down from the plateau,
and my favorite, the *I tien tien fung*, which Guy Murchie

describes as "a sigh in the sky of China." How like human beings it is to tag all the delicate shadings of a force with vivid nicknames.

I can tell now by the hip sway of the locust limbs out front, or by the spin of dust and leaf along the curb, or by the torn cotton-candy appearance of high clouds plucked apart by the invisible, how brisk the winds are. All April, while rivers overflow their banks in St. Louis and Germany and the down-tugged jet stream wreaks havoc with Virginia, I try to find a scrap of an afternoon or morning calm enough to take off in, let alone take the check ride for my license, an aerial exam that may last hours. I'm not alone in this pickle; we're all anxious and itchy, wishing days just to be up alone with our thoughts, getting used to the normal splutter and growl of the engine, laying our hands on the throttle in swift, gentle embraces, learning how not to be ashamed of fear, discovering the sky to be where we last left it.

One day, I watch a sparrow blown backward at full flap for five minutes before it clings gratefully to a gutter-spout, crouching, feathers all in disarray. "What a good day for crosswind training," I say to Tom, yelling to make myself heard over the rattle of wind around the light, almost flyable trailer. Its Venetian blinds chatter like bamboo sticks. I figure Tom has more flight time logged than any sparrow. Up we go to discover the crosswind limit of an airplane, and it's just where the book says it will be, at the point where there is no use trying to land because the controls are at full stretch, and the plane is still coming in crooked. It's amazing how easily you can come to the limit of a brilliant design. Just when we're set to fly off to Patrick Henry to try to land, the winds drop a smidgen, and Tom thrashes the plane safely onto the runway, though three feet from touchdown the 20-knot wind from the right shifts suddenly to a 20-knot wind from the left, which leaves even tundra-cool Tom sweating a little.

Part of my amazement has to do with *our* design limits, as well, how many inner trends and forces are at work on us, though they're usually beyond detection. I'm thinking of radiation, chemical compromises, bacteria and viruses, molecular zippers, and especially the cottage industry in every organ and cell. My body is so much smarter than I am and leads so much more ambitious a life. If I had to first think through the Krebs cycle every time I inhaled, my enzymes would be out of luck, but how simply my caretaker body does it, carrying on elaborate and ingenious tasks anonymously, as if I were not here at all, as if I were a toddler who could not be trusted with its own upkeep and health. I often think of a plane, like a microscope, as an instrument of inquiry, a probe with which to better scan the invisible. I don't know why we live so much by effect, detecting the world through sign, spoor, and symptom, instead of making direct contact with it, but that's how it seems to be. When I wonder who the pilot in the airfoil of my flesh really is, I mainly picture a team of specialists, not a cranial Tzarina with four stripes on her sleeve. I'm not one of those people who worship machines, or think the world would be cleaner without them. I admire machines, and I can live without them: I'm a mechano-moderate. In part, because I know my body is a machine, albeit one of indefinable delicacy. Of course, a plane has a more complicated sex life than a human being has, but the machinery part of a machine doesn't stand between me and the marvel. It just reminds me how inventive we latter-day lemurs or floppy fish can be, given a little fabric and a yearning. Icarus fell from the sky, but never from the thermal of his desire. Wear wax wings of one sort or another long enough, and you'll get to know what melting hope feels like.

Along the primped streets of Williamsburg, the past is orderly and clean, the gardens pruned, the bricks scrubbed, and the birds permitted to nest in glossy brown replicas of eighteenth-century bird bottles. You can buy licorice bark to gnaw as you listen to a garbed apothecary recall the life he would have lived on Duke of Gloucester Street ("Dog Street," as the locals call it) two centuries ago. Each yard is enclosed by a spotless white picket fence, and each gate closes itself thanks to a pendant ball on a chain. In the glazed terra-cotta bird bottles, twentieth-century sparrows nest with eighteenth-century cunning. The air swirls with maple seeds: ultralights spinning whirligig to the ground or swiveling rudderless across the parking lot and vest-pocket gardens. Because the maple seeds have no ailerons to coordinate, they all fall in a flat spin. That makes me smile the same smile I do when considering a dragonfly's dihedral biplane. The sky is deep as a pop-up storybook today, the clouds untidy nebulas. The morning's post brought the results of my FAA written exam: 100 percent. And next week, on the first calm day for nearly a month, I go up with Tom to spend two hours proving that I can fly the squirrelly high-winged marvel of a Cessna trainer, and at long last he will dub me a fully fledged *pilot*, adding as examiners always do, and wisely, that the grubby little wing of paper I hold in my fist is really only a license to learn. But that's nonstop trumpet flourishes to a Faustian like me, for whom the real thrill will begin when I can drive to an airport, rent a plane, and follow my yen upward to where patterns become clear, and thoughts can prowl.

I also like the ground school of an airport, which in summer means learning about the black widow spiders nesting beneath a floorboard in one of the Pipers, or the mud-dauber wasps busily searching every plane for an exposed Pitot tube, fuel-tank vent, stall-warning screen, or other small hole to pack up, or the birds tucking bits of grass, string, or pine needles into tail assemblies and carburetor intakes and propeller housings (which is why most planes have their noses stuffed with styrofoam or rubber plugs), or the mice which tend to leave oddments of cloth and paper shreds in wheel fairings and are sometimes overly fond of wooden spars and rib cord stitching. A small blockage can mean a large problem for a pilot. It doesn't seem like a blade of grass or daub of mud would do much damage against a revving, tons-heavy machine, but if you block the flow of air, fuel, or information to the plane, forced landings will follow. So we check every opening carefully before a flight, and very close to the time we fly, since some critters are quick masons. But that vigilance also teaches you about the habits of the critters, like the minute, bright-red wheel lice whose unlikely niche is an airplane's rubber tires.

Nothing is as special as floating over the known world, which you are both part of and above. When my heart is a drudge, I want to leave my anonymous, astonished neighbors, the law-abiding hickories, the taxis called Terminal Cab whose meters are always throbbing, the slum of papers on my desk, the students lying out on the grass like the war wounded at Gettysburg, all the normal hash of people and circumstance, and take to the sky. There is no other cure for it, this fidgeting of the will, no cure but rushing up into the blue basin of the sky, where time and cloud maneuver, and one has a view of Creation wide, bright, and flowing. Otherwise the world would be as small as a postage stamp. Otherwise the winds, like invisible sheep, would bleat and attitudinize unnoticed. Otherwise the condition we in chauvinistic shorthand call *human* would be tight as a noose. Otherwise there would be no release from the tidy local orders of aster, garter snake, sweetheart, and wild strawberry, though I'm devoted to their mysteries in almost terrifying detail. As I've learned this year, in many climates of the heart, it's only when the red, white, and blue airport lights mix like a scrambled flag beneath you, and you climb away, that real astonishment begins.

The Words We Use

"It is the words we use, finally,
that matter. . . ."
LOUIS SIMPSON

ABEAM. When an aircraft is roughly 90 degrees to the left or right of an object or point. Abeam indicates a general position, not a precise location.

ABORT. To stop a maneuver, as in to abort a landing.

ACTIVE. The runway in use. At uncontrolled fields, one often hears a pilot say he or she is "taking the active," which means taking off (but it doesn't say in which direction).

AFFIRMATIVE. Yes.

AILERON. A movable control surface, one of a pair located in or attached to the wings on both sides of the plane. The ailerons are used to control the plane in a turn or roll by creating opposite lift forces on opposite sides of the plane. Example: when the right aileron is up and the left aileron is down, the plane rolls to the right.

AIR WORK. Flying practice.

ANGELS. A military term for thousands of feet of altitude. Example: 37 angels = 37,000 feet.

ANGLE OF ATTACK. The angle at which the wing meets the air.

ANGLE OF INCIDENCE. The angle at which the wings are set with reference to the lengthwise axis of the airplane.

ANVIL. The spreading top of a cumulonimbus cloud in full maturity.

APPROACH CONTROL. The air traffic controller, addressed as "Approach," handles aircraft approaching the airport. Example: "Tucson Approach, this is 1900 U. . ."

APRON. An area for parking or handling aircraft, usually paved.

297

ARTIFICIAL HORIZON. A gyro-operated flight instrument that shows the pitching and banking of an aircraft with respect to the horizon. Most versions use a miniature airplane or an abstract wing to represent the real airplane.

ATTITUDE. Most often used to mean the pitch and bank of the airplane vis-à-vis the horizon, ground, or some other reference line.

BACK PRESSURE. Pulling the control wheel toward one's chest, which brings the plane's nose up.

BACK SIDE OF THE ENERGY CURVE (also: **REGION OF REVERSE COMMAND**). A demonstration of why it requires the same amount of power to fly very fast as to fly very slowly.

BALLOON. Putting the flaps down adds more camber to the wing surface; as a result, the airplane's nose may pop up. The plane "balloons" upward. The term can also refer to a landing attempt when the pilot levels off too high or too fast and the plane bounces up momentarily.

BELOW MINIMUMS. Weather conditions worse than those decreed, by government regulations, to be suitable for flight.

BUFFETING. The beating effect of a disturbed airstream on a plane's structure during flight.

BUSTING MINIMUMS. Exceeding the legal limits for various procedures or maneuvers. A favorite way to bust minimums is to descend below minimum altitude on an instrument approach in bad weather.

CALCULATING THE MOMENT. The moment arm is the horizontal distance in inches from a reference line to the center of gravity.

CARBURETOR ICE. In moist air, the cooling effect of the evaporating fuel will cause ice to form at surprising temperatures (as high as 65 degrees F). The ice forms in a narrow air passage above the throttle and may stop the engine completely or seriously dilute its power. Most planes have a device with which to heat the carburetor.

CAVU. Acronym for "ceiling and visibility unlimited." It is pronounced as a word and frequently is used as a noun or an adjective, as in CAVU weather.

CHANDELLE. A maneuver in which the airplane makes an

abrupt, steep, climbing turn, gaining altitude and reversing its direction of flight simultaneously.

CITABRIA. An aerobatic plane, whose name is also aerobatic (spelled more or less backward).

CIVIL EVENING TWILIGHT. Although the sun may drop below the horizon, the rays are bent by refraction; thus, when the sun appears to be at o degrees, it's really at about .8 degrees. "Civil evening twilight" is a celestial navigation term for the appearance of the sun at the horizon until 6 degrees below. From 6 degrees to 18 degrees below is "nautical evening twilight." During civil evening twilight, only the moon and the planets, and occasionally first magnitude stars are visible. During nautical evening twilight, the second and third magnitude stars are visible. After that, when the sun drops below about 18 degrees, the fifth magnitude stars become visible.

CLEAR AIR TURBULENCE. Turbulence in air where no clouds are present, often in the vicinity of the jet stream.

CLEARANCE DELIVERY. Air traffic control clearance which pilots receive before taxiing for takeoff.

CLIMBING OUT. The climb made directly after takeoff.

CONE OF CONFUSION. The cone-shaped area just over a VOR station, in which signals are uncertain.

CONSOLAN. A long-distance, low-frequency navigational aid used mainly for transoceanic flights.

CRAB. To tack into the wind, as a sailboat does, so that, although the plane may be flying somewhat sideways, it is making a straight path over the ground.

CULTURAL FEATURES. Man-made features visible from the sky, which can be used as checkpoints (cities, bridges, dams, railroads, racetracks, etc.).

DECISION HEIGHT. During an instrument landing, the height at which one must decide to land or declare a "missed approach."

DEPARTURE. The act of leaving an airport. Also the air traffic controller one addresses as "Departure" and summons in the air when leaving the immediate environment of the airport.

DF STEER. Direction-finding guidance given to aircraft in distress. The headings offered will lead the plane to an airport.

DISPLACED THRESHOLD. The "threshold" is the beginning of the part of the runway that is usable for landing. If it's "displaced," as many are, then it's located at a point on the runway other than the runway end.

DOWNWIND. See *Traffic pattern.*

DRAG. The force that retards a body moving through a fluid.

DUAL. Flight instruction.

EMINENCE. A high-pressure system characterized by generally fair weather, in which the winds rotate clockwise.

EXPEDITE. What an air traffic controller says when he means "Hurry up!" Example: "Cessna one-two-three-four-five, expedite departure."

FACTOR. Most often used to refer to other aircraft at the same altitude and general area one should be looking out for. A pilot might say: "Ithaca Tower, is that traffic still a factor?"

FBO. "Fixed Base Operator." A central place at the airport where planes are rented, sold, and/or fueled. It usually includes a pilots' lounge, telephones for filing flight plans and inquiring about weather, vending machines or restaurants, and pilots' supplies.

FIX. An aircraft's position, determined by a landmark, a navigational aid, or some other agreed-upon site.

FLAPS. Hinged portions of the trailing edge of both wings between the ailerons and the fuselage, whose purpose is to increase lift, drag, or angle of descent.

FLARE. To descend in a smooth curve during landing, making a transition from a steep descent to flight almost parallel to the earth. From the point of view of the pilot, one is bleeding off airspeed while staying at the same height over the runway, so the airplane's nose rises up.

FLAT APPROACH. Coming in too low on final.

FLICKER VERTIGO. A special type of vertigo caused by a plane's propeller or a helicopter's rotor. This movement causes the light to flicker in a very fast rhythmic cycle (ten to twenty times per second).

FSS. Flight Service Station. A facility operated by the Federal Aviation Agency to give flight assistance. One gets the latest weather from them, files a flight plan with them, and also requests various services from them in the air.

FULL RICH. A mixture-control setting of highest amount of fuel to air.

G'S. The "g" stands for gravitational acceleration, 32 feet per second, of a body falling in a vacuum. In Air Force tests, men have survived accelerations of 30 g's without permanent injury. Women sometimes report prolapsed wombs at high g levels.

GET OUT OF MY EAR! What one air traffic controller was overheard saying to another on his frequency.

GETTING THE PICTURE. Picturing in one's mind the position of the aircraft vis-à-vis the horizon, ground, or sky at various airspeeds and landing configurations, so that even if some of the instruments fail, one would know, by visual reference, enough information to land safely.

GLIDE PATH. The flight path of an aircraft in a glide, seen from the side.

GLIDE SLOPE. The angle between the horizon and the glide path of an aircraft (3 degrees).

GLORY. A series of concentric colored rings around the shadow of an observer, cast upon a cloud or fog bank, due to the diffraction of reflected light.

GO AROUND. Either a noun or an imperative: to abandon a landing attempt and return for another try.

GREASE IT ON. To land with expert gradualness and delicacy.

GROUND. The ATC one addresses as "Ground," who directs the movement of planes when they are on the ramp or taxiing around the airport.

GROUND LOOP. A violent, whirling turn of an airplane on the ground, usually pivoting on a wing tip after a very crooked landing.

GROUND SCHOOL. A school that gives flying instruction. Classroom work.

HANDOFF. Passing the radar surveillance of a plane from one controller to another before the plane enters the new controller's airspace.

HAVE NUMBERS. What a pilot says who is approaching an airport and has heard the tower speaking with other planes about the runway in use, wind conditions, etc.

HEAVY. A large aircraft.

HOLD SHORT. Instruction to taxi up to, but not onto, the runway.

HOLDING PATTERN. A racetrack-shaped pattern over a navigational aid, or at the intersection of two airways, around which a pilot flies while waiting for further instructions.

IDENT. An ATC request for a pilot to better identify his airplane (on radar) by pressing a special button on the plane's transponder.

IFR. Instrument Flight Rules.

INTERSECTION. The point where two VOR radials converge.

JET STREAM. A meandering river of high-velocity winds, 50 knots or more, imbedded in the normal wind flow aloft, often 1,000 to 3,000 miles long, 100 to 400 miles wide. The core of the jet stream is generally found at 20,000 to 40,000 feet.

KNOT. Speed equal to one nautical mile (6,080 feet) per hour. It refers to speed and velocity only and isn't used as a measure of distance. A knot equals 1.15 statute miles per hour.

KNOWN ICING. Definite, reported icing conditions.

LAND ON THE NUMBERS. An instruction to land near the beginning of the runway, precisely where the large runway numbers are painted in white.

LEAN. Reduce the fuel in the fuel-air mixture.

LET DOWN. To descend from cruising altitude before beginning an approach or landing.

LOOKING. What a pilot says when he or she doesn't have the "traffic" in sight yet.

MACKEREL SKY. A sky patchy with cirrocumulus or altocumulus clouds, which resemble the scales and stripes on a mackerel.

MAKE SHORT APPROACH. An ATC instruction to change the usual traffic pattern and make a short final.

MANEUVERING SPEED. The maximum speed at which the flight controls can be used to their full extent without damaging the aircraft's structure. In severe turbulence, for example, one must slow up to maneuvering speed.

MAYDAY. The international distress signal. When repeated three times, it indicates imminent and grave danger and an immediate request for assistance. The word itself evolved during World War II, from the French flyers' *M'aidez,* "Help me!"

MILE-HIGH CLUB. An informal club of people who have made love at or above 5,000 feet.

MIXED ILLUSION. The combined reactions of a human body in flight to the different motions and maneuvers of an aircraft.

MOAS. Military Operating Areas. Flight through them is permitted at certain times and certain altitudes. Each has a name (Lady MOA, Rappa MOA, Fuzzy MOA, Sells Low MOA, etc.), and probably is not intended to invoke the flightless birds of New Zealand.

MUSH. To gain little or no altitude while flying in a semi-stalled condition or at a high angle of attack.

MY POP TEASES FAT GIRLS. A mnemonic for the prelanding checklist: Mixture, Prop pitch, Throttle, Flaps, Gear.

NEGATIVE. No. Example: "Negative transponder" = "This plane is not equipped with a transponder."

NO JOY. Means: "I do not see the traffic you warned me about." Some pilots use "Tally ho" for "Have the traffic in sight."

ON TOP. Flight above the cloud deck.

OUT OF SEVEN FOR SIX. Leaving the first altitude for the second, each one referred to in thousands of feet.

OUT OF THE ENVELOPE. A weight and balance calculation which falls in the unsafe range.

PAN PAN PAN. The international urgency signal. When repeated three times, it indicates uncertainty or alert, followed by the nature of the urgency.

PANCAKE. To level off and stall an airplane too high over the runway, so that it falls rapidly and hits hard.

PAPER WORK. Most often used to refer to one's licenses, credentials, or file.

PILOT IN COMMAND. The pilot responsible for the operation and safety of an aircraft. Usually sits in the left seat.

PIREPS, AIRMETS, SIGMETS. A Pirep, "pilot report," is a report of weather conditions encountered by a pilot in flight. Airmets and Sigmets are issued by the government, with Airmets reporting weather of less severity than Sigmets.

THE PROBABLE CAUSE. Most likely reason an airplane crashed. It's the jargon used by the National Transportation Safety Board.

THE RABBIT. Ground lights designed to help a pilot breaking out of the clouds. High-powered flashers leap toward the runway threshold; in some systems, there is more a rolling ball-of-fire effect.

RED LINE. The never-exceed speed, beyond which structural damage to the airframe is likely to occur.

ROGER. "I have received all of your last transmission." Does not mean "Yes."

ROTATE. To lift the nose wheel from the runway during take-off.

RUN-UP. Just before takeoff, one runs the engine up to a higher RPM setting for a minute or so, while testing various instruments and operations.

SAY AGAIN. "Repeat the last transmission."

SCUD RUNNING. The risky practice of flying underneath low clouds.

SIDESTEP MANEUVER. Making an approach to one runway, then landing on a runway parallel to it.

SIGN. Aircraft tail number.

SPIN. A rapid descent during which the airplane's nose is pointed down, while the airplane revolves around the line of descent.

SQUAWK. Request by a radar controller to engage the transponder, so the airplane's exact position can be determined.

"Squawk 1432" = "Put the code 1432 into your transponder."

STALL SERIES. Exercises in recovering from a variety of stalls.
Example: approach to landing stall, departure stall, etc.

STAND BY. Wait.

STEP ON THE BALL. Push the rudder pedal on the side that the
turn-and-bank ball is out of the center, to bring the airplane back into coordinated flight.

STOP SQUAWK. Controller's request to turn off the transponder.

TOP IT OFF. Fill the tanks as full as possible.

TOUCH-AND-GO. A landing in which the airplane touches down
but does not come to a stop before making another takeoff.

TRAFFIC. A term used by ATC to refer to one or more airplanes. At an uncontrolled airport, a departing pilot announces his or her intentions, to all traffic in the area,
over the Unicom frequency: "Wane traffic, Cessna six-
six-six-six-Sierra departing runway seven."

TRAFFIC PATTERN. The five positions in an airport traffic pattern are Downwind, Base, Final, Crosswind, and Upwind.
In this way, you always know where other planes are located. If a plane says that he is "turning crosswind for
seven" and you are "downwind for seven," then you know
that the other plane is behind you and to your left.

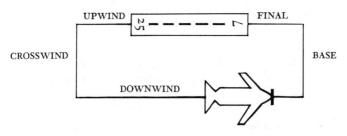

A controller usually asks an incoming pilot to "report
downwind."

TRANSPONDER. A device which, by responding to a coded radar
pulse, identifies an aircraft on a radar screen.

TRUE VIRGINS MAKE DULL COMPANY. Mnemonic for how to arrive at a correct compass heading when planning a cross-country flight. True course $+/-$ Variation $=$ Magnetic course. Magnetic course $+/-$ Deviation $=$ Compass heading.

UNABLE. Indicates inability to comply with a specific instruction, request, or clearance.

UNDER THE HOOD. A hood shaped like a welder's mask (but without eye holes), which restricts an instrument student's vision to the panel instruments.

UNFAMILIAR. What a pilot may say to a controller when he or she is new to the airport and needs help in figuring out where the taxiway, FBO, or some other site is.

UNICOM. A nongovernment facility at certain airports which may provide airport information. Airplanes flying into and out of towerless airports announce their intentions over the Unicom frequency.

V SPEEDS. The key speeds for an airplane. Example: stall speed with or without flaps, best rate of climb or best angle of climb speeds, never exceed speed, maneuvering speed, etc.

VASI LIGHTS. Visual Approach Slope Indicator. Ground-based lights which help guide a pilot to the runway. The ingenious lights are designed in such a way that if you see red over white, you're on glide slope. If you see red over red, you're too low. If you see white over white, you're too high. The jingle that goes with it is "Red over white, pilot's delight. White over white, you're sky high. Red over red, you're dead."

VFR. Visual Flight Rules.

VOR. Variable Omni Range. A type of radio beacon that gives radials, like spokes of a wheel, in all directions from the transmitter.

WAKE TURBULENCE. The disturbed and mostly downward moving air behind an aircraft: counter-rotating vortices from each wing tip. If a small plane takes off behind a large plane, it is advised to wait at least three minutes for the wake turbulence to settle down.

WALK AROUND. A preflight inspection of the airplane.

Weather. A weather briefing ("Have you got weather?"). Also used to mean bad weather ("Is there any weather around Lexington?").

Wilco. I will comply with your instructions.

Wind shear. A change in wind speed or direction in a very short distance, resulting in a tearing or shearing effect.

Wind sock. A fabric sleeve designed to catch and swing with the wind, to show wind direction and force.

The winds aloft. Winds at high altitudes, which are unaffected by surface features and must be taken into consideration when flying cross-country.

With you. What a pilot says to a controller after a handoff. Example: "Departure, Cessna one-seven-seven-six-Alpha, with you at three thousand feet."

Words twice. A request to repeat each word twice because communications are difficult.

Zero zero. A condition in which there is no visibility horizontally or vertically (fog to the ground, for example).

Zulu time. Greenwich Mean Time, used throughout the aviation system and sometimes referred to simply as Z. It has nothing to do with Africa. When they were dividing the planet into meridians, they began with A and ended with Z (at the Greenwich Observatory). In the aeronautical alphabet, Z is Zulu.

Diane Ackerman was born in Waukegan, Illinois, in 1948. She received a B.A. from Pennsylvania State University, and an M.F.A., M.A., and Ph.D. from Cornell University. In addition to her collections of poetry, *The Planets: A Cosmic Pastoral*, *Wife of Light*, and *Lady Faustus*, she has also written a prose memoir, *Twilight of the Tenderfoot*, and a play, *Reverse Thunder*. Her poetry and prose appear regularly in *The New York Times*, *The American Poetry Review*, *The Kenyon Review*, *The Washington Post*, and elsewhere; and her work has been awarded the Pushcart Prize (1983–1984), the Black Warrior Poetry Prize (1981), and the Abbie Copps Poetry Prize (1974). She is the recipient of grants from the National Endowment for the Arts and the Rockefeller Foundation. In addition to being a licensed pilot, Ms. Ackerman is also an accomplished scuba diver and horsewoman. She divides her time between Ithaca, New York, and St. Louis, Missouri, where she is currently director of The Writers' Program at Washington University.